Michael Veitch is well known as an author, actor, comedian and former ABC television and radio presenter. His books include the critically acclaimed accounts of Australian pilots in World War II, *Heroes of the Skies*, *Fly*, *Flak* and *44 Days*. *Barney Greatrex* is his seventh book. He lives in the Yarra Valley, outside Melbourne.

T0363303

BARNEY GREATREX

FROM BOMBER COMMAND TO THE FRENCH RESISTANCE – THE STIRRING STORY OF AN AUSTRALIAN HERO

MICHAEL VEITCH

BASED ON RESEARCH BY ALEX LLOYD AND ANGUS HORDERN

hachette
AUSTRALIA

Barney Greatrex's story is drawn from research and interviews conducted for the 2015 documentary *For School and Country* by Alex Lloyd and Angus Hordern, and with further research and interviews by Michael Veitch.

hachette
AUSTRALIA

First published in Australia and New Zealand in 2017
by Hachette Australia
(an imprint of Hachette Australia Pty Limited)
Level 17, 207 Kent Street, Sydney NSW 2000
www.hachette.com.au

This edition published in 2019

10 9 8 7 6 5 4 3 2 1

NATIONAL
LIBRARY
OF AUSTRALIA

A catalogue record for this book is available from the National Library of Australia

ISBN: 978 0 7336 4090 2 (paperback)

Cover design by Luke Causby, Blue Cork Designs
Front cover images courtesy of Barney Greatrex (Avro Lancaster heavy bomber), and Imperial War Museum/CH 10714 (No. 61 Squadron RAF crew walk towards their Avro Lancaster B Mark I at Syerston, Nottinghamshire, before taking off for a raid on Hamburg, Germany)
Back cover image courtesy of Barney Greatrex
Author photo courtesy of Gina Milicia
Text design by Bookhouse, Sydney
Typeset in 12/17 pt Simoncini Garamond by Bookhouse, Sydney
Printed and bound in Australia by McPherson's Printing Group

MIX
Paper from
responsible sources
FSC
www.fsc.org   FSC® C001695

The paper this book is printed on is certified against the Forest Stewardship Council® Standards. McPherson's Printing Group holds FSC® chain of custody certification SA-COC-005379. FSC® promotes environmentally responsible, socially beneficial and economically viable management of the world's forests.

To the airmen of all nations and of all wars

CONTENTS

Part Two

Part Three

PROLOGUE

Barney Greatrex could bear the tension no longer. Wincing through the cigarette haze, he once again took in the handful of faces that surrounded him in the small wooden hut buried deep in the French forest: hard, swarthy, Gallic faces, outwardly calm, but long inured to explosions of sudden, brutal violence. Even then, Barney had noted, their expressions hardly changed.

Pale sunshine pushed its way feebly through the small, grubby window, cutting shards of watery light through the permanent fug of smoke and stale sweat. Barney swallowed. His knee fidgeted. A raw sense of dread washed over him.

The stranger sat among them too, all but indistinguishable from the others. Like them, he talked quickly, gesturing forcibly with his hands, smiling, even offering up an occasional brittle joke. But he was not one of them, and everyone knew it.

It was his eyes that gave him away, thought Barney: darting from face to face, from moment to moment; preparing – for what?

A sudden bolt from this bare little room that threatened to suddenly close in on him? Where, though, could he run? Outside was nothing but trees. These endless woods besieged them like a gloomy army, and the hard men of the Maquis knew their every meandering path, and every dank hiding hole. In any case, reflected Barney, he'd probably never even make it to the front door.

Careful not to catch his eye, Barney studied the stranger's face. Like the others, it was aged far beyond his thirty-five or so years, but – he was almost sure – it was still unsuspecting. He risked another glance. How, he thought, could he tolerate this atmosphere? This grinning pall of false cordiality that dangled like a noose in front of him?

Barney sent his eyes to the ceiling, then the floor. For how many weeks had these flimsy walls served as his home as well as his prison? How many weeks had these faces been his closest companions as well as his jailers? And when was it that he had first counted himself among their number?

He strained to pick up the conversation humming around him. His French, though a little better now, could barely glean the gist of it. The only thing of which he was certain was that no one was saying what they thought. With an almost involuntary spasm, Barney shoved back on the thin wooden chair, scraping it noisily over the bare floorboards. Unused to the young, blond Australian airman doing anything very much besides sitting quietly and observing, the others glanced up for a moment, then lost interest. Barney excused himself and went to the door. Outside, the air, though fresh, brought little relief.

Walking a short distance from the hut, he picked up an axe and began to chop wood. The rounds of pine, still too green to burn, exploded satisfyingly under his blade, blocking out – momentarily – the sound of the voices inside the hut.

The irony of the scene was not lost on him. Like the man with the sallow skin and the darting eyes, Barney too was a stranger, thrust into an alien world of danger and uncertainty, over which he had no control whatsoever.

A month earlier, he had watched the south coast of England passing below him through the perspex astrodome of the great black Lancaster bomber, the familiar outline of Beachy Head dissolving into a wintry evening haze. Less than three hours later came the frenzied few seconds that he had long dreaded but long expected: the punctuated conversation over the aircraft's intercom as the night fighter stalked closer: 'Nine hundred yards, skipper . . . eight hundred . . .' The voice of Reg, his now dead wireless operator, still rang in his ears. Then the sickening tear of cannon shells splitting metal, the sudden fire, and those surreal moments as the doomed aircraft gripped him in its centrifugal death spin; the miracle of his escape, the shock of a freezing black wind, the parachute blooming white above his head in the night sky; the snow, then the almost unbearable realisation that, out of his crew of seven, he alone was now alive.

A few days later, cold, hungry and exhausted, he had emerged from another forest – much like this one – to take the biggest gamble of his life: opening the back door of a small house in a tiny mountain village and stepping inside. The middle-aged Frenchman who met him stood frozen to the spot, as if encountering a ghost.

•

Still they talked inside the hut. Even away from it, Barney found the tension no less palpable. What could they be talking about? What was there to discuss? The stranger sounded cheerful, even familiar. Was it possible he did not realise his identity as a German spy had been unmasked? Or perhaps, Barney thought, clinging to a sudden, desperate hope, it was all a mistake. What if these men had been wrong? What if the man's unlikely story had, after all, checked out and even now they were joking about how a tragic misunderstanding had been narrowly avoided? But no. Even with his miserable French, Barney could sense some macabre charade approaching its denouement, whereupon it would be kicked over like a flimsy theatre set and the stranger's fate would be sealed.

Barney went on chopping, his sweat alternately cooling and warming him against the early spring breeze.

Then, to an exhale of relief, the sounds of more chairs scraping and feet shuffling towards the door. More voices. The party was breaking up. Nothing would happen, he decided, not today. Barney swung his axe once more, then suddenly a pistol shot rang out, followed quickly by another. Two spiteful jabs punctuating the cold, clear air, then the sound of something soft but heavy falling hard.

Without thinking, Barney bolted to the door of the cabin as it swung open before him. A man's dead body rolled out, an oozing smear of blood staining the wooden floor behind him. Barney almost stumbled into him. He looked into the man's dead eyes, wide open at his feet, a moment of hideous confusion frozen forever on his lifeless face. Barney felt a tight wave of nausea – even anger – course through him. Now blood started to gush from the back of the man's head, expanding quickly in a black-red balloon. Revolted, Barney turned away.

A nearby woodsman, a friend, had heard the shots and had warily approached the cabin. He now stood at the open door, shaking with fear and glancing anxiously back towards the woods like a guilty child about to be caught. In his grim, dark voice, Bébert growled that he would kill him if he breathed a word of what he saw. Everyone knew it was no idle threat.

Well into the night that followed, Barney, wielding a pathetically inadequate implement, would be hacking into the partially frozen ground to dig a moonlit grave and quietly developing a lifelong amazement at the weight – the dead weight – of a lifeless human body. Eventually, this too would become simply another surreal moment in an ordeal of terror, luck and survival about which he would keep all but silent for the next seventy years. As his small shovel wedged out another clod of frozen earth in the darkness, he glanced up at a dark, skidding sky, and once more pondered what part of his utterly unremarkable upbringing in the Australian suburbs could possibly have led him to this.

PART ONE

1

AN AUSTRALIAN FAMILY

As noble as the name may seem, the Greatrexes in fact came from England's rising industrial class, originally as leather tanners. Sometime in the late eighteenth century, they ventured down from Cumbria in England's far north-west to bring their entrepreneurial skills to Birmingham, one of the epicentres of the industrial revolution then sweeping the country. By the 1850s, in the village of Walsall, they had built one of the most prosperous leather-making companies in the country, producing everything from saddles to the finest in ladies' gloves, which were exported all over Britain and to the wider world.

The Greatrexes established themselves in Ashfurlong Hall, an ancient and impressive stone manor that is today listed as a national asset by the British Government. In the 1870s, the family built another large home, Moss Close, which survived until the 1960s, when it was demolished. A photograph adorning the wall of the home of Barney's brother, Antony, shows a large and obviously well-to-do Victorian family posed in front of its imposing stone edifice, surrounded by myriad servants and carriages.

It was Barney's mother, Elsie, who was responsible for luring the Greatrexes to Australia. Descended from the French Clapin family, who had been honoured for service in Napoleon's *Grand Armée*, but who had migrated to Sydney in the 1840s, the young Elsie grew up in the remote western New South Wales town of Cobar, where her father managed a copper mine. One day in 1906, a representative of the Greatrex Ltd Company of Walsall called by in the form of a handsome young Englishman named Basil Valant Ryder Greatrex. Basil led an enviable life before World War I, travelling across the Empire (first class, of course), looking after the family's extensive business interests in India, Africa, New Zealand and Australia. But it was the open and adventurous plains of Africa that worked their spell on the young Basil, a place – according to his family – for which he quietly pined for the rest of his life. A superb horseman, Basil would undoubtedly have cut a dashing figure to young Elsie, who at the very least seems to have determined not to spend the rest of her days in Cobar. Training as a nurse, she boarded a ship in 1911 and set off as a single woman – almost unheard of at that time – to America, where she worked in hospitals across the country until arriving in England on the eve of World War I.

It was here, by means that still remain a mystery to her descendants, that she contrived to reacquaint herself with Basil

Greatrex, now a serving army officer. In London, in 1915, they were married, but Elsie had no intention of remaining in England for a moment longer than necessary.

Basil had happened to be in his beloved South Africa when the Great War broke out, and with his skills in horsemanship and a background in saddlery he had spent some time organising an irregular South African mounted cavalry unit, the Natal Light Horse. Convinced, however, that this would lead to very little action indeed, he had headed to London, where he joined the British Army and would once again meet the spirited girl from Cobar, Elsie.

Basil was put in charge of organising a contingent of cavalry for the Gallipoli campaign and was sent to the Dardanelles. Once there, however, he was informed that his horses were of no use whatsoever and that he and his men would instead function as dismounted cavalry. He was subsequently sent to the relative backwater of the Macedonian front, where he spent the remainder of the war. This confusing Balkans campaign was initially designed to prop up beleaguered Serbia, but after simmering away intermittently for a few years it evolved into a more or less static front where the greatest enemy was diseases such as typhus and dysentery.

'My father was a typical English gentleman,' remembers Barney's brother, Antony. 'Very calm, very reserved. I don't think I ever recall him raising his voice.' Perhaps it was this sangfroid that assured he survived what was possibly his most dramatic incident of the war, on the return journey to Britain. The genies of independence unleashed throughout the Middle East were felt strongly in the imperial seat of Egypt at war's end, and Basil, with an eye to protecting both his men and his beloved horses, on one occasion risked his all. Confronting a riot determined to loot the army's stores of horse-feed grain, Basil, then a lieutenant, simply stepped in front of the mob with his hand raised. Probably astonished by the man's impudence, the rioters stopped dead and listened as the young British officer explained that this feed was essential for his horses and that, after all, helping one's self to it simply wasn't done. His nerve won the day, the rioters dispersed and Basil was promoted immediately to captain and mentioned in dispatches. 'He was lucky he wasn't knifed on the spot,' remarked Antony when retelling the family legend.

Elsie, meanwhile, had spent an eventful war working in a London hospital with the groundbreaking New Zealand paediatrician Sir Truby King, under whose direction she developed a passion for the proper care of infants that would remain with her for the rest of her life. One evening, however, a pregnant Elsie came arguably closer to being killed than her husband ever did at the front. While she was walking in a London street near the hospital, a bomb from one of the intermittent zeppelin raids landed close, blowing her over and causing her to lose the baby. Only in his later life did Basil reveal to his family that it was a girl, and a loss from which his wife never fully recovered.

The Middle East was not the only place to undergo sweeping change following the war. The decline of the horse saw the rise of the motor age, presenting an opportunity that

Basil's father, Albert – reportedly a charming man but with no great head for business – spectacularly failed to exploit. With a refusal to adapt to the mechanical age, the company lurched into decline and was sold to a man called Hilditch, who proceeded to quickly run the once great Greatrex Company into the ground.

With no job and his family business practically bankrupt, Basil had little choice but to accede to his wife's desire to return to Australia. So, in late 1919, before posing for some splendid farewell photographs that still exist, they boarded ship and arrived, virtually penniless, at the dawn of the twenties in Sydney. If, after having lived a life of independence and adventure before and during the war, Basil found it irksome to now be forced to inhabit the spare room of his new wife's parents' home in a country he had expressed no great desire to live in, he never showed it. According to Antony, Basil was always the consummate English gentleman and rarely complained. Besides, he quickly proved his business skills to be superior to those of his father. He established a small engineering import company, which thrived, and survives today.

In 1920, Basil and Elsie welcomed their first child to the world, Barnaby Ryder, to be dubbed immediately and forever as Barney. Antony followed in 1923 and their sister, Pleasance, in 1926. After the loss of Basil and Elsie's first girl seven years earlier in London, the arrival of Pleasance was greeted with particular joy. This was also the year in which the Greatrexes moved to Narelle Avenue, Pymble, on Sydney's Upper North Shore. Although deep in suburbia today, it was in the 1920s, according to Antony, still largely agricultural. 'We were one of only three houses in the entire street,' he says. 'There was just paddocks all behind us, and hardly even any trees.'

Their upbringing, recounts Antony, was 'very middle class'. While by no means rich, the Greatrexes were comfortable, with Basil's business managing to survive the terrible years of the Great Depression, albeit with difficulty. In an interview conducted in 2011 by fellow old boys of Sydney's Knox Grammar – Barney's school for the decade prior to the war – he remembers the Depression 'being talked about the whole time. I always recall one stage my father had to ask the council to postpone his payment of the school fees, which I think were about 17 pounds a quarter.' The family, however, managed to hold on to some luxuries, including the family car. This was fortunate, as one of the Greatrexes' few rituals was a weekly trip to the beach, undertaken without fail every Sunday.

Antony describes the family as close, but to modern sensibilities the atmosphere sounds decidedly austere. Basil and Elsie never entertained nor – unusually for the times – attended church. There were no children's parties permitted, and even birthdays and Christmases passed by uncelebrated. Although Basil and Elsie were undoubtedly caring parents, they showed little in the way of affection towards either the children or indeed each other. Antony cannot recall witnessing so much as a moment's display of tenderness between his mother and father. It would be wrong, however, to assume theirs to be an unhappy family. If affection was not forthcoming, at the same time – Antony is at pains to point out – the sound of a raised voice never shattered the atmosphere of calm.

Left largely to their own devices – as children then tended to be – the young Greatrexes availed themselves of the open spaces at their back door, planning long and adventurous treks on rickety bicycles, or piling hoards of timber packing cases their father used for his import business into castles and cubby houses of doubtful construction. The boys, however, were not particularly close, and Antony has few memories of playing with his brother. It was either alone or with their respective friends that the adventures of childhood were undertaken by the two Greatrex boys. 'We were never great mates,' says Antony. The three-year age gap notwithstanding, Antony believes Barney probably looked down on him, 'because I always found school a struggle'.

Now suspecting himself to have been partially dyslexic, Antony found his education a never-ending challenge, changing schools six times and failing to pass exams. Elsie, however, persisted and patiently sought out a place where her younger son could fit in, or at least cope.

Barney, by contrast, quickly found his niche at the prestigious Knox, just a couple of train stops away in the suburb of Wahroonga. Founded by a group of Presbyterian ministers and laymen in 1924, Knox was quick to establish for itself a powerful reputation under the driving force of its original headmaster, Neil Harcourt MacNeil. Born in Victoria as the fifth child of a Scottish Presbyterian minister, MacNeil travelled to Oxford as a Rhodes Scholar in 1914. He enlisted at the outbreak of World War I in the Highland Light Infantry, in which he eventually rose to the rank of captain. He saw a great deal of action on the Western Front, was badly wounded at the disastrous 1915 Battle of Loos, won the Military Cross for bravery and was twice Mentioned in Despatches. As if this was not enough war for any one man, after convalescing he went on to train as a pilot and transferred to the Royal Flying Corps, taking part in air operations over Arras with 16 Squadron.

After the war, MacNeil returned to Oxford to read Modern History before taking up the job at Knox, where he seems to have had a depressingly prescient view of the future of the boys under his care. Convinced of the inevitability of another conflict, he went about making sure they would at least be ready for it by instilling into the school a strong military focus. Not only did he appoint half his teaching staff from the ranks of veterans of the Great War but he also instigated an unusually professional school cadet corps, along with a former Sandhurst officer to run it as authentically as possible.

According to a more contemporary Knox headmaster, John Weeks, 'Unfortunately war is a place where survival is critical and that survival comes about through self-discipline and the ability to work as a team. MacNeil knew there was more war to come and, sadly, that his boys needed to be well trained for that eventuality. Hence, early in the school's history, he introduced cadets to a high standard so that those concepts could be instilled for their survival.'

The Kirby Shield was a local competition between various school cadet units, and Knox won it four times during the 1930s. To further cement a lasting military tradition, every holidays the boys travelled north for a week's training with the army at their base at Singleton, even taking their weapons with them on the train.

For Barney, it would provide a crucible for the eventful years that lay ahead. In later life, he remembered the formidable MacNeil, as well as the camps and bivouacs he instigated among his cadets, designed to replicate those of a professional army. 'MacNeil was the number one,' he said in the 2011 interview by fellow Knox old boys. 'Definitely more than the ordinary masters. He was a bit, I think you'd call it "dour". You know, Scottish background, but he certainly knew how to run the place, and I think he did it extremely well.' Five years after leaving school, sheltering in the hard conditions of a French Maquis camp in winter, surrounded by the Germans, Barney would have many reasons to quietly thank his former headmaster for the levels he went to in preparing him for that moment.

Upon enrolling in 1929, Barney's star at Knox shone early as he devoured subjects both in the sciences and the humanities as well as thoroughly enjoying life in the cadet corps. He was even awarded the coveted job of running the armoury, where he was in charge of the school's considerable collection of World War I–era Lewis guns and .303 rifles, which MacNeil ensured were used to a high level of proficiency. Barney distinctly remembered being handed a large and ominous set of keys by the feared master Captain D. T. Okey. 'Look,' he was told in no uncertain terms, 'here are the complete keys to the armoury. If you lose them, you'll never hear the end of it!'

'So I didn't lose them,' recalled Barney.

Matriculating easily, Barney was accepted into the University of Sydney in 1940 to study engineering. He was proving once again to be an exceptional student when world events conspired to interrupt his studies.

2

THE FARAWAY WAR

Barney Greatrex would spend a long and gruelling nineteen months preparing to play his small part in the terrible conflict that exploded in 1939, leaving the world utterly changed by the time it came to its exhausted, shattering conclusion six years later in 1945.

Although World War II's origins were in Europe, Australia's sensibilities at the time leaned completely towards its cultural and historical origins of Great Britain, and to a generation of young men and women it was axiomatic that, as part of the Empire, Britain's fight was also their own.

Going to Sydney University straight from school, Barney felt for a time that the war was indeed far away. The newspapers talked about the fall of Poland and France, and then, later in 1940, young imaginations everywhere were fired by the exploits of Britain's Royal Air Force (RAF) in their epic sixteen-week defence of their small island in the Battle of

Britain. If Australians played but a small part in that saga, the role of the Second Australian Imperial Force (Second AIF) on the ground in Africa fighting the Italians at places with exotic names such as Sidi Barrani and Bardia provided easy headlines for Australian newspapers.

Then, in the new year of 1941, Barney and his fellow students began to read about the heroic Australian stand at an inconsequential Mediterranean port called Tobruk. In time, this action would take its place alongside the legendary Australian engagements of the Great War, fought by Barney's father's generation. As the months went by, though still far off, the war seemed to be expanding incrementally, and it began to seem inevitable to Barney and millions of others that they would soon be called to play their own part in the cataclysm. Then, at the end of Barney's second year of study, the war arrived on Australia's doorstep virtually overnight when Japan launched its lightning, make-or-break grab for a south Pacific empire with coordinated attacks on Pearl Harbor and other targets including Hong Kong and Malaya on 7 December 1941. All of a sudden, the war didn't seem so very far away at all.

Barney recalls that after the dawn of the Pacific War there was 'enormous pressure' on boys of sixteen to eighteen to join up or get involved, but which service would he choose? 'I looked at it all,' he later recounted in the Knox interview, 'and I thought to myself that the thing to do was get into the air force.' His reasons were more pragmatic than patriotic: 'It appeared to me that once you joined up in the RAAF, you were very likely to be promoted to sergeant almost straight away.'

Before the war, Australia managed to train roughly fifty pilots per year. But an agreement signed in Ottawa in December 1939 between Great Britain, Canada, Australia, New Zealand, South Africa and several of the other dominions of the British Commonwealth led to the formation of one of the largest, most ambitious and most efficient accelerated military training programs ever undertaken.

Air power, it was realised early, would be decisive in this highly mechanised conflict, and while the industrial might of Britain could be relied on to churn out fleets of modern aircraft, providing the men to fly them was a far more difficult prospect. Nor did the cramped layout of the British Isles, its doubtful climate and its proximity to enemy attack make it the best place to transform untrained civilians into skilled airmen. The Dominions, it was decided, would be required to fill the gap of mother England's need for trained airmen. Hence, the British Commonwealth Air Training Plan was conceived, then rushed into existence across five countries and three continents, from which an astonishing 800 trained airmen would be provided to the United Kingdom every month.

In Australia alone, where the plan became known as the Empire Air Training Scheme, nearly forty separate schools were established providing instruction in all aspects of flying modern military aircraft: elementary and advanced flight training, navigation, bombing, air gunnery and wireless operation. At places as diverse as Victor Harbor in South Australia and Cunderdin in Western Australia, Sandgate in Queensland and Bradfield Park in the suburbs of Sydney, hitherto sleepy weekend airstrips were overnight transformed into the busiest aerodromes in the world – far busier in fact than the biggest airports of the day. Sometimes they had arisen from nothing at all save a wide open piece of paddock, where, after a few weeks' attention by the bulldozers, graders and construction contractors, the march of drilling boots and the drone of aircraft engines could be heard day and night.

In all, it was a massive undertaking, but by war's end over 37,000 young Australian airmen would be trained under the machine-like operation of the Empire Air Training Scheme, providing thirty-six per cent of the entire British and Commonwealth aircrew total. Intakes would be divided into numbered courses, of which the timetable was so relentless that if a student became ill it was almost impossible for him to catch up. Instead, he was assigned to the following course and usually had to begin all over again.

After the beginning of the Pacific War in December 1941, the shock realisation that Australia's own air defences were woefully inadequate led to the exportation of trained airmen being temporarily halted, but only until February 1942, when the obligations to Britain recommenced. The question on every cadet's mind was where would he be sent, and it was usually not until the very last day of his course that he would find out – when his name was read from a list by an impatient corporal on parade.

Ten thousand Australian-trained airmen were destined to be sent to the United Kingdom to fly with Bomber Command, of which 3486 would lose their lives, accounting for nearly thirty-two per cent of the entire RAAF casualties for the war. Even these statistics, however, fail to give the true picture of the dangers. At various stages of the war, flying the RAF's bomber offensive gave its young volunteers a dismal one-in-three chance of survival. Worse odds by far than for any other unit of any other branch of the Western Allied armed services in any theatre of World War II. It was estimated that only by joining the German U-boat service could one be presented with a more certain path to self-destruction.

Barney Greatrex, however, had little idea of this when he walked into No. 2 RAAF Recruiting Centre in Sydney's Martin Place one afternoon in September 1941. Like millions of other young men of the early war years, he simply wanted to 'get into it', and the sooner the better.

3

THE IMPATIENT STUDENT

Almost without exception, each of the thousands of young men who stepped forward to put themselves in harm's way by joining the air force in World War II did so with their sights firmly set on becoming a pilot. This was, after all, the most glamorous job in the most glamorous service, fuelled by newsreel images of dashing Oxbridge-educated Spitfire and Hurricane pilots who, after unbuttoning the top button of their service tunic, jauntily took to the skies in the great mechanical thoroughbreds of their day to decimate the enemy. In reality, the vast majority of these men hailed not from the great English public school system at all, nor were most of them even officers, and any sangfroid was soon replaced by shattered nerves and exhaustion. That, however, was not something the newsreels felt obliged to portray.

In Australia, the pervasive desire to emulate the famed airmen of the Battle of Britain caused a glut in the hastily assembled training program that took months to clear. Having signed on the dotted line, clutching a certificate and a badge that told the world they had indeed put their best foot forward, most volunteer airmen were then told to go home and wait. Sometimes it was for weeks, often longer. Eventually, however, the telegram would arrive, directing them to present themselves at one of the six Initial Training Schools spread across the country, where they would spend several weeks learning the basics of aerodynamics, navigation, and the fine art of marching up and down an asphalt square and saluting.

Barney Greatrex had to wait a seemingly interminable five months before his introduction to military life commenced on the last day of January 1942, when he presented himself to No. 2 Initial Training School in Sydney's Bradfield Park. Here, he was kitted out in a coarse, dark-blue woollen uniform, given the service number 413758 and inducted into the Empire Air Training Scheme's No. 21 course. Whereas many of his fellow recruits suffered an initial shock to the system, Barney found that his time with the Knox Grammar cadets and, later, the Sydney University Regiment made the transition to the rigours of the military relatively easy.

As the men proceeded to be instructed in the theoretical basics of flight in long lectures in stuffy classrooms, in the mess and the dormitories every evening Barney's new companions talked of little else but their brilliant forthcoming careers as combat pilots, preferably at the controls of fast, single-engine fighter aircraft such as the Spitfire. Almost all of them were to be bitterly disappointed. The Battle of

Britain was long over by the end of 1941, and the need for single-engine fighter pilots had severely diminished, even in endangered Australia. Despite their own country now facing the most dangerous crisis in its history, years of neglect by successive Australian governments had led to the RAAF having almost no aircraft of any type of its own to face the enemy when it appeared on their doorstep to the north. Hence, for some considerable time, it was still to Europe that most new Australian airmen continued to be sent, and not as pilots but as aircrew for the RAF's voracious and expanding bomber offensive, providing the navigators, gunners and bomb aimers required by a large, modern four-engine bomber such as the Lancaster.

Anecdotally, the means by which men were selected for these roles was varied, even arbitrary. Almost all were given the chance to state their preference at the outset in an interview, with the vast majority opting for fighter pilot training. 'Well, son, we have a wonderful array of fighter planes for you to fly,' was the droll response from a weary instruction officer to one hopeful young man, 'and they all have four engines.' Others recall simply being lined up and having their names read out under various categories: 'The following will be trained as air gunners . . . the following as navigators . . .' and so on. Others recall it as being even more random, with one's alphabetical listing determining at which end of the aircraft you would be sitting. 'Those with names beginning L–Z will be trained as wireless operators and air gunners,' reportedly announced one clipboard-clutching sergeant to an astonished group of men on parade one morning at Somers in Victoria.

For some, the disappointment was agonising. Having volunteered, many assumed their often lifelong desire to be a pilot was something akin to a right, and the realisation that this was not to be was crushing. Perhaps, however, if some of these headstrong young men had examined the statistics, they would have realised earlier that at most only thirty-five per cent of those accepted for aircrew training would have the opportunity to become pilots. Twenty-five per cent would be trained as navigators, and forty per cent as wireless operators/air gunners. Those who could not contain their disappointment were told not to worry, as they could always apply to 're-muster' for pilot training later. 'Later', it would transpire, turned out to be after the completion of an operational tour, which many would not survive.

Then there were the many handed the dream of training to be pilots but who would fail to meet the exacting standards and would find themselves re-mustering downwards to the other varied but also vital roles of the aircraft.

Barney Greatrex, though, had an altogether different experience. At his initial interview, when a jaded personnel officer once again prepared to write 'single-engine pilot' in the preference box, the officer all but dropped his pen when Barney expressed a desire to be the man whose job it was to lie down in the nose of the aircraft and release the bombs. Some men, particularly the quieter and more cerebral types, would occasionally request to be navigators, but it was almost unheard of for a well-qualified young man to request to be trained as a bomb aimer, a position that in fact did not exist in its own right at the time Barney joined up.

Early in the war, the multi-tasking 'observer' was expected to fill a variety of roles, such as navigating, monitoring the aircraft's mechanical systems and releasing the bombs as closely as possible to the target. Later in the war, with the advent of large and more complex four-engine bombers such as the Lancaster and the Halifax, the new and specialised roles of navigator, flight engineer and bomb aimer would all be created. Meanwhile, Barney would have to train to be the bomber crew's all-rounder, an observer.

Years later, Barney would reveal the reason for his preference, and once again it was pragmatic. 'I couldn't help noticing that the bomb aimer was in a marvellous position to get out of the plane,' he said. As the young cadets pored over magazine images of Britain's new four-engine Avro Lancaster, Barney noticed the forward escape hatch placed virtually under the bomb aimer's position in the nose. This, he determined, would give him the greatest chance of survival in an emergency. Three years later, it would prove to be an extraordinarily prescient decision.

Barney's training could now be fast-tracked, as no time needed to be spent on testing out along with hundreds of others for his potential as a pilot. His initial observer training would require him to become versed in all aspects of navigation, bombing and even air gunnery, with the bomb-aiming component to come only later at his Operational Training Unit.

In March 1942, he began a twelve-week course at No. 1 Air Observers School at Cootamundra in south-east New South Wales. Upon arrival at this somewhat bleak establishment, he was presented with his government-issue 'form A.73', a small, blue, cloth-bound volume issued to all airmen into which they were required to record the details of every moment spent in the air, down to the minute. This logbook became almost a sacred tome to any airman, and was meticulously checked by an officer on a monthly basis. Woe betide any airmen who failed to fill it in to the required standards. Barney's, still a precious memento of the Greatrex family today, faithfully records the beginning of his flying career on 9 March 1942, when in a careful – even cautious – hand he recorded his first ever flight, describing it appropriately as *Air Experience*. We can tell that this initial trip lasted one hour and ten minutes, was conducted in a de Havilland 82 Tiger Moth biplane – one of the most ubiquitous trainers of the war – and that his pilot on that occasion was one Sergeant Sinclair, who was in all likelihood as nervous as Barney.

The weeks that followed were a blur of almost daily flights and lectures, learning the difficult and intricate science of air navigation under the most intense crash-course imaginable. The relaxed pace of peacetime flight instruction vanished under the relentless machine of the Empire Air Training Scheme, where oceans of information that previously would have been digested over months were now required to be mastered in weeks, even days. Every professional peacetime flying instructor in the country was recruited for the task, with some even being dragged out of retirement to teach the basics to this new army of airmen and send them off to war. Their qualifications and experience, not to mention their temperaments, varied enormously. Some were placid and laid back; others were 'screamers', barking confusing and bewildering instructions without mercy, and seeming to delight in striking off young men who failed to make the grade. A large number of instructors were themselves serving RAAF officers, begrudgingly putting in their mandatory stint before being sent into active service, often wanting to be anywhere but where they were and taking out their frustrations on their students.

As Barney and all his fellow cadet airmen discovered, you kept up or crashed out, sometimes literally. Air accidents cruelly cut short the lives of a horrendously high number of nervous and inexperienced young airmen, barely across the basic information of how to handle their powerful aircraft. By the end of the war, a total of 2832 RAAF trainees had been killed in accidents, often lost before even leaving the country and having the chance to get at the enemy.

In his neat black writing, Barney recorded his progress: 'March 29, short triangular cross-country; April 4, advanced cross-country; April 14, advanced map reading.' On Anzac Day of that year, he successfully carried out a 'long cross-country' flight with a Sergeant McHugh in the cockpit, and a few days later underwent his first night flight, steering his pilot from the aerodrome at Cootamundra to Jerilderie and back, on a trip lasting two hours, thirty-five minutes. By this time, however, he was flying in that other training warhorse, the twin-engine, fabric-covered Avro Anson, a primitive aircraft by today's standards but a step up from the open cockpit of the Tiger Moth. On completion of this first course of his training, Barney had flown an incredible sixty-eight hours in daylight and seven at night in just under two very intense months.

From Cootamundra, he then proceeded to a bombing and air gunnery (BAG) course at Sale in Victoria, where he was introduced to the Fairey Battle light bomber, a truly woeful aircraft that had rolled off the production line in the mid-1930s into immediate obsolescence. Slow, and poorly armed, the RAF's Battles were annihilated en masse by the Germans when they were foolishly sent up against their Messerschmitts in France in 1940. After such devastating losses, the only use anyone could think of for the remaining ones was to crate them up and send them as far from the enemy as possible, preferably to the other end of the earth – i.e. Australia – where they perhaps could find some role in training. Hence, almost every Australian air gunner who served in Bomber Command at some stage had to put up with being thrown around the back of a Battle bomber, almost all of which reeked of vomit and leaking engine coolant, while attempting to fire an almost useless World War I–vintage Lewis gun at a tin drogue being towed by another time-expired Battle several hundred metres away. Not particularly surprisingly, the air gunnery skills acquired under such circumstances proved quite useless once the airmen arrived in England to commence operations, and many men were required to start all over again under the auspices of the RAF. Luckily for Barney, he never had to operate a gun in action.

The only salient memories Barney could recall of his six-week BAG course was a brief introduction to the use of a bombsight – again, completely superseded by the one he would actually have to use on operations – and the afternoon he dropped a piece of equipment over the side of the aircraft. While attempting to change one of the round and heavy Lewis gun magazines in mid-flight on a drogue-firing exercise, his pilot executed a sudden turn and the thing slipped out of his hands. He last caught a glimpse of it being carried away by the aircraft slipstream and tumbling towards a Gippsland beach far below.

Reporting it as missing by his own hand upon his return, Barney had strips torn off him by the gunnery sergeant, who demanded he proceed forthwith to go and look for this irreplaceable piece of government equipment. With no choice but to acquiesce to this ridiculous exercise in humiliation, Barney spent some hours filling in time, wandering aimlessly through the tertiary sand dunes over which he had flown that morning. Suddenly, his foot struck something solid. Looking down, he gasped in amazement as there was the missing magazine, looking none the worse for its journey from several thousand feet up. The respective looks of glee and astonishment on the faces of Barney and his sergeant remain, sadly, unrecorded.

Saying farewell to Sale without a great deal of regret, Barney proceeded to the final part of his instruction in

Australia, a night astro-navigation course at Nhill in the Western District of Victoria. Here, at least, he actually learned something and completed another eleven days and eleven nights flying hours, guiding his aircraft by holding a sextant while obtaining his bearings by the stars.

In August 1942, after seven months of intensive training, Barney found himself having come full circle to where his air force career had begun, at Bradfield Park, not far from his home in Sydney. Here, along with around fifty other young men of No. 21 Course, he stood to attention on the same asphalt square he had bashed up and down so often, to receive his new rank of sergeant, his coveted half wing brevet with a small B in the centre, denoting the role he was now qualified to perform: bomb aimer.

By the time Barney finished, more airmen were being sent to New Guinea and beyond to bring the war to the Japanese, and he and his fellow graduates still had no idea whether they would be flying in Europe or in the sweltering tropics. Primarily because of his father's upbringing, Barney's overwhelming preference was to be sent to England. It was a choice, though, over which neither he nor his fellow cadets had any control. Standing to attention, clutching the precious wing that would soon be sewn onto their tunic, the men with beating hearts listened as an officer read from a clipboard: 'The following will be travelling to operational units in New Guinea: Anders, Anderson, Andrews . . .' Then he proceeded to read from another list: 'The following will be travelling to operational units in the United Kingdom: Ambrose, Arthurs, Astin . . .' It seemed to Barney to be ad hoc at best.

Finally the man came to the Gs: 'The following will be travelling to operational units in New Guinea: Graham, Grieson . . .' The two men on each side of Barney let out an audible groan, while he waited for his name to be called, and began to have visions of jungle strips and dripping tropical humidity. But the officer remained silent and instead announced 'Greatrex, B.' would be heading to Europe. 'Those two boys were standing either side of me and were sent straight to New Guinea,' reflected Barney years later. 'While Greatrex went straight to England! So it was all just luck, you see.'

Over the next two years, there would be times he wished he could have taken his chances in the green jungles and the blue waters of the Pacific.

4

TO THE OTHER SIDE OF THE WORLD

In September 1942, virtually a year to the day since joining up, Barney began a voyage from Sydney to the United Kingdom that was to be anything but straightforward, taking seventeen weeks and at times verging on the comical. 'It wasn't like just getting to Mascot and flying there,' he said later. Nor would it be in the comparative luxury of one of the great liners such as the *Queen Mary*, which had been pressed into service for the duration of the war.

As he and a small group of about fifteen fellow sergeants from his course made their way through the chicanes of wire fencing and military bureaucracy at the wharf at Woolloomooloo in Sydney Harbour, small groups of mothers and sweethearts waved, or even snatched a final farewell kiss when the embarkation warrant officer could be impressed to look the other way. With kitbags across their shoulders, the men made their way down the long wharf at Woolloomooloo past vast grey warships and passenger vessels of every size. Their faces fell, however, as waiting for them at the far end was a small, somewhat battered and rust-stained cargo vessel, dwarfed by the other ships like a toy. With Britain crying out for more and more airmen, every inch of space onboard anything that could float was being utilised, even on an old refrigerated meat vessel like the one now in front of Barney and his mates.

Finding a bed or a hammock wherever they could, the men came out on deck for a final glimpse of their home town. Below them, frozen sides of meat, bound for England via South America and New York, were being loaded into the refrigerated holds. The irony of the cargo in light of their own situation was not lost on them. At last, in the late afternoon and with little ceremony, their small ship headed out of the heads before turning south. In silence, Barney and his mates in their blue uniforms watched the lights in the houses of the Sydney suburbs begin to come on as the dusk arrived. Silently, all of them wondered how long – if ever – it would be before they again saw such a familiar and comforting sight.

More meat was loaded in Melbourne, Adelaide and Perth before the little ship, now considerably lower in the water, ploughed into the Indian Ocean for the long trip to England. She got as far as Durban, and then promptly broke down.

'We all had to get out and go and camp in the sand dunes,' recalled Barney of this ignominious start to his war. Among the delights of the makeshift camp in which the men found themselves was a swarm of sandflies, which left rashes on thighs, groins and armpits that took weeks to heal.

After a week of torture, another ship was found, which made it only as far as Cape Town before she too broke down. Here, at least, they were billeted in relative comfort until a third vessel successfully negotiated the Cape of Good Hope and proceeded north to New York via stops in Brazil and Trinidad. If nothing else, the young men from their relatively protected pre-war Australian upbringings were seeing the world.

Nothing, however, could have prepared the young airmen for the world of New York City. Given ten days' leave to explore Manhattan, Barney, along with just about every other Commonwealth airman who passed through the great city during World War II, was feted, fussed over, escorted and ushered into nightclubs. The RAAF men sat in groups in their unfamiliar blue tunics and forage caps, an endless curiosity to Americans who, for the most part, had never seen, nor especially heard, an Australian before. Barely anyone from down under at that time was not, at some stage, complimented by an American on their excellent English, their hosts being completely unaware of not only where Australia happened to be on the map but also what language constituted its native tongue.

For the Australians, they were happy to mischievously fuel the myths of pet kangaroos, but the music and the nightlife were certainly things none of them had experienced before. So was the cold, which had begun to creep into their bones after crossing the equator. For all of them, it was the first white Christmas they had ever experienced, but the freezing temperatures of New York in winter were something even more astounding. One young pilot famously reported braving the frigid conditions while wandering around Harlem one afternoon, following the sound of a particularly expertly played trumpet. Venturing down a laneway and opening a side door, the curious young airman was met by none other than a rehearsing Louis Armstrong, who promptly asked him in and insisted he come as his guest, front row, to that evening's concert at an upmarket club on the Upper West Side.

Eventually, though, the partying had to end, and Barney was ordered to be ready to depart on short notice, to join the great armada of men and weaponry heading east from the New World to liberate the Old.

•

In a convoy of forty vessels of varying sizes, Barney headed into the North Atlantic. Around them, US and Royal Navy destroyers darted like gnats to ward off the ever-present threat of U-boat attack. Only the largest and fastest vessels, such as the 'Queens', *Mary* and *Elizabeth*, could outrun any submarine in the world and sail in relative safety on their own. For the rest, the terrible, constant threat of the 'crump' of a torpedo hitting their ship in the middle of the night, and the gnawing obsession of how, if at all, they might escape their steel tomb before it took them under in a death too ghastly to contemplate, made the notion of sleep nominal at best.

Barney's vessel was a requisitioned British passenger ship, more used to languid peacetime Mediterranean runs, now stripped of all fineries such as carpet, mirrors and comfortable furniture and pressed into the service of hauling back and forth across the slate-green waters and under the blackened skies of one of the most treacherous sea lanes in the world. Accompanying Barney and his handful of fellow Australians were several thousand nervous American soldiers, also heading further than almost any of them had ever been, to begin taking the war to the Germans, who were now reaching the zenith of their terrible reach across Europe.

Most men were given an onboard job, both to assist with the running of the ship and to ward away boredom and the debilitating spectre of submarine attack. Barney drew what must have been something of a short straw, being put in charge of the disposal of the ship's garbage. Feeding thousands of men in constantly rotating meal sittings resulted in literally tonnes of kitchen refuse, which was manually disposed of over the side. Upon Barney's signal, the bins were released in sync with the waves least likely to wash it all back onto the deck. Very often, he got it wrong, so he was constantly being covered with icy water and kitchen scraps. The waves, recalled Barney, were 'absolutely enormous', more wild and terrifying than anything he could have imagined. Even then, he began to perceive his senses being tested for what lay ahead.

Finally, on 15 January 1943, the convoy pulled into a battered and grimy wartime Glasgow. Unlike in America, little fuss was made of their arrival. These were just more unfamiliar faces in unfamiliar uniforms arriving to fight a seemingly implacable enemy in an interminable war. On the vast platforms of the Glasgow railway station, hordes of men stood in the freezing late afternoon darkness, trying to decipher the broad Scottish brogue of the female announcer, hoping the train they eventually boarded was taking them to London and not Inverness.

Heading south, the view from the grimy window brought Barney face to face with the realities of a nation at war, as city after city revealed the broken walls and ghostly, shattered houses of bombing attacks, particularly as they travelled through the more industrial midlands and on to the capital. Barney and his companions sat silently as the tableau of war rolled past. Soon, they knew, they would be the ones inflicting damage such as this. For the first time, their grisly purpose in going there began to sink in, leaving an uneasy taste in their mouths.

5

WAITING FOR WAR

With trained airmen arriving in Britain faster than they could be absorbed, the RAAF in October 1942 had been required to establish a holding depot, No. 11 Personnel Despatch and Receiving Centre, in the English seaside holiday town of Bournemouth. Here, spread out across a series of quaint and usually dilapidated Victorian-era hotels, the thousands of young Australian flyers eager to get into the war could do little besides stroll the local gardens, become acquainted with the local pubs and the local girls, and – often for months – wait. Occasional lectures, as well as a promotion to flight sergeant, broke up the tedium for Barney, but the normal routine continued to revolve around looking for one's name on the daily-updated postings board. Some airmen began to despair, fearing the war would run out before their number came up. They needn't have worried. The terrible potential of Bomber Command under its new chief, Air Marshal

'Bomber' Harris, was beginning to be realised, and would incur an increasingly alarming casualty rate. Barney and his friends, plus many thousands to follow, would be required to fill its ranks.

A handful of letters Barney sent home to his parents still survive, and they convey the sense of a young man impatient to begin the part he has travelled so far to play:

> . . . over here we are still waiting for OTU [Operational Training Unit] training and it's certainly very hard to find something to do here. The uncertainty of being posted has, in my case, gone on now for almost 9 weeks and another 5 weeks is on the cards too!

On at least one occasion, Barney would get a sense of the terror of an air attack when, on leave in London, he witnessed the aftermath of a minor raid:

> It was a typical 'hit and run' affair. Jerry achieving abso-lutely nothing but deeper anger among the ordinary people. It was all over in 30 seconds with piles of broken glass from shop windows lying all over the roadway, a few killed and injured with air raid wardens fussing about everywhere.

On 2 April 1943, Barney at last gave a cry of joy as he read the newly placed postings list on the big wooden board. There, finally, was his name, alongside his next destination: No. 10 (Observers) Advanced Flying Unit in distant Dumfries, Scotland. The very next day, he was on his way north, where he would reacquaint himself with flying after a long absence and begin his introduction to the use of a non-obsolete bombsight.

Barney was lucky to have been posted away from Bournemouth when he was. Despite being on the English coast across the Channel from occupied France, Bournemouth had escaped the devastation suffered by larger south coast towns during the Blitz and by 1942 had settled into something resembling the sleepy seaside atmosphere of the pre-war years. Strolling its parks and lounging in its canvas deckchairs overlooking the beach, Barney undoubtedly felt a long way from the war he had crossed the globe to fight. All that was to change, however, one sunny spring Sunday seven weeks after he had departed.

A fortnight earlier, in mid-March, Operation 'Chastise' had splashed across the world's front pages when a group of specially trained Lancaster crews daringly attacked some of the great dams of western Germany, breaching two of them: the Möhne and the Eder. Apart from the large number of civilian casualties inflicted, the Nazis regarded these 'Dambuster' attacks as a particular affront to their sense of invincibility, and retaliation was planned. While Britain's industries had demonstrated they could keep up with the supply of aircraft, the same could not necessarily be said for the men who flew them. What better way to strike at Bomber Command, they reasoned coldly, than to kill them en masse, while still in training?

Just before 1 pm, at a time designed to catch as many people outside enjoying a lazy sunny afternoon as possible, twenty-six single-engine Focke-Wulf 190s took off from their base at Caen, each with a single 500-pound bomb strapped to its underbelly. Flown by pilots experienced in lightning-fast, low-level attacks, the formation bolted across the Channel in minutes, made landfall just to the west of the Isle of Wight, followed a railway line into Bournemouth and then fanned out over the town. The raid lasted barely a minute but brought catastrophe to Bournemouth. One of the first bombs fell on a children's hostel. Then a bus depot was hit, then a cinema, a department store, and the offices of the department of trade. By far the greatest devastation was wrought on the Metropole Hotel, in which fifty-four people – including seven Australian airmen enjoying a Sunday lunch – were killed when a bomb entered through a first-floor window and exploded against a steel and concrete staircase. Bodies, and parts of bodies, were strewn across the adjacent street.

In bitter irony, the local Pleasure Gardens were then strafed by the Focke-Wulf pilots, who were particularly keen to mow down anyone in uniform but also killed women and children. The spire of a church was hit, which promptly collapsed into itself. Carnage and destruction were everywhere.

The German pilots made one single deadly pass over Bournemouth in a meticulously planned and executed attack that destroyed around fifty buildings and damaged thousands more. One hundred and thirty-one people were killed outright and many others would die of wounds, a great deal of those being airmen, who would now never reach their operational squadrons. Had he been made to linger there a little longer, Barney could well have been counted among their number.

That night, it was agreed that a scheduled concert to be given in the town's Winter Gardens by the Bournemouth Municipal Orchestra and conducted by no less than Sir Adrian Boult would not, as had earlier been proposed, be cancelled. The people of Bournemouth, in shock, their town still smoking, came out in defiance to listen to the performance of that most English of music, 'Nimrod' from Elgar's *Enigma Variations*, denying the Germans, at the very least, the propaganda victory of its cancellation.

The true devastation of Bournemouth that day was kept secret until well after the war, and the actual number of casualties was probably higher. Barney, meanwhile, would go on to resume his long preparations for operational flying, and in a letter to his mother, Elsie, he expressed relief at being finally back in the air:

> For about 3 months I have really only been filling in time. Now we have taken up training again and are actually flying. From September last year to April this year is a long stretch of idleness, especially after intensive training we did at home. Don't for heaven's sake imagine we all rush off and start bombing Jerry – it takes months and months of training for the specialised job we now do.

Barney barely knew the half of it. Having last flown in Australia seven months earlier, taking to the air in Britain was a very different proposition. At home, the wide open spaces of New South Wales made navigating from one land-mark to another relatively straightforward. Many Australian airmen who flew in the United Kingdom recall their first horrified glance at a British aviation map, with every single inch crowded out with towns, roads and rivers. From the air, it was even more bewildering, as every village and every church steeple looked identical to its neighbour. Finding your destination, or even your way back to your own rather insignificant-looking aerodrome, was suddenly problematic. Then there was the shock of the realities of British weather, with its constant squalls, low skies and utter unpredictability. Hopefully, however, for Barney this would be sorted out in the last step of his training before joining his OTU. Here, also, he would meet his crew.

6

FORMING A TEAM

Having completed course after course in myriad aspects of gunnery and navigation, amassing skills he would never be called upon to use in operational flying, Barney could have been forgiven for thinking himself somewhat over-qualified by the time he reached his penultimate destination before beginning ops, No. 27 Operational Training Unit in Lichfield, Staffordshire, at the end of May 1943. It was here he would say goodbye to the array of small and usually superannuated aircraft he had trained in thus far, and meet his first real aeroplane, the Vickers Wellington twin-engine bomber. This excellent machine had served as Bomber Command's backbone in the early stages of the war but was now being supplanted by the four-engine 'heavies', such as the Halifax and the Lancaster. It was also at his OTU that Barney had to find himself a crew, and in Bomber Command tradition this was achieved in the most haphazard way imaginable.

No. 27 OTU was a largely all-Australian outfit, established a year earlier to give the closest approximation to battle experience to fresh airmen before sending them to an operational squadron. In fact, nothing on earth could emulate the hell they were to endure, but at least the OTU gave the young airmen a sense of the importance of working as part of a team. And it was in the forming of that team that, counterintuitively, the relentlessly regimented patois of the British military suddenly gave way to an astonishing exercise in free-form logic, the so-called 'crewing up'.

Barney remembered it only vaguely in his interview but captured the simplicity of the process itself. 'We were all put into a big room,' he recalled, 'and told to form up as crews. Make a crew. And that was all.' In almost every other air force in the world, including the United States, bomber crews were formed by a dry but random process of administration. But in a flash of British eccentricity, the RAF allowed their men to work it out for themselves. At the beginning of their final period of instruction, around 70 men, most of whom had never met, and whose lives for the previous couple of years had been prescribed down to the minute by air force regimentation, were now told to get together and make one of the most momentous decisions of their lives: deciding who to go into battle with on a tour of thirty operations. No direction was given beyond a time limit usually of an hour, during which the men would be expected to coalesce into a seven-man crew to operate a Lancaster: pilot, navigator, bomb aimer, wireless operator and two gunners. The only exception was the flight engineer, who usually joined later at the Operational Training Unit stage. At the end of the allotted time, all airmen still unassigned would be then directed to form a crew by an impatient officer. There were, however, usually very few such stragglers, as on the whole the system worked brilliantly.

No airman of Bomber Command ever forgot his crewing up: ten navigators, ten pilots, ten wireless operators, etc., and double that number of gunners all together, usually in an aircraft hangar, mingling like high schoolers at a ball, trying to catch some look of quality or character in another's eye, something to give one a sense that this person might just be worth risking your life with. The pilots – who, regardless of rank, were always in command of the aircraft – were usually approached first, with a 'You looking for a navigator?', or 'Fixed up with wireless op?'. A little background was exchanged while the men looked each other up and down, before a usually mutual decision was arrived at. One airman might also suggest a friend and dash off into the fray of blue uniforms to pluck him out before he too was picked.

Although dominated by Australians in their distinct darkblue uniforms, No. 27 OTU also had its share of English, Scots, Northern Irish and every representation from all parts of the Empire: New Zealanders, Canadians, Rhodesians, and a smattering of airmen who had escaped from occupied countries such as Holland and Norway. Australians were a popular choice, particularly pilots, who – at least to the British crews

– appeared more as individuals and less bound by class and military traditions.

In surprisingly short order, the process was usually complete. Looking around nervously, Barney for the first time examined the faces of his brand new crew: an Englishman, a Canadian, a Welshman, an Irishman and, including Barney, three young men from Australia. Like many Bomber Command crews of the time, it was a fair representation of the international nature of the fight against Hitler's empire.

The youngest member was Barney's flight engineer, a new position brought about by the advent of the four-engine bombers, which required constant maintenance and monitoring of their complicated fuel, oil and electrical systems while in flight. The engineer was often the last to join, sometimes not meeting the rest of the crew until their first taste of flying Lancasters following OTU. Often they were drawn from the ranks of the mechanical ground staff and had the least flying experience of anyone in the crew. At age just twenty, Sergeant Maurice 'Mauri' Worth came from a place no one had heard of called Widnes and spoke with a distinctive Lancashire accent.

Barney was joined by two other Australians, Pilot Officer Allen Collins as navigator, twenty-seven years old and from Canterbury, close to Barney's home in the suburbs of Sydney, and who had for some reason picked up the nickname 'Curly', and wireless operator Flight Sergeant Reg Gill, twenty-five, from Launceston in Tasmania. These were joined by the Lancaster's two air gunners, Flight Sergeant Paddy

Rankin, twenty-two, from Dublin, in the rear turret, and a Welshman from Cardiff, Phillip Jones, in the mid-upper, who, at the ancient age of thirty-five, must have been one of the most venerable airmen in Bomber Command.

The senior ranking crew member, in Barney's case, also happened to be his pilot, a Canadian from Saskatchewan, and a more impressive leader it would have been very hard to find. At age twenty-three, Johann Walter 'Wally' Einarson wore on his tunic the blue and white stripe of the Distinguished Flying Medal (DFM), had come up through the ranks from sergeant to now bear the double sleeve ring of a flight lieutenant, had already completed a full tour of operations earlier that year and was now volunteering for his second, where he would go on to win the Distinguished Flying Cross (DFC).

The citation for Einarson's DFM, a decoration open only to non-officers and never awarded lightly, reads:

> This pilot has displayed the greatest possible determination to locate and bomb his target on all possible occasions. He has taken part in many long and dangerous raids on a variety of targets in Germany and Italy ... His calmness and courage have inspired great confidence in his crew and contributed to the success of many missions.

The war had already left its mark on Wally Einarson. While serving at his OTU, his Whitley bomber lost an engine and he was forced to ditch in the Firth of Forth. His crew took to the emergency dinghy and were picked up after a wet and miserable night on the water.

Eight months earlier, his twin brother, Harry, also a bomber pilot, had taken off in Lancaster Q-Queenie from his 207 Squadron base at Bottesford in Lincolnshire. It was supposed to be a relatively quiet night of 'gardening', a code for the laying of sea mines in the shipping lanes used by the enemy. Flying over the North Sea to Denmark, the younger Einarson dropped his mines off the Danish port of Thyborøn and was heading for home when attacked by a Dornier 217 night fighter. A fierce battle ensued, and Einarson's gunners returned fire. The German aircraft was mortally wounded but managed to find land, over which its four-man crew bailed out safely. Einarson's Lancaster, however, was not nearly so lucky and, along with its crew, vanished into the North Sea sixteen kilometres off the coast of Denmark. Of the thirty-four aircraft sent out that night, theirs was the only loss.

Whether Wally Einarson was spurred on by the loss of his younger brother to so brazenly dare fate and volunteer for a second tour, no one will know. Barney seems to have liked him immediately, describing him, despite his loss, as 'a very jolly, happy-go-lucky sort of person, who contrasted with the other members of the crew who were quieter and more reserved'.

After a month spent bonding with his new crew on all manner of practice missions flown day and night, learning their habits, their strengths, their weaknesses, even the smell of their sweat, Barney in July 1943 joined No. 1660 Heavy Conversion Unit in Swinderby, Lincolnshire, to come to grips with the aircraft he had pored over in photographs as a raw cadet back in Australia, the Avro Lancaster.

Although other types of aircraft were operated by Bomber Command during World War II – the Halifax, the Wellington, the Stirling and the Mosquito, to name a few – it is with the mighty Lancaster that it has become synonymous. When looking at the plane's statistics, it is not hard to understand why. Built originally as an improvement on a woeful predecessor, the short-lived Avro Manchester, the 'Lanc' soon established itself as a truly superb aeroplane. It was immensely powerful, mechanically reliable and, according to its pilots, a wonder to fly. Its four Rolls-Royce Merlin engines were the same that powered those other legends, the Spitfire and the Hurricane, and each delivered over 1600 horsepower. It was a forgiving aeroplane, could manoeuvre well for an aircraft of its size, but above all it could carry an enormous bomb load of up to 22,000 pounds, exceeding by a staggering factor of five the weight the designers intended it to carry. By way of comparison, the mainstay of the American bomber fleets, the famous B-17 Fortress, could not quite manage to haul 5000 pounds of bombs into the air.

At the conclusion of his air force training at the end of August 1943, exactly nineteen months since joining up in Sydney, Barney Greatrex's logbook records him as having completed a total of 313 day and night flying hours. Along with his crew, he was posted to B Flight, 61 Heavy Bomber Squadron at Syerston, Nottinghamshire. Finally, he was ready to begin flying bombing missions against Germany. No aspect of his extensive training, however, could prepare him for what was to come. Little did he know it, but Barney and his crew would be tested during one of Bomber Command's most difficult, costly and controversial campaigns of the war, staged in the long, dark, sub-zero winter nights over the Nazi capital, Berlin.

7

THE REAL THING

Barney's assigned squadron had already seen a good deal of war, having been reformed from a World War I fighter squadron in 1937, and was in action within the first weeks of this second global conflict. As part of what many considered to be Bomber Command's backbone, No. 5 Group, 61 Squadron had already taken part in several attacks of note, including the first large-scale raid on the German mainland in May 1940, then the first strike at Berlin in August that year, at the height of the Battle of Britain.

The squadron even covered itself in the rare glory of winning a Victoria Cross, when a young Scottish pilot named Flight Lieutenant William Reid performed one of the most astonishing feats of bravery imaginable on a trip to Düsseldorf in November 1943. Attacked by a Messerschmitt 110 on the way to the target, Reid was wounded in the head, arm and back when the windscreen of his Lancaster was smashed.

Ascertaining that the rest of his crew were unhurt, he pressed on another 480 kilometres towards the target and bombed accurately. On the way home, they were attacked again, this time by a Focke-Wulf 190, which raked Reid's Lancaster from stem to stern, killing his navigator and wounding his wireless operator. Losing blood, in agony and freezing to death, he managed to get his aircraft back to Syerston and land, despite one wheel collapsing on contact with the runway. As if this were not enough for the career of any bomber pilot, after a stint in hospital Reid joined the famous Dambuster 617 Squadron and was later shot down and taken prisoner for the rest of the war.

Barney and the crew were impressed by Syerston's established pre-war facilities, which were the envy of men stationed on the many temporary bases, hastily constructed in the early part of the war.

Not much fuss would have been made of Wally or Barney or the rest of the crew on their arrival at Syerston. Simply a brief meeting with the squadron adjutant, who would have looked them over, signed their names off on a list and allotted them an accommodation hut, recently vacated by a similar crew who had failed to return. A couple of weeks were spent getting to know the base and flying cross-country trips of one or two hours' duration, and generally being ignored by most of the other crews on the base. With the casualty rate of Bomber Command airmen being so high, it did not pay to form friendships with other crews, and most confined their socialising to the small group of seven men with whom they were required to fly into danger and catastrophe no less than thirty times, who would to each other become as bonded as family.

At around 10 am on 4 October, Barney's name, along with the rest of his crew, appeared on the battle order for that night. Reading it several times over, just to make sure, he swallowed hard with the realisation that he was about to be tested in his first op. Tonight, he knew, would be the real thing.

The rest of that day, Barney's head spun with all he had learned over the past very crowded year and a half. Minute details about fuses, wind directions and bomb selector switches raced through his mind as he visualised that long-anticipated but dreaded moment when, over the target, he would be effectively controlling the aircraft and releasing the bombs. A mistake at this point, he knew, would wreck the entire purpose of the trip, effectively risking his own and his crew's lives in vain. He took comfort from the fact that in practice it had all worked well enough. This, however, would be no practice.

With the announcement of a raid that night, the station went into lockdown, the gate guards preventing all comings and goings and the telephone lines disconnected to all but the most senior staff. Closed-door meetings would take place between flight commanders and the commanding officer (CO), who would be informed of availability of aircraft and crews.

All crews would, as soon as possible, conduct a short test flight to assure aircraft and equipment were all serviceable. Telephone conferences would take place between 5 Group

HQ and all senior officers on all bases designated to attack the target. Routes, diversions, take-off times, fuel and bomb loads, and a hundred other details were all calculated down to the finest degree.

Barney's briefing, as it would on all his trips, began with his pre-op meal taken late in the afternoon. On days such as this when it was 'on' for that night, normal time seemed to drop away into an irrelevance, reflected by the fact that most aircrew preferred bacon and eggs as their potential last supper. 'Can I have your egg if you don't come back?' was a common joke, its grim humour underlining the rawness of their mortality.

Barney would then report to the squadron's bombing section, where the bombing leader would issue him a green canvas navigation bag in which to store pencils, rulers and maps of the target's topography as well as known surrounding searchlights, flak belts and other defences. A dire warning would also be issued about the danger of 'creep back', when the itchy fingers of successive bomb aimers hit the release button a fraction early, resulting in the area of destruction ballooning away backwards from the target.

Still, the target itself remained a mystery. The skipper, by this time, would have a rough idea of at least the flight duration by the amount of petrol loaded into the aircraft's tanks, for which he would have to sign. Half-filled tanks meant a short trip; full tanks usually meant a long haul into the heart of Germany or beyond.

Finally, at the appointed time, all airmen headed for the main briefing room. In front of them was a large curtain covering a map of Western Europe. When all the crews flying that evening were inside, and the doors were locked, the curtain was drawn back by the squadron CO, and all eyes were drawn to the coloured lines of tape marking the prescribed routes to the target and back. If it was a 'hot' or well-defended target, a groan would go up from the old hands who had been there before. Tonight, however, everyone would be leaping into the unknown, as this would be the first major attack on the great German city of Frankfurt.

Along with his navigator, fellow Aussie Allen 'Curly' Collins, who was already busy with his own charts, plotting distances and turning points, Barney listened more intently than to anything he had ever listened to before in his life. Tonight, the CO told them, a new chapter in the war against Germany would be opened by showing them that none of their cities were immune to attack by Bomber Command. If cities such as Frankfurt had felt safe by their relative distance from Britain, tonight they were in for a shock. A little over 400 heavy bombers would be taking part in an attack on the city centre and the dock areas along the River Main. If the attack was carried out successfully, it could have a major impact on the course of the war – dramatic words that all but the newcomers such as Barney had heard before. His heart beat hard in his chest.

Then the briefing team arrived, specialised navigation, intelligence and meteorological officers all imparting information to give the crews the best chance of getting there and back alive. The intelligence officer spoke about known enemy defences of flak and fighter bases. Presently, the bombing leader spoke. Barney noted down meticulous details about the bomb load as well as its composition: a mixture of incendiary, high explosive and the large 4000-pound 'cookie' blast bomb hung dead centre in the Lancaster's capacious bomb bay. He noted the fuses that would be used, and the altitude at which they must be released for optimum effect.

Next came his aiming points. Pathfinders would mark the target areas with specifically coloured flares – two green, one red – which had to be noted and memorised. Barney also furiously studied the map and aerial photographs of the area, making careful notes on his own copy, registering any physical features that might stand out at 17,000 feet, even in the dark. The Germans were likely to set off dummy flares to confuse the bomb aimers, but these he must ignore. On his notepad, Barney underlined code words such as 'Parramatta' and 'Wanganui' – so designated by the Australian head of the Pathfinders, Wing Commander Don Bennett – referring to the newly developed airborne ground-tracking radar H2S, or special sky-markers that were to be used if the target happened to be obscured by cloud.

Above all, he was told to listen to the instructions of the Master Bomber, who, circling the target, would direct the attack over open voice, ordering adjustments in bombing and correcting aiming points, like a conductor of some macabre orchestra of destruction. The men were even told his name – which he was to announce – to avoid the chance of being mistaken for English-speaking German stooges. He was warned again to avoid 'creep back', and to wait till he was right over the target to release the bombs. 'Even when you're right on the money, give yourself another couple of beats, just to make sure,' said the bombing leader. Barney's hand shook slightly as he noted down every detail.

The CO then returned to the small stage at the front of the room, instructed everyone to 'stay on their toes' and wished them all the very best of luck. Finally, there was a quiet word from the OC of B Flight, which was composed largely of new crews, or, like Barney, those on their very first trip: 'Just stick to the flight plan, remember what you've been told, listen to your skipper, and always be on the lookout for fighters.' Barney would have taken this advice to heart, as the most lethal part of a tour was always the first five trips, before the crews could get the hang of it. As the saying around the bases of Bomber Command went, 'Survive your first five – double your chance of staying alive.'

With the briefing concluded, Barney gathered his maps and equipment and proceeded to empty his pockets of every personal item that could possibly assist the enemy in the event of being shot down. These were placed into a bag with his name on it, which, hopefully, he would retrieve upon his return. Then he was issued with his escape kit, including extra 'escape maps' printed on silk and easily concealable, currency of the countries he would be flying over, and a small passport-size photograph of himself wearing civilian clothes, which could be incorporated into forged passes and documents. This last item was to prove particularly useful in the months ahead.

Then to the crew room, where Barney was kitted out with flying suit, parachute and Mae West life preserver in case of coming down over water. A thermos flask of coffee and sandwiches were issued to each crew member for the trip, and then a small van took them out to the aircraft. Through the front windscreen, Barney saw his aircraft looming larger in the dusk like a great black beast as the small van, laden with silent, anxious airmen, rattled towards it.

Barney's Lancaster for his first op was coded N for Nellie, a relatively old 'kite' that had already survived a couple of tours. A good omen, perhaps, but on the other hand, thought Barney, all luck had to run out sometime.

Upon reaching the aircraft, Barney's first job was to stick his head into the open doors of the bomb bay and literally count the bombs. If they tallied with what was written on the form being handed to him by the waiting armourer, he was required to sign for them (a sensible piece of British military bureaucracy, he thought, no doubt designed to prevent him spiriting away the several tons of high explosive and flogging them on the black market!).

The crew would then board the aircraft and commence a series of pre-flight checks. The gunners would test their hydraulically powered turrets, the navigator would go over his charts and each man would check oxygen and intercom.

'All okay, skip,' each would answer in turn. Then came the pre-flight dialogue between pilot and engineer:

'Altimeter set to zero; pitch – fully fine; supercharger in M ratio; flap cover neutral; undercarriage lever locked down; main switch to ground . . . contact starboard outer' – and one of the great Merlin engines would cough and roar into life – 'check revs – 2800; throttle back to six pounds of boost; watch for mag drop,' and so on.

When all was running as it should, the aircraft was shut down again to a strangely deafening silence. The only man who did not test his equipment was the wireless operator. Even at this distance, the Germans were listening, and the simple act of turning on his big Marconi set could be detected by the ever-vigilant enemy, hundreds of kilometres away.

The seven-man crew would then leave the aircraft via the main aft door, stand outside on the grass . . . and wait. This, said many Bomber Command veterans, was the hardest part of all. Suddenly, and for the first time since learning of the trip that morning, there was nothing to do but wait for your signal to go, and contemplate what might be a terribly short future.

All around the aerodrome, Barney and the crew heard the pleasant English gloaming being split with the sound of aircraft engines. On 'big' nights, some men said, you could hear – even feel – the roar, deep and distant, from dozens of similar aerodromes to Syerston, dotted across the flat north-west of England, as literally thousands of aircraft engines warmed up in preparation to take off and attack their distant targets.

The crew would try to make conversation, ignoring the tension they felt in their gut. Some ritually urinated on the tail wheel for good luck. Others tried to pee but couldn't. Finally, the signal came, from a green Aldis lamp on a small van parked near the runway either flashing for the order to line up or shining steady for take-off. Sometimes, a flight commander not operating that night would race around in a jeep to each aircraft with a final, 'Righto, start up and good luck.' On hearing the engines come to life, the anxiety would briefly drop away. N-Nellie joined the queue of great black bombers lining up for take-off as the last light of the day disappeared.

Skipper Wally had to be careful not to overheat the touchy Merlin engines, which had a tendency to warm quickly when idling. Then, at precisely 1830 hours on a cool October evening, he opened up all four throttles, and the fully laden aircraft began to proceed and then roar down the runway. In his rear turret, Paddy watched the base recede and returned the wave of the few WAAFs and non-flying officers who always gathered by the runway to wish each plane off before it leaped seemingly vertically from the tarmac.

8

BARNEY'S TOUR BEGINS

Having been frantically busy all day, now, as the Lanc sped towards Frankfurt, Barney found that out of all the crew he had the least to do. It was a common experience of all Bomber Command bomb aimers. Allen was busy navigating, working out the complicated course to Frankfurt using nothing but a pencil, a wristwatch and mental arithmetic; the two gunners, Paddy and Phillip, could now test their guns, squeezing off a few rounds from their quick-firing but short-range .303 Browning machine guns; Reg was busy with his wireless set, sending and receiving plot positions, wind and weather updates; and Wally the skipper maintained a dialogue with Mauri the flight engineer on fuel consumption, oil pressure and temperatures as the coast of occupied Europe loomed ahead. Barney, however, was permitted to simply lie in his relatively comfortable padded position in the nose as the aircraft sped through the darkness towards the target.

He tested the rarely used front turret and, after a couple of hours, was required to start dropping bundles of 'window' from a special chute adjacent to his position.

This ingeniously simple device – strips of aluminium foil cut at lengths to match the wavelength of the German radar frequencies – was designed to create phantom contacts on the operators' screens, confusing and overwhelming the German night fighter defences. In the beginning, it had worked brilliantly, throwing out the enemy's carefully planned 'box' night fighter defence system. But countermeasures were developed, and its success was never thereafter assured.

On occasions, bomb aimers were called on to assist the navigator by calling out over the intercom any ground features he could make out or by monitoring the cathode ray oscilloscopes of the various navigation and airborne warning devices, with bewildering codenames such as H2S, Fishpond, Gee and G-H. They were imperfect at best – particularly the terrain-reading H2S, which, while a gargantuan leap of technology for its day, could barely distinguish between lakes and fields, or hills and buildings, giving its operators only a vague picture of what was beneath them.

As they now closed in on the target, however, Barney became the paramount member of the crew, positioning himself over the viewfinder of his Mark XIV bombsight. Beside him, on his right, was his all-important bomb selector panel, with its array of sixteen switches, dials and gauges. This 1940s-style mechanical 'computer' (it was the first time most of its operators had heard the word) used a combination of gyros and compressed air to calculate air speed and wind direction with reasonable accuracy, making the necessary corrections to calibrate the sight. With this information, Barney was able to fuse and select which bombs to release in which order.

At this point, Barney essentially took over the aircraft, by directing the pilot to fly straight and level. 'Bomb doors open,' he called, and a thump was heard underneath as the big aircraft's cavernous bomb bay revealed its payload. An illuminated vertical line appeared in Barney's sight, with a 'hilt' crossing it. 'Left, left a bit, skipper, a little to the right now, steady . . .' The rest of the crew remained silent as Barney's voice reminded them of why they were there, guiding the aircraft in small, incremental movements. Willing him to hurry up, some spat out a 'just drop the bloody things!' in frustration.

Only when the target passed across the hilt of the glowing sword did Barney press the 'tit' of a small hand-held release and call out, 'Bombs gone!' Instantly, the aircraft surged upwards, suddenly relieved of thousands of pounds of explosive.

Now, however, came the most trying part of the run: the twenty-second wait for the photo flash flare, timed to illuminate the scene for the aircraft's downward-pointing camera to capture the mandatory 'bomb shot' as proof that the target had been hit. Without such evidence, a crew's endeavours would remain unverified, and the trip could be struck from their tour and not count towards the magical thirty. But continuing to fly straight across the target with no leeway to weave made that twenty seconds pass like an eternity.

Finally, the flash went off and the photograph was taken. Barney immediately called, 'Bomb doors closed, skipper! Let's get the hell out of here,' to his greatly relieved crew. Now for the ordeal of the trip home.

All things considered, Barney's first trip went smoothly. Despite the relatively long flight of six and a half hours, night fighters were not encountered and Frankfurt's defences were overwhelmed, having previously been pitted against only smaller attacks. Out of the more than 400 aircraft taking part, ten were lost, including five Halifaxes and three Lancasters, representing 2.5 per cent of the total force – completely acceptable losses in Bomber Command's grim ledger. They would not often get off so lightly.

On the ground, however, it was carnage. The only clue Barney gives to the nature of this first trip are the words 'fire tracks' in his logbook. The weather was clear that night, and the Pathfinders marked the target well, making Barney's job easy.

Made a free imperial city in 1372, Frankfurt-am-Main was considered by some to be the finest intact medieval city in Germany, housing countless treasures of European art and culture. In little over half an hour on this night in October 1943, it was engulfed, in the words of the city's own report of the attack, in 'a sea of flame'. The old wooden structures along the wide River Main burned like tinder, wiping out centuries of human habitation in minutes. Worse, in the basement shelter of a former hospital being used as an orphanage, a bomb – possibly even one of Barney's – made a direct hit, killing ninety children and more than a dozen of the nuns caring for them. Later in the war, even worse was to befall Frankfurt.

The only surviving letter from Barney's operational period, written in October to his mother, conveys a more sombre tone, devoid of the boyish impatience of his training and perhaps beginning to accept the reality of his nightly incursions into hell:

We're doing the 'real thing' now. I wasn't going to tell you but I think you would rather know what I am doing and then you have no qualms as to what the risks are. I have been on several trips – over there – and have sent several 'cookies' on their mission. The first was the worst, I think everyone gets the jitters a bit before setting out and honestly I was no exception. When you see all Jerry's searchlights looking for you and the yellow flashes as the ack ack fires you feel terribly naked but soon the novelty wears off and you just concentrate on the target and try to get it bang-on and be able to say that it was a jolly good prang. Before Ops we get a proper tea – generally a fried egg & bacon with apple pie & ice cream and plenty of milk to drink. Then we all fill our thermos flasks with tea, before getting togged in our long silk-wool underwear and electrically heated clothing. After landing we again get an egg and sausage. At this meal everyone Messes with the

Sergeants – the CO had breakfast with us, as he always takes a great interest in how everything went. Then we all creep back to bed and get in six or seven hours sleep – a slice of your cake goes well at this stage, if we have any!

•

Bomber Command operations were like nothing else in the world: seven men, flying in darkness, relieved only by the dim orange glow of a lamp over the navigator's table or the faint green luminosity of the pilot's instruments, five or six kilometres high in bitter cold with the thundering roar of engines shutting out all other sounds except the occasional metallic crackling of a fellow crew member's voice in one's earphones. Although each man was bonded utterly to every other, it was an intensely lonely experience. There was no single moment of security from take-off to touch down; instead, the terrible constant wait for catastrophe and death that would come in an instant, all while having to give one's utter concentration to the job.

Having taken so long to start operations, Barney must have felt like he was now making up for lost time, crowding a lifetime's flying into a few short weeks. A couple of days after Frankfurt, he attacked Hanover, along with 504 other aircraft. This night, despite the elaborate and frequent changes of course designed to confuse the Germans, the Luftwaffe night fighter controller correctly guessed the intended target and despatched his aircraft accordingly. Arriving as the raid was progressing, the night fighters tore through the bomber stream, shooting down fourteen Lancasters and thirteen Halifaxes.

The weather was clear, and the Pathfinders marked accurately. Lacking the jitters of his first operation, Barney blocked out everything else on the bombing run to the target to concentrate on the correct combination of coloured target indicator markers (TIMs), which again and again he checked against his briefing notes. As he carefully called to Skipper Wally, who obeyed his instructions perfectly – never over- or under-correcting – he pressed the tit, and the aircraft seemed to moan with relief as the bombs fell free. Later, in his logbook, he once again recorded 'fire tracks'.

Barney was not mistaken, as, that night, Hanover burned. The target was the city's industrial centre, particularly the Continental tyre works, but Bomber Command's 'area bombing' practice was a blunt and indiscriminate weapon. Five-hundred-pound high-explosive bombs tore off the roofs of buildings, and then bundles of incendiaries – little more than half-metre lengths of pipe packed with burning magnesium that set alight everything they touched – rained down.

A large fire quickly developed in the centre and spread rapidly to the south of the city. Electricity failed, and gas and water mains ruptured, rendering fire hydrants useless. One thousand two hundred people were killed, crushed by burning masonry or asphyxiated as the voracious fire sucked the oxygen from the air. It was Hanover's deadliest attack of the war, but it would not be its last.

The faraway city of Leipzig was the next target, sending Barney on his longest trip to date – over seven and a half hours return. Loaded to absolute capacity with bombs and fuel, the plane took off into appalling weather on a trip that should in reality have been cancelled hours earlier. The 358 Lancasters of Nos 1, 5, 6 and 8 (Pathfinder) Groups became badly scattered in the high winds and icy conditions on the long and difficult run to the far side of Germany. Dozens of aircraft either turned back or failed to find the target. For those that prevailed, the bombing was ineffectual. Sixteen Lancasters were lost, each with their crew of seven highly trained men.

In November, Barney took off and for the first time headed due south towards France, with 313 other aircraft. The target was the railway marshalling yards on the main line between France and Italy, chosen to expedite Italy's departure from the war. On a trip lasting nearly nine hours, it was another milestone of endurance for Barney. In the difficult weather conditions, the Pathfinders dropped their markers slightly ahead of the target, which was surrounded by a steep valley. Even so, photo results showed major damage to the local railway network – damage that the Germans, however, quickly managed to repair. For the first and only trip of Barney's tour, no aircraft were lost on this night.

A period of leave in mid-November followed, and it was nearly a fortnight till he was airborne again. His next mission would involve him in the RAF's infamous Battle of Berlin.

9

THE DARK WINTER

The head of Bomber Command, Sir Arthur Harris, claimed that he could end the war by wrecking Berlin 'end to end' in a massive bombing campaign targeting its industry as well as its civilian population, and in the winter of 1943–44 he was given the chance to try it. If, Harris believed, he could repeat on Berlin the devastation wrought on Hamburg the previous July when a firestorm destroyed most of the city and 40,000 of its inhabitants, the Nazis' morale would collapse, followed swiftly by the regime itself, thus winning the war for the Allies. In each one of these objectives, he failed. Berlin was not wrecked, its inhabitants' morale remained intact, the war went on, and over a thousand RAF heavy bombers and their crews – the cream of Bomber Command – were sacrificed in the attempt.

If anyone's morale did begin to collapse, it was that of the airmen themselves, subjected as they were to months of flying in appalling winter conditions against a revived and confident enemy who inflicted unprecedented casualties upon the exhausted bomber fleets. The battle was not in fact confined to attacks on the capital but also took in a range of other German targets, many of which filled the logbooks of Barney Greatrex and his crew. The last op of the campaign, flown in late March 1944, was the RAF's most deadly of the entire war, when, against the formidable fighter defences of Nuremberg, no less than ninety-five heavy bombers were shot down in one catastrophic night. By that time, however, Barney's circumstances – and his war – had altered dramatically.

Bomber Harris began his assault on Berlin on 18 November 1943, when 440 Lancasters climbed into a wretchedly cold winter sky for the more than seven-hour trip to the capital. It was a virtual exercise in pointlessness. The harsh winter weather totally obscured the target, which was marked only vaguely by the Pathfinders, and the bombing was scattered and inaccurate. Barney, on leave that night in Nottingham, heard the massed throb of aircraft engines overhead, all heading due east towards Berlin. A few nights later, he would be joining them.

Barney later entered in his logbook, '22/11/43 OPS Berlin. Cloud at 12000.' A gigantic fleet of 764 bombers took off that night on this, the second major raid on Berlin in Harris's winter campaign. Unlike the earlier effort, the bombing this night was destructive and effective. Again, the target was covered in cloud, the weather being so bad that most of the

German night fighters stayed on the ground. Nevertheless, twenty-six British bombers failed to return.

For Barney and his crew, it was the most arduous trip of their tour so far. Their Lancaster, loaded to capacity with five tons of bombs and another five of fuel climbed through rain and even snow to be buffeted by sub-zero winds in the upper atmosphere. The cold was unbelievable. Even with their electrically heated suits, various layers of silk and woollen gloves, frostbite was common. The aircraft's internal heating system struggled to keep the temperature above minus twenty. Skin stuck fast to even the slightest contact with metal. Thermos flasks failed. Rations such as chocolate and fruit, needed to restore energy, froze to inedible blocks of stone. The toll on the body just to stay warm left the men enervated and exhausted. For the gunners, Paddy and Phillip, it was particularly arduous, as their vital role in looking out for the menacing shadow of a fighter slipping beneath the aircraft could not be relaxed for a second. When it happened, the long, dull silences over the intercom were shattered with the cries, 'Fighter to port, skipper! Corkscrew now!' Wally would instantly throw the Lancaster into a hard bank with full left rudder, sometimes even throttling back on the bottom engines while pushing up the revs of the outer two, twisting the aircraft even further. Some of the crew would vomit at the violence of the sudden manoeuvre. The danger of the aircraft succumbing to structural failure – losing part of the tail or even a wing – was great, but so were the consequences of being blasted by a night fighter's cannon shells. The statistics tell us that the overwhelming majority of bombers struck by fire from German night fighters were brought down.

Unlike many of the targets of Barney's tour, with Berlin there was nowhere to hide. Despite the complex changes of direction taken en route to confuse the German defences, sooner or later the Lancs had to turn towards their intended destination of the great capital, and usually for the last hundred miles or so it was obvious to the night fighter controllers that this was indeed the target. At this point, they directed their fleets of twin-engine Junkers 88s and Messerschmitt 110s with their Lichtenstein bomber-hunting radar sets towards the stream.

Over the target, Barney found the conditions gruesome. A small gap between the front turret and fuselage became a freezing wind tunnel that allowed the minus-forty-degree winds to blast him as he lined up on the target, or on what he could make of it – their own H2S sets could barely pick out any recognisable terrain. Fires somewhere below glowed through the dense banks of cloud, but the aiming point was anyone's guess. Like many bomb aimers on the Berlin raids, Barney didn't even bother using his sight. When somewhere over the flames, he could only hope for the best and press the release button. There was a slight metallic twang as the great 4000-pound 'cookie' blast bomb fell away, and the engines changed their note from strain to relief. 'A strange way to fight a battle,' thought Barney as he waited the interminable seconds for the photo flash to ignite – not that it would be yielding anything of use for the intel officer back at Syerston. This was a battle with no blood, no ground to take, no gun in hand – just a calculation of wind speed and direction from a small, primitive computer inside a grey metal case, and the simple depression of a button on a release as he lay on a padded cushion high above an enemy he never saw. 'That's it, skipper,' he would say, knowing that, seconds later, his tons of explosive would crash down onto factories, houses, hospitals . . . God only knew what.

Despite the virtual 'blind bombing' of many of the crews, this second raid turned out to be the deadliest on Berlin for the entire war, razing a vast area of the city, including parts of Spandau, Charlottenburg and the famous Tiergarten park. Unusually dry weather led to a series of firestorms that tore through the older parts, including the Berlin Zoo and the diplomatic quarter, destroying the French, Italian and, in grim irony, British embassies. Three thousand homes were destroyed, and the city authorities estimated 175,000 people to have been bombed out. Any visitor to Berlin in more recent times cannot help but be affected by the broken spire of the half-ruined Kaiser Wilhelm Memorial Church in the busy centre, standing as a ghostly reminder of Berlin's mid-twentieth-century nadir, destroyed on this night.

After the terror and exhaustion of his first attack on Berlin, Barney, though never a religious man, offered a prayer of thanks when, in the early hours of the morning, he felt Lancaster P for Peter's wheels grip the tarmac after the long flight back to Syerston. His night, however, was not quite done yet. Now, the crew must undergo the debrief, deliberately held as soon as possible upon their return, denying shock and exhaustion the chance to erase details from their minds. Still in their flying gear, the men, pale and blinking, emerged into the harsh light of the debriefing room, where an intelligence officer took each of them in turn through the trip. How intense was the flak, and where was it? Did you encounter fighters? How was the weather? How clear was the target? Did the Pathfinders manage to mark the target clearly? How accurate was your bombing? Did you see other aircraft going down?

With a cigarette shaking slightly between their fingers, sipping from an enamel cup of tea bolstered by a generous swig of rum or whisky, first the pilots, then the rest of the crew went through it again, moment by moment. Finally, with the words, 'That'll be all, well done, now get a meal if you like and then some rest', they could help themselves to yet another helping of fresh bacon and eggs that the tireless kitchen staff had prepared, then fall, exhausted, into their beds for several hours of dreamless sleep. When, later that same morning, Barney with still red eyes stood under a bleak winter sky before the operations board to once again read his name on the battle order for that very night, he could hardly believe it.

It was another attack on Berlin, and tonight the Germans would be waiting for them. Abandoning the ruse of alternative targets altogether, the main force of 383 aircraft headed straight for the 'Big City', as it was dubbed, cutting more than an hour off the previous night's trip, almost daring the German night fighter force. The Luftwaffe were up for the challenge, and they arrived over the capital to meet the Lancasters and Halifaxes just as the raid was beginning.

This night would also be a battle of the intelligence experts and the countermeasure science 'boffins', employing various ingenious methods to throw the Germans off guard. Broadcasting over the Luftwaffe's radio frequency from England, and sometimes even from within specially equipped bombers flying with the formation, fake German-speaking fighter controllers issued bogus orders, drawing them off or even getting them to land on account of fog at their bases. At one stage, in frustration, one of the real German operators, a male, was replaced by a woman – a move instantly replicated by another female voice in England. Messerschmitt pilots later described flying in confused circles, trying to determine the real voices from the pretend. Just north of the city, RAF Mosquitoes dropped the same type of flares that the German night fighters used to illuminate a bomber stream, luring them away in search of a non-existent enemy.

Once again, Barney swore as the accursed winter weather confounded his attempts to aim. 'Clouds at 12,000' is again wearily entered in his logbook. The sky-marker flares dropped by the Pathfinders floated down through the solid cloud cover but could only offer an approximation of the target's location and in any case were soon blown off by the wind. Instead, Barney aimed at the glow from the still-burning fires from the previous night's raid, adding further destruction and chaos to the city below. Another 2000 houses were destroyed, and up to 1500 people, it is estimated, were added to Berlin's death toll this night. Despite the efforts to throw the Germans off the scent, another twenty Lancasters were shot down.

Following this trip, Barney and his crew were given a two-day respite before once again paying a visit to the Nazi capital. It was another disastrous night for Bomber Command, and one on which Barney and his crew very nearly added themselves to the casualty list. In their case, however, the Germans had little to do with it.

More complex tactics were employed against the Germans this night as a force of 600 bombers took off from England on the evening of 26 November. Close to Frankfurt, 157 aircraft split off on a diversionary raid to Stuttgart to draw off some of the assembling fighters. Six of those, mainly Halifaxes, were lost. Meanwhile, the main force headed to Berlin, by which time they had become somewhat scattered, so the bombing was widespread but not concentrated. One casualty, however, was again the Berlin Zoo, from which most of the animals had already been relocated to other zoos around the country, but several large and dangerous creatures, including panthers and jaguars – no doubt already driven mad by the experience – escaped and had to be hunted down in the streets and shot.

Another 800 people died this night, but neither did the aircrews of Bomber Command emerge unscathed, with the scattered nature of the formation providing easy targets for the night fighters on the trip home. Twenty-eight Lancasters – over six per cent of the total force – were shot down, with another fourteen crashing through lack of fuel or on landing back in England, resulting in several hundred more highly trained young British and Commonwealth airmen failing to complete their 'tour'. The shaken crews who returned re-calculated the terrible odds stacked against them. With nightly losses rising to the six, seven and even eight per cent mark, only luck, they realised, would enable them to defy the stark mathematical impossibility of surviving their thirty ops. More and more faces Barney had begun to recognise in the briefing room or in the Mess simply began to vanish, to be immediately replaced in what one writer called 'a magic lantern show of changing faces'.

For a change, the weather this night was clear, giving Barney the first impression of the scale of the task in front of him. Below him, showing relatively clearly in a dull quarter moon through his freezing perspex bubble in the aircraft's nose, sprawled the vast mass of the city of Berlin, by far the largest he had ever seen. Even from that height, he could make out the parks, the churches and the great avenues such as the Unter den Linden, appearing as straight, dark arteries running through the all-but-blacked-out grey of the metropolis. It seemed to stretch to the horizon, and the sight was overwhelming. How, he thought, could they ever subdue a city such as this? Even a force of hundreds of Lancasters felt like ants gnawing at the sides of a great and obdurate beast. On the run-up to the target, the fighters, ominously, disappeared as the flak batteries took over. Miles below him, German gunners – some of the more than 50,000 extra troops brought in to defend the capital – loaded shell after shell in the breeches of their 88-millimetre guns, their muzzles pointed almost vertical.

No sooner had Barney spotted the red and blue marker flares and heard the voice of the circling Master Bomber stressing 'all aircraft, bomb on the blue, repeat, bomb on the blue' than he finalised the calculations in his bombing computer, selected and fused his bombs, and once more began his dialogue with Wally the skipper. 'Okay, skip, bomb doors open. Line her up . . . come over to the left a bit . . . that's it . . . steady . . . a little to the right . . .'

Just as he reached for the hand control tit, extracting it from its clip on the bomb selector panel, an enormous flash almost directly in front of him threw the aircraft up like a tossed ball. Choking cordite, sucked in through the gaps in the plane's nose, seeped into his oxygen mask and made breathing almost impossible. Barney felt something hot and sharp near his collarbone. The skipper's soft but firm Canadian accent sounded in his headphones. 'You okay there, bomb aimer?'

Looking around, Barney saw a piece had been torn out of the perspex blister and air was now whistling oddly through the front turret just above his head. It took a moment to gather his senses, still reeling from the shock of the exploding shell. 'Er, yes, skip, I'm okay. Not too much damage here from what I can see.' Blinking hard, he ignored the ringing in his ears and returned to the bombsight, which was still functioning. The shell had seemingly missed everything vital, and Barney continued with his bomb run. 'Come round the right a bit, skipper,' he directed. 'Target dead ahead, steady . . . steady . . .'

Barney jammed the little button in his right hand, and the Lancaster lurched upwards. 'Bombs gone! Stand by for photo flash.' Every man froze in the aircraft as Barney counted down the seconds, watching the blinks and flashes of more anti-aircraft fire erupting from the ground. 'Come on . . . come on . . .' he willed. Then, suddenly in his headphones, the urgent voice of Allen in the mid-upper turret: 'Lancaster right on top of us, skip! Turn to port now!'

With his excellent all-round view high atop the aircraft's backbone, Allen's value as a lookout was worth as much as the two Browning machine guns he operated in his gloved hands. Even when formations of Lancasters were perfectly coordinated at their assigned heights for the few deadly minutes over the target, mid-air collisions were frequent. This night, with the formation buffeted and out of order at the end of the long flight to Berlin, it was particularly perilous. Allen, peering into the night sky, rotating his turret constantly over the target area and trying not to look at the fires below to preserve his night vision, was probably a little stunned by the 88-millimetre shell exploding at the front of the aircraft. As usual, Skipper Wally had done a quick roll call over the intercom – 'Navigator okay, skip', 'Wireless operator okay, skip', and so on – but the flash had spoiled Allen's ability to cut through the wintry gloom. Seconds later, in his peripheral vision, he sensed rather than saw the weak moon suddenly vanish, followed by the great black shape of a Lancaster, oblivious to what was underneath, descending towards them almost directly overhead. So close was the other aircraft that

Allen could see the dull glow of the motors' exhaust stubs, and even make out the pilot's face, barely illuminated by the soft green light of his instrument panel. 'Port, skipper, port!' shouted Allen, dropping all pretence at staying calm.

Wally instinctively hit his left rudder bar hard and turned the wheel over. The speed of his response undoubtedly saved both aircraft and their crews, but a second later a ghastly metal-tearing crash reverberated through the aircraft, and then suddenly the noise of the engines seemed to drop away. 'Jesus!' shouted someone over the intercom.

As much as he tried to slide under the Lancaster, Wally's quick manoeuvre couldn't prevent the port wing of the adjacent bomber slamming into the starboard wing of his own. Barney could barely bring himself to peer through the small window above his bomb position. Sparks were cascading between the two wings, which for a moment appeared to be locked together. Shining metal, hacked by the spinning props of their two starboard engines, hung in shreds from the leading edge of the other Lancaster's wing. With another terrible lurch and a sound like a metallic roaring, the great black aircraft slid away into the night. Barney could just make out the now frantic expression on the face of the neighbouring pilot and the red letter codes on the side of his fuselage: 'PO', denoting 467 Squadron, an all-Australian unit based at Waddington in Lincolnshire. 'Another bloody Aussie,' thought Barney. For the briefest of seconds, he pondered whether he might know the man, and what he might say to him regarding his careless flying if he ever happened to meet him.

This same thought, however, could well have been on the mind of the other young man. Such collisions were frequent, particularly over the target as the great black fleets came together in concentration to release their loads on the target flares. Whether the other pilot was foolishly descending over the crowded target area or Wally had neglected to control the ascent of his suddenly lighter aircraft was never determined. In any event, such matters were immaterial, as now they had to get home.

10

BY THE SKIN OF THEIR TEETH

The wing of the rogue Lanc had smashed Wally's two starboard engines and torn gaping holes in the wings of both aircraft. By a miracle, there was neither fire nor explosion. Wally's starboard outer instantly lost its propeller, which flew off into the darkness, while the remaining right-hand motor shuddered violently, threatening to shake itself off its mount. If that happened, Wally would likely lose the entire wing. Flight engineer Mauri instantly cut power to both damaged engines and began as best he could to pump what fuel remained in the starboard wing tanks to the port. By this time, however, the aircraft had begun to dive. With such a sudden loss in power, the big Lancaster stalled and started to drop from the sky like a stone. 'Hang on, everyone,' Wally called over the intercom, as the nose lurched downwards steeply.

With only two engines now operating, the noise inside the aircraft was quite different from the usual deafening, monotonous drone of the four Rolls-Royce Merlins. Wally had to use the two working port engines gingerly to prevent the aircraft from going into an unsalvageable spin or breaking in half.

Down and down the Lancaster went. Mauri made his way the short distance from his position to the cockpit and helped Wally try to wrestle back the controls. Gargantuan strength was needed to pull the aircraft out of its lopsided dive. 'Come on, come on, you bastard!' muttered Wally between gritted teeth as the two men grappled with the control column. In front of them, the altimeter began to wind downwards like a deranged clock, yet still the strength of the two men was not enough to overcome the forces of the wind on the Lancaster's large control surfaces. Finally, Mauri put one booted foot onto the control panel and pushed as only a man whose life depended on it could. At just 3000 feet, the aircraft began to respond. First an inch, then another was gained back, and the nose began to lift. The altimeter slowed and, half in amazement, the two desperate airmen watched the gauges begin to return to something like normal. Elsewhere in the plane, five other men who had sworn they were living their last moments sighed quietly to themselves and wondered how much more of this war they could take.

With a chance to assess the damage, Wally and Mauri realised they were flying a very lame bird indeed. What they could see of the starboard wing was a mess – two dead engines, one missing its prop, and an expanse of torn and shattered metal. In the dark, Mauri tried to focus through the perspex greenhouse of the cockpit canopy. In the dim moon, he could make out the dead outer starboard motor, but nothing beyond that.

'What does she look like, Mauri?' enquired the skipper, as he regained some control.

'Hang on, skip . . . Jesus!' As Mauri's eyes adjusted to focus on that part of the wing beyond the far right-hand engine, he realised with alarm that it wasn't there. 'We've lost the wing at the starboard outer, skip,' he said.

Wally paused for a moment before giving a cool reply: 'Okay, thanks for that, Mauri.'

As they would later learn, the wayward Lancaster's props had sheared off a great chunk – twenty-eight square feet (around two and a half square metres), in fact – of the tip of their aircraft's right wing. How it was actually still flying was something the crew could not bring themselves to ponder.

The Lancaster was a superb aircraft; it could fly reasonably well on three engines and was even manageable on two, but with both right motors out the aircraft wanted to pull dramatically to the left and fly in a never-ending circle. In compensation, Wally had to keep his foot jammed hard applying full left rudder. To give themselves a chance of flying in anything like a straight line, he also needed to reduce some of the power to the remaining motors. This, however, affected their ability to maintain height, and with almost no lift being generated at all from the maimed right wing it was almost an impossibility.

Assessing their chances of making it back to England as slim at best, Wally tried everything to increase the odds. 'Righto, everyone, we need to lose weight. Throw out everything that isn't bolted down.'

For once, Barney found that he was very busy indeed. Scrambling back behind the cockpit and over the dreaded main wing spar, which formed a waist-high barrier at the fuselage's mid-section, he, Reg the Australian wireless operator and – when he could be spared from giving vital course headings – Allen the navigator passed everything they could pick up down towards the open door just forward of the tail. Ammunition, emergency escape packs and rations, axes, fire-extinguishers, spare oxygen bottles: all were hurled out into the void. At one stage when he dared to look out, Barney, in horror, noticed the moonlit countryside of eastern Germany a perilously short distance beneath him.

Mauri continued to pump as much of the aircraft's remaining fuel as he dared from the right wing tanks to the left, but as he did, Wally noticed the Lancaster lurching down on its now heavier left side. Manoeuvring his horribly unbalanced aircraft as best he could, he discovered that in fact he could maintain altitude, and at one stage he even gained a little height. They were, however, flying low and slow and alone over enemy territory. If one stray patrolling night fighter happened to pick them up on their airborne radar, they were doomed, and each man knew it. Ever vigilant in their turrets, Paddy and Phillip strained their eyes to cut through the dark, praying there would be nothing to see.

Looking at the map, Allen contemplated making a beeline for the relative safety of the open ocean due north and east of Denmark, but Wally was loath to keep the aircraft in the air a minute longer than necessary and decided to follow their assigned course home. 'Just keep me clear of Hamburg and the Ruhr,' Wally said, knowing the flak defences of those major centres to be formidable.

'I'll do my best, skip,' replied Allen, making a calculation with his wristwatch and a small notepad. 'Turn onto 282 . . . now.'

Holding his breath, Wally gingerly pulled the wheel over and kept his eye on the compass. Its two engines seeming to issue a note of protest, the Lancaster turned slowly onto the course heading and settled into the uncertain journey ahead.

As the hours passed in silence, Barney watched the white line of the Dutch coast catch the moonlight, followed by the usual display of anti-aircraft fireworks the Germans always put on to let passing British aircraft know they were there. This was usually the light stuff and too low to worry about, but not this night. At just a few thousand feet, oxygen wasn't needed, which was just as well as all the bottles had been thrown out anyway.

'How we doing back there? Rear gunner?' asked Wally at regular intervals, mainly to keep his men on their toes.

'All okay back here, skip.'

'Mid-upper?'

'All good, skip – coast of England looks lovely up ahead.'

In fact, Phillip couldn't see it yet, but he said he could for the sake of everyone's morale.

As they pushed over the North Sea, Reg began tapping out emergency signals on his Morse key, requesting a bearing and notifying England of the crippled state of their aircraft. As all of them knew, in such a condition as theirs, getting back onto the deck was often the most dangerous part. Another pale ribbon of sand flashed underneath them as they crossed the very welcome English coast.

'Okay, skip, head for Woodbridge,' said Allen. With its 9000-foot (2743-metre) runway, the RAF's emergency aerodrome in Suffolk had been built to accommodate returning and damaged bombers such as Wally's, even with vital hydraulic braking systems damaged or shot away. In such circumstances, once over friendly territory a pilot would give his men the option to bail out in relative safety, but Wally, glancing down at his altimeter, knew this was no longer an option. It would all be up to him.

Ordered out of his usual place in the nose, Barney assumed the emergency brace position with his feet up against the main spar and hoped for the best. It was not for no reason, however, that Wally Einarson wore the ribbon of the DFM on his tunic. 'All crew in brace positions,' he called over the intercom, as he watched the long black streak of Woodbridge's gargantuan runway seem to almost envelop him as he descended onto it. What the Lancaster would do when its wheels touched, whether its brakes would fail or its undercarriage collapse, Wally had absolutely no idea.

'Wheels down,' called Mauri with relief.

Still applying a great deal of rudder to prevent the unevenly powered machine from bolting sideways and cartwheeling, Wally dropped revs as much as he dared, suddenly unsure of the stalling speed. 'Here we go, boys,' he said reassuringly.

Eyes closed, with his head in his arms, Barney resigned himself to whatever was coming. In reality, something inside him was too exhausted to care. Almost directly underneath him, the big rubber tyres – first one then the other – landed with a thud and a deep squeak. With Mauri pulling hard back on the two working throttles, Wally gingerly hit the brakes to find they bit. Fishtailing slightly, but maintaining control, Wally avoided the swing and realised in a single unexpected and intoxicating moment that they were going to make it.

Standing outside the aircraft a short time later, the crew could now afford to make light of their ordeal, even joking about their skipper's prowess as a pilot. 'Is that all that happened to her, skip? Jeez, I thought we were in trouble!' and so on. In reality, the six men were grateful beyond words to Einarson, and silently in awe at how he had managed to handle the aircraft, hour after hour, all the way from Berlin. Using a small service torch, the men examined the wrecked starboard wing. It was worse than any of them could have imagined. Across the metal skin, some gigantic monster seemed to have gouged out great chunks, leaving trailing gash marks with its teeth. The useless motors appeared to have been taken to with a hammer, and, beyond the starboard outer, the wing vanished completely, leaving nothing but torn and exposed metal, even revealing the starboard main wing fuel tank, which, amazingly, remained unruptured.

As the aircraft cooled down in the winter air, it gave off a soft hiss as if panting slightly and exuded the smell of scorched engine oil. Picked up by a van, the men were congratulated by the station commander and asked who they were and what base they were from. They were then made to sign the inevitable paperwork before at last being allowed to retire.

It had been the most dramatic moment of the war so far for Barney, and still the night was not quite over. Finally taking off his flying jacket, he heard something metallic hit the floor. At his feet lay a small, grey steel pyramid about the size of a matchbox. Examining it closely, he could just make out small letters, then realised it was the cone of the 88-millimetre flak shell that had exploded just before the collision. Only now did he recall the brief feeling of something hot around his collarbone. Sure enough, on checking his thick lamb's wool flying jacket (Australian lamb's wool, he noted proudly), he found a small perforation and a scorch mark. Just a few inches higher and he would have copped it in the face. He showed the others. They too looked in amazement, and advised him not to ever bother buying a lottery ticket, as every ounce of his luck had been expended.

In the morning, with Wally's Lancaster P-Peter unflyable (in fact, it underwent an entire wing replacement and flew again), the sublime gave way to the ridiculous as a small

British farce ensued. Bemused to say the least, Barney and the crew listened on as the respective station commanders bickered as to who, exactly, was responsible for returning the crew to Syerston and who, exactly, was going to pay for the petrol. As tempers flared, the men cooled their heels for most of the day, until being eventually ferried the 170-odd miles (274 kilometres) back to Syerston in a passing Halifax.

Very little fuss was made of their ordeal upon their late return to Syerston. The intelligence officer even seemed slightly annoyed at having to conduct a debrief at this unscheduled hour. Two months later, though, in *The London Gazette*, the following citation appeared for the awarding of the DFC:

January 23, 1944.

Flying Officer Johann Walter EINARSON, D.F.M. (Can/J. i7276), Royal Canadian Air Force, No. 61 Squadron.

This officer has completed a very large number of sorties including five attacks on Berlin. On the last occasion one night in November 1943, his aircraft was hit by anti-aircraft fire and sustained damage. Nevertheless, Flying Officer Einarson pressed home his attack. Soon after the bombs had been released, the aircraft was struck, the starboard wing tip and part of the aileron were torn away and the aircraft went into a steep dive. Flying Officer Einarson succeeded in regaining control and afterwards flew safely to an airfield in this country. Throughout his tour of operations this officer has invariably displayed a high degree of skill, courage and determination.

Although, for morale purposes, the official citation omitted to mention that they had been 'struck' in fact by a friendly aircraft, Wally Einarson would have another ribbon to sew onto his battle dress tunic, that of the DFC. Barney, for his part, would simply have another story of survival to tell, and another almost absurdly understated entry in his logbook to fill in: '26/11/43 OPS BERLIN. COLLIDED WITH A/C FROM 467 SQD. 28 SQ FT STARBOARD WING OFF.'

11

BACK ON OPS

In December 1943, the weather got worse, and Barney's tour quietened down somewhat, with only two trips being flown on 16 and 29 December – both, once again, to Berlin. Reflecting the almost overwhelming sense of scale Barney had felt when, at least briefly, the clouds had cleared over the Big City on the night of the collision, Bomber Command too must have begun to realise that the German capital was not going to be subdued as planned. On 2 December, another 458 Lancasters climbed into the night to attack, and forty of them did not return, representing 8.7 per cent of the force. One Australian squadron, 460, on this night lost five of its twenty-five Lancasters, one of which was carrying two prominent newspaper reporters from the London *Daily Mail* and Norman Stockton from the Sydney *Sun*. His body is buried alongside the airmen on whom he was reporting, in the Berlin War Cemetery. Again, the German fighter controllers guessed the target early and shook their heads in disbelief as their radar images showed the British bombers not even attempting to conceal their destination. Damage to Berlin that night was negligible.

It was not for another fortnight that the weather made any further attempt at Berlin possible. Sitting in the briefing room, waiting once again for the curtain to be drawn back to reveal the target, Barney Greatrex realised that in just two months he had completed the journey from novice to veteran. There was no sharp edge of nerves now – that had diminished after the first couple of trips. Now there was just a solid lump of quiet but immovable fear sitting at the bottom of his gut.

He glanced around at the new faces that every day now were taking the places of the old. With some of the newer ones, he did not even make eye contact. Nor was he any longer shocked by the grim turnover. True feelings were best locked away, to the point where the loss of a crew and its seven men, with whom one may have chatted the previous morning over eggs and bacon, was treated as little more than an inconvenience, with a 'Too bad . . . sorry about old so-and-so . . . rotten luck', and so on.

The false jollity of the station commander did nothing to wash away the general air of cynicism in the room. 'Well, tonight,' he announced, drawing the curtain, 'you lucky fellows are off to . . . you guessed it . . . Berlin!' An unconcealed groan went up and expletives were mouthed. 'We've got them wobbling on their feet and now we just have to deliver the knockout,' the officer assured them, using the tired old boxing analogy and spouting the bravado of the daily BBC radio reports of supposedly massive damage being done to the enemy capital. Barney didn't believe a word of it. Half the time, he didn't even know what he was aiming at, let alone hitting, and the other crews felt the same. Yet, on 16 December, in a new aircraft with call sign V for Victor, he took off with 483 aircraft and once again headed to Berlin.

It was another nightmare op. The German fighters encountered some of the Lancasters as early as the Dutch coast, and more were waiting at the target. In the nose, Barney watched silent flashes of tracer being fired from fighters and returned by the bombers' gunners. Occasionally, a great flash would appear in the night sky. 'Scarecrow at ten o'clock, skip,' answered by, 'Thanks, bomb aimer, I see it'. It was believed that the Germans had a devilish weapon designed to sap airmen's morale in the form of a gigantic shell sent skywards to replicate an exploding aircraft. Sometimes two or three in a trip seemed to be used. These 'scarecrows', as the RAF dubbed them, were an impressive sight, but all believed them to be a ruse. After the war, it was discovered that the Germans in fact had no such weapon, and these 'scarecrows' were in fact actual aircraft exploding mid-air, hit by anti-aircraft or fighters, vaporising in a blast of fuel and bombs, invariably taking seven brave men with them. Night fighters, however, remained the bombers' hoodoo. So far, apart from one or two sightings, Barney and the crew had managed to escape their seemingly omnipresent attention. Barney was starting to wonder how much longer his luck would hold.

Barney would record that Berlin was again cloud-covered to 10,500 feet over the target. He and the rest of the force bombed on the Pathfinders' cloud markers, but later analysis revealed that almost no industrial damage was done, and the Germans were unable to conclude what had even been the aiming point. Unless, of course, it had been the now destroyed National Theatre, a building housing the country's political and military archives, or a train crowded with forced labourers from the east, seventy of whom were killed when a bomb made a direct hit as it stood idle at a railway station.

The fighters were largely avoided by the main force, who took a northerly route over Denmark, but low cloud caused mayhem on their return to their bases in England. Twenty-nine bombers crashed or were abandoned by crews bailing out. This, in addition to the twenty-five lost to enemy action this night, accounted for the deaths of another 148 men.

On the third-last night of 1943, Barney made his fifth trip to Berlin – another inconclusive re-run of the previous four. At least, though, he was surviving. He didn't dare to think about the prospects of surviving his tour. He hit the Big City again on New Year's Day – another messy raid that neither aimed for nor hit anything in particular, the bulk of the bombs of the 420-strong force landing in the Grunewald forest, south-west of the city. Still, twenty-eight Lancaster crews were marked down as 'missing' the next morning.

On 5 January 1944, Barney and his crew undertook their longest trip to date, with a nearly nine-hour round trip to Stettin, in what is now Poland but was then a German Baltic city near the Polish frontier. Whatever was being aimed at, the practice of 'creep back' pulled the bombing to the west of the city, wiping out hundreds of houses, sinking eight ships in the harbour and killing 244 people. For a change, Barney could see it all, writing the dry observation of 'ground detail' in his logbook.

It was a much more active night for Barney's boss, 61 Squadron's CO, Wing Commander Reggie Stidolph, from Rhodesia. This remarkable officer had so far done his best to expend most of his nine lives in three theatres of war: the Western Desert, the Burma campaign and then in Europe with Bomber Command. Flying Blenheims earlier in the war, he often sustained hits to his aircraft, but they were never quite mortal. His luck nearly ran out, however, this night over Stettin when attacked by a very fast Messerschmitt 210, which his wireless operator picked up on their 'Monica' radar, and which the gunners failed to see until they were being fired upon. Holes were blasted in the tail fin and elevator, and one engine was ablaze. His gunners eventually fired back, and reported the night fighter pulling away with smoke pouring from one engine.

Bringing his crippled Lancaster, dubbed 'Just Jane', back on two engines after ten hours of flying, Stidolph later discovered that a mere eight and a half gallons remained in his tanks – enough for half a circuit of the base at best. He was awarded an immediate DFC, and his signature adorns the monthly flight time tallies of Barney's logbook.

•

Because of bad weather – too bad even for Bomber Command – as well as enduring a minor accident, Barney enjoyed a comparative rest from operations, flying just once over the next four weeks. With the Big City deep in the grips of what for Berliners must surely have been one of the most dreadful winters imaginable, Arthur Harris was forced to pause his attacks, possibly even realising that his much-vaunted promise to crack the city wide open might not, after all, come to pass.

Barney and his crew spent several weeks propping up the bars of the local Nottingham pubs, quietly looking to the heavens and thanking the weather. Only once, on 21 January, did the battle order summon them aloft, again to Berlin.

Owing to the city's usual winter garb of impenetrable cloud, just where the bombs of the 769 attacking aircraft actually fell is a mystery. Photo flashes in such conditions were not required and would have been useless anyway, but the German authorities recorded no bombs falling on the Berlin area this night at all. It has been suggested that the entire force, relying largely on their terrain-reading H2S radar, could have been hopelessly off-target. Thirty-five aircraft, however, remained unaccounted for the next morning.

Shortly afterwards, Barney took to his bicycle to explore some of the surrounding byways, as well as some of the favoured watering holes of Lincoln. On one such afternoon, he took an icy country corner a little too hard in the short afternoon light and landed nastily, breaking a tooth on the hard turf. This was followed by a nasty bout of impetigo, a superficial facial infection. Flying into the face of anti-aircraft guns and Nazi night fighters had so far not managed to lay a glove on Barney Greatrex, but a quiet English country lane laid him up in the squadron hospital for a fortnight.

While he was recuperating, the attacks on Berlin resumed, including two on consecutive nights at the end of January that again brought patchy results, the main concentration of bombs seeming to fall on housing districts. It would not be until 15 February that Barney would resume operations, and as he took off that night for another battle over Berlin, he reflected, with some dismay, that after what seemed like an eternity since beginning operations he was still only halfway through his tour. What he did not know, however, was that this would be his last trip to the Big City.

Harris this night, possibly with a sense of despair, threw all that he could at Berlin, mustering an enormous force of nearly 900 four-engine bombers, including a record number of 300 Halifaxes. It was also a record for the amount of bombs dropped – 2642 – and damage was extensive, with hundreds of fires reported, destroying nearly 1000 houses. Civilian casualties were diminishing, largely due to a thorough evacuation program, but even on a night like this, Berlin and the Nazi regime showed not the slightest sign of the cracks Harris had so long predicted.

When the crews filed into the briefing room on the afternoon of 19 February, a somewhat macabre cry of reprieve went up as the curtain revealed a target that was not Berlin for a change but the even more distant Leipzig. Their relief was misplaced. This was a terrible raid for Bomber Command, with the predicted winds not appearing and many aircraft arriving over the target early and then having to circle to wait for the Pathfinders to mark it. Four aircraft were lost in subsequent collisions and, with aircraft circling overhead, the German flak had a field day, shooting down twenty bombers. But Barney's luck continued to hold. As he felt the Lancaster's wheels touch the runway back at Syerston, he began to wonder if he might just make it through his tour after all, but quickly suppressed the notion out of superstition.

He felt the same after trip number nineteen to the German ball-bearing works at Schweinfurt, where the force of 734 were divided into two sections, staggered by a two-hour interval. The first section took most of the casualties from the night fighters. Barney was in the second and, once again, made it home.

It was in fact rare that Barney was placed on the battle order two nights in a row, but after a fitful sleep on the morning of 25 February, his shoulders sunk as he read his name once again. He and the crew were 'on' again that night. He had not the slightest idea that chilly winter morning that it would be the very first part of the greatest and most terrible adventure of his life. As Barney himself recalled years later, 'February 25th, 1944 is a date which is not likely to fade from my memory.'

12

BARNEY'S FINAL TRIP

'Gentlemen, tonight we are visiting Augsburg,' announced the CO with his usual irritating jauntiness at the briefing. For once, there was no eruption of catcalls and groans from the collected airmen of 61 Squadron, simply a curious echoing of the name. Augsburg? Barney had no idea what to expect from this old German city he had barely heard of as he had never been there before, and nor had anyone else in the room.

The reasons behind Bomber Command's selection of targets during World War II were varied, ranging from a need to pinpoint specific industries, such as the ball-bearing manufacturers at Schweinfurt, to vast campaigns of largely indiscriminate destruction such as those visited upon Cologne, Hamburg and, less successfully, Berlin. Then there were the places that were attacked largely because they were next on the ever-shortening list drawn up at the beginning of the war by high-level strategists within the RAF and the British

Government. Exactly what was being attacked at Darmstadt in September 1944, for example, remains obscure, but the horrific firestorm, mass civilian casualties and utter destruction of this beautiful baroque centre at least allowed Bomber Command to cross it off its list of doomed German cities.

The attack on Augsburg in Germany's south seems to fall somewhere in the middle of these. There was some industry located there, such as part of the MAN diesel engine works and the Messerschmitt aircraft company, but these were largely missed by the force of 594 aircraft that attacked it on 25 February. The bombing was considered accurate, with the beautiful heart of the ancient city being completely destroyed, along with nearly 3000 houses, countless art treasures, sixteen churches and a number of hospitals. With the temperature being minus eighteen degrees, the River Lech froze, confounding the efforts of the fire services to extinguish the myriad fires that took hold of the old wooden buildings. Around 700 people were killed and tens of thousands bombed out. Twenty-one British aircraft were lost, and the Germans were quick to publicise it as an extreme example of the RAF's 'terror raids'. However, Barney Greatrex's bombs for once played no part in the destruction. By the time the bombers were over Augsburg, Barney was on the ground – cold, frightened and very much alone.

Zero hour that evening was 1830 hours. Climbing from Syerston in Lancaster LL775, O for Orange – a kite they had used on most of their recent trips and which was now becoming familiar – Barney contemplated the milestone of this, his twentieth operation, two-thirds of the way through his tour. The end of it was now beginning to seem possible, even tangible. In his headphones, navigator Allen 'Curly' Collins announced in his always cheerful voice their first course heading, to Reading, near Oxford. Barney remembered a burned golden winter sun setting in a sea of cloud, diffusing the English countryside with a soft blanket of pink. From his view from the perspex observation blister in the canopy, he found the notion of war at that moment quite alien. Then, looking to port, he saw the black outlines of two other Lancasters climbing, like him, through 19,000 feet.

In the cockpit, Skipper Wally Einarson was also pondering his future, which at this moment felt strangely positive. Few airmen possessed the mettle to voluntarily put themselves through a second tour in Bomber Command, but Flight Lieutenant Einarson was one of those. Pilots vary in their recollections of the pressure applied to volunteer for a second tour. Some say it was subtle; others less so. Either way, most men were more than happy not to tempt fate beyond the thirty. As an incentive, second-tour pilots had only to complete twenty extra trips before being allowed to stand down, making this one to Augsburg Einarson's last. His crew still had another ten to survive and silently contemplated adjusting to life with a new skipper. No one, of course, dared discuss this, with Einarson or even among themselves. In the rampant super-stitions of bomber crews confronting their mortality on a nightly basis, raising such a topic would be seen as tempting fate well beyond the margin of safety.

A mile or so to their port side, Beachy Head slipped away below. 'How we going, navigator?' asked Wally as the sandy line of the French coast appeared faintly ahead. All was well, reported Curly, despite their being a few minutes late. This wouldn't be a problem as they were in the first of three waves, with a three-minute lag between each. They would eventually simply merge into the second wave of bombers.

As they approached France, Barney slipped into his position in the nose, making one of his few regular announcements, but one that always tempered the atmosphere: 'Enemy coast ahead, skipper.' The cloud cleared over France, giving way to a dense haze that rose to 21,000 feet, making visual observation difficult. Looking down through the nose blister, Barney could just make out some of the street lights as they passed over the champagne city of Rheims. For the next hour, the usual strict intercom silence was observed, broken only by Curly's course heading corrections to Wally. 'Okay, skip, course coming up . . . turn onto 162 . . . now,' and so on.

Three hours into the flight, just short of the city of Nancy, where they would swing south towards the bottom of Germany, wireless operator Reg Gill's voice broke the silence. 'Er, skip . . .' Something in his tone of suppressed urgency sent a chill through Barney. 'Getting a reading here of . . . something . . . approaching us from behind.' With his eyes attuned to the subtleties of the wavering lines of the cathode ray tube in front of him, Reg could not be sure whether what he was seeing was ground interference from the Germans or something more sinister.

The senses of each member of the crew sharpened, but particularly of the two gunners, Paddy and Phillip, who now began combing every inch of the sky to the rear with even more intensity. After a pause that seemed to last an eternity, Reg spoke up again. 'Yep, something there, skip. One thousand yards.'

This time, Wally replied. 'Gunners? Anything?'

'Not a thing, skip.' This was not surprising, considering the thick, cloying haze that enveloped them. Still, they rotated their turrets with the hand-grip controls, fingers poised on the trigger to fire at anything they saw emerge from the gloom.

Suddenly, Reg's voice sounded more emphatic. 'Nine hundred yards now, skip ... 800 ... 700 ...' Just as Wally began to ask the gunners something, Reg's voice cut in again, this time with unconcealed urgency. 'For Christ's sake, get weaving, skip, the kite's only 600 yards to the port quarter.'

Years later, Barney would reflect, 'These were the last words I heard spoken in the aircraft.' Whatever it was Wally might have been planning to do, he had left it too late.

Just under an hour earlier, 200 kilometres away, a Messerschmitt 110 twin-engine night fighter had taken off from its base at Finthen aerodrome near the German city of Mainz. Its three-man crew included Oberfeldwebel (Sergeant) Heinz Fitzner as both air gunner and flight engineer; wireless operator Oberfeldwebel Friedrich Meyer, and pilot Oberleutnant (Senior Lieutenant) Wilhelm Engel, who, in early 1944, was well on his way to being a night fighter ace. Scrambled to intercept the bomber stream picked up by the ground radar, the plane was sent in a south-westerly direction. Making wide-ranging figure-of-eights, Engel cursed the mist, willing the night to clear.

'Enemy formation now heading south-east,' his operator informed him in his headphones.

'Anything?' he asked wireless operator Meyer, who was glued to the Lichtenstein airborne radar screen.

'Nothing,' was the reply. Facing the prospect of a wasted flight, Engel cursed. 'Just a second,' returned Meyer, 'contact up ahead. I think it's a big one, maybe a Lanki.' Engel's night vision, always sharp, focused through the windshield. 'Closer now . . .' said Meyer. Then Engel saw it: the big black shape with the distinctive twin tail.

He held back a little. No evasive action on the part of the Lancaster could be observed, so he guessed he had not yet been seen. 'Attacking,' the pilot said to his crew, and he dropped altitude slightly. He knew the routine: drop behind, and then come up from below and fire into the wing tanks between the motors, hoping that the four machine guns in the rear turret were not about to blast him at close range. He knew many crews that had already suffered that particular fate. At just a few hundred yards, he opened up with his cannon. It was a lucky shot, and his very first rounds hit home, igniting the wing immediately.

Barney felt the aircraft shudder. Suddenly, the lighting system went out. Glowing lights of tracer bullets, like incandescent insects, flashed by just forward of the nose. The stink of cordite filled his nostrils. A flash, then a bright glow to his right made him turn to the small observation window. In an instant, he caught sight of the two starboard engines ablaze. Then, like being on a terrible roller-coaster, the aircraft began to drop.

Decades later, Barney would learn the identity of the German pilot who attacked Lancaster O-Orange over Nancy that night. But for now, it was just a sudden and anonymous strike from the shadows. Barney looked behind him and barely made out the figure of Mauri Worth, the flight engineer, gesturing towards the escape hatch, indicating there was no time to lose. Expecting him to then come forward and use it himself, Barney was alarmed to see Mauri turn away towards the interior of the crippled aircraft and disappear. It was the final glimpse he would ever have of any of his crew again.

With only the port motors running, O-Orange began to spiral down in an intense half-glide, a death spin that Einarson was unable to control. Instantly, Barney was thrown against the left-hand side of his bomb compartment as the extreme centrifugal forces took hold of the aircraft and himself. No sound could be heard above the shrieking whine of the overstrained engines. The stress on the airframe meant that its integrity could fail at any second. Every loose object was now flying around inside the fuselage. On and on it went, the aircraft still seeming to drop like a stone.

Having no idea of what height he was at, Barney expected to meet the ground, and oblivion, at any second, but instead summoned what strength he could to pull at the escape hatch door at his feet. It moved slightly in his hand, but with another jolt of the aircraft Barney actually found himself pinned against it. In an impossible position, he struggled, pulling at the thing against his own weight desperately, but sensing hope begin to fade. Then, in an instant, it moved again, then seemed to fly away by itself to reveal a gaping black hole into the night sky. Without thinking, Barney dived headlong through it, hitting his head on the side and blacking out.

Oberleutnant Engel watched O-Orange descend, ablaze from 21,000 feet, and duly noted the time and location. No enthusiasm was expressed by either him or his crew. All of them had long lost their taste for the kill. He had, however, failed to notice the single parachute that emerged into the night sky as the plane plummeted down towards its destruction.

•

Four days later, in far-off Sydney, a post office delivery boy placed a pale yellow envelope in the hand of Barney's mother, Elsie. Trembling slightly, she opened it and felt a black tide of shock course through her as she scanned the first lines of a government telegram:

413758 WARRANT OFFICER B R GREATREX MISSING STOP REGRET TO INFORM YOU THAT YOUR SON WARRANT OFFICER BARNABY RYDER GREATREX IS MISSING AS RESULT OF AIR OPERATIONS DURING NIGHT 25th FEBRUARY 1944 STOP

Barney in 1921, aged eighteen months; one of many photos taken by his father, Basil, a keen amateur photographer. *Courtesy of Antony Greatrex*

A pensive young man, Barney in his Knox Grammar uniform. *Courtesy of Barney Greatrex*

Barney (left) with a friend in their Knox Grammar Cadet uniforms. The authentic military training instigated by the school would serve Barney well for what was to come. *Courtesy of Barney Greatrex*

Barney outside the family business, Basil VR Greatrex Pty Ltd, in central Sydney just before the war. *Courtesy of Antony Greatrex*

Barney, Basil and Pleasance (left to right) walking along a Sydney street in 1939. *Courtesy of Antony Greatrex*

Renowned Australian photographer Max Dupain made several portraits of Barney. This one depicts him in his RAAF cadet uniform, March 1942. *Courtesy of Barney Greatrex*

Barney in training with some of the men who would form his crew: (left to right at rear) Reg Gill, Maurice Worth, Wally Einarson, Allen Collins and Barney Greatrex; and kneeling are Gunners Thring and Nicholas. *Courtesy of Barney Greatrex*

Barney and crewmembers Reg Gill, Allen Collins and Maurice Worth (left to right) making light of reality; flying over Germany was a nightly catastrophe. RAF Skellingthorpe, November 1943. *Courtesy of Barney Greatrex*

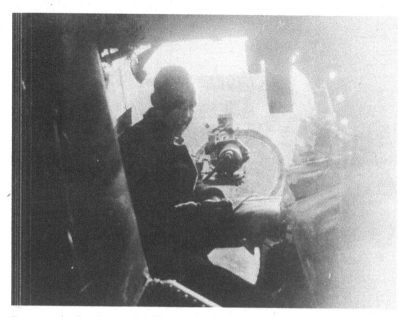

Barney in his bomb aimer's 'office' in the aircraft's nose, right behind his Mark XIV Computing Bombsight. *Courtesy of Barney Greatrex*

Flight Lieutenant Wally Einarson in the cockpit of a Lancaster bomber. *Courtesy of Barney Greatrex*

Bomb doors open, ready to load several tons of high explosive destined for Germany. Reg Gill and Curly Collins pose for an unofficial snap in front of their Mark I Lancaster. *Courtesy of Barney Greatrex*

Barney snapped this 61 Squadron Lancaster 'coming in' to RAF Skellingthorpe the morning after another trip to Berlin. *Courtesy of Barney Greatrex*

Barney on leave in Torquay with Curly Collins and two WAAFs in January 1944, at a time when the whole of Britain seemed to be in uniform. Life for Barney would soon be very different. *Courtesy of Barney Greatrex*

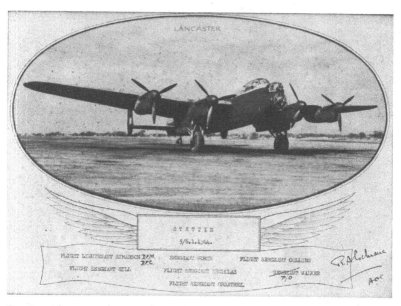

Stettin raid commemorative photograph, 5/6 January 1944. *Courtesy of Barney Greatrex*

AIR FORCE CASUALTIES

From Air Ministry Casualty Communiques Nos. 287 and 288.

ROYAL AIR FORCE.
Previously reported Missing, now presumed Killed in Action.

Sqdn. Ldr. A. C. L. A. Stuart (W.A.).

Missing.

Wing Comdr. J. F. Dilworth (Sydney); Sgt. L. E. Mears (W.A.).

ROYAL AUSTRALIAN AIR FORCE.
Killed in Action.

Flt. Sgt. A. E. D. Davey; Flt. Sgt. H. S. McGill; Flt. Sgt. C. A. Rye; Sgt. A. G. Wilson.

Previously reported Missing, believed Killed in Action, now presumed Killed in Action.

Sgt. N. E. Bellman; Flt. Sgt. R. T. Gregory; Flg. Off. S. T. J. Rundle.

Missing.

Flt. Sgt. J. Ansell; Flt. Sgt. A. E. Arnold; Flt. Sgt. D. T. Balmanno; Flg. Off. D. L. Boyd; Flt. Sgt. W. D. Carlile; Plt. Off. A. J. Collins; Flt. Sgt. R. T. Gill; Plt. Off. B. R. Greatrex; Flt. Sgt. P. W. B. Gurdon; Flt. Sgt. W. J. Howie; Flg. Off. J. P. Hutchinson;

Plt. Off. R. C. Martin; Flg. Off. C. E. Melin; Flt. Sgt. R. G. O'Neill; Flt. Sgt. J. G. Russell; Flt. Sgt. C. W. Sisley; Plt. Off. D. B. Snape; Flt. Sgt. J. A. L. Carmichael; Flt. Sgt. J. G. L. Glazebrook.

Killed on Active Service.

Flg. Off. P. W. Hart; Flt. Sgt. M. C. Simpson.

Previously reported Missing, now reported Prisoner of War.

Wt. Off. A. E. Daley; Flt. Sgt. N. L. Ginn.

ROYAL NEW ZEALAND AIR FORCE.
Previously reported Missing, now presumed Killed in Action.

Flt. Sgt. J. G. A. Fisk; Plt. Off. G. V. Helm; Plt. Off. D. C. Henley; Flt. Sgt. I. H. R. Smith; Flt. Sgt. D. M. Stewart; Flg. Off. C. A. Watson.

Previously reported Missing, believed Killed in Action, now presumed Killed in Action.

Flt. Sgt. D. J. A. Hannan.

Missing.

Flt. Sgt. D. A. Chisholm; Plt. Off. A. P. Chisholm; A. Flt. Lieut. K. B. O'Connor; Flt. Sgt. L. N. Atkinson.

Killed on Active Service.

Flg. Off. J. D. McMillan; Plt. Off. R. G. C. Payne.

N.Z. NAVAL CASUALTY.

Sub-Lieut. (A) R. A. Cranwell, R.N reported missing, presumed killed service (mother in Epsom, Auckland).

Temp. Sub-Lieut. (A) Douglas Web N.V.R., killed on active service (father church).

Temp. Sub-Lieut. (A) A. E. Martin, V.R., died on active service on 3 Ma in Ashburton).

A saved clipping from *The British Australian and New Zealander* from May 1944 reports Barney and his crew as having failed to return. *Courtesy of Antony Greatrex*

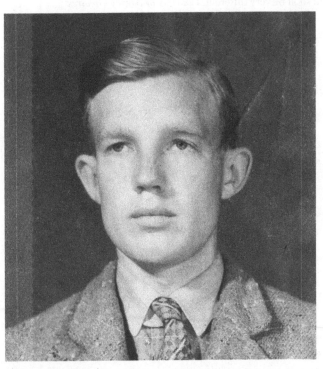

Barney's 'escape photo', a part of every airman's emergency pack for use in forged documents if shot down. For Barney, it would prove invaluable. *Courtesy of Barney Greatrex*

PART TWO

13

THE BIGGEST GAMBLE OF HIS LIFE

Years later, when finally allowing himself to talk about his astonishing war, Barney Greatrex never quite knew what woke him up as he fell towards the ground after knocking himself out cold while bailing out. Whatever it was, though, it saved his life. Regaining his senses, Barney found himself falling through the air, apparently just a few hundred feet above a snow-covered pine forest. Instantly, his brain fired, just in time for him to pull his ripcord. A violent jolt, and over his head a comforting, crumpling sound of unfolding silk. Then the silence. After hours of the usual white noise of the engines, followed by the panic of the night fighter attack, the sudden silence was what he remembered as being the greatest shock to his system. There was little time to reflect, however, as the ground was coming up fast to meet him.

Quickly, Barney tried to conjure whatever he had learned the day of his one and only bail-out drill session – a cursory exercise that comprised little more than leaping from a raised wooden platform into a rather small pen of sand and rolling forwards. For some reason, he remembered brushing the sand out of his hair, and drew up his legs. The tops of trees became visible at his feet, followed by a small clearing. Suddenly, and without realising it, he was rolling over and over in a bed of soft new snow. Face down, he felt the cold bite his skin, but finally, thank God, he was still. As he lay there, his shocked brain informed him that this was the first time in his life he had ever seen snow. It was also the first time he had used a parachute.

Gingerly, Barney tested one leg, then the other, then his arms, and to his considerable disbelief he found himself apparently in one piece. The same could not be said for his aircraft. In the dark, he picked up the smell of burnt oil first, then the petrol. As his eyes adjusted, he realised he had come down barely a hundred yards from the aircraft, which now lay burning in two grotesque pieces in a freshly made crater. In the light of the fires, Barney could only stare in silence at the ghastly broken carcass of his Lancaster. He looked around for more of his crew to emerge, like himself, gathering up their big bundles of parachute, but no one appeared. He slowly began to comprehend that the twisted remains of the bomber in front of him was now also the tomb of six men to whom he felt closer than family.

Suddenly realising the aircraft may still be carrying its bombs, which had yet to explode, Barney moved away to a small road that cut through the woods. For the first time, he felt a sharp pain and a lump on his head, sustained in his sudden exit from the aircraft. There was a small amount of blood, but the cut was superficial. Looking up, he noticed that the sky was clearer than he had seen it in weeks, and he looked for the Pole Star. At this point, he later said, 'nausea and a deep despair' overcame him as he thought of his magnificent pilot, Wally, whose luck had finally run out on his very last trip. The pity of it was too much to bear. He bent over and vomited violently. He looked at his watch. It was 9.30 pm, just three hours since having taken off from England.

Barney's reverie was broken by the sound of approaching motors. Dashing into the forest, he saw a truck pull up next to the flaming wreckage and soldiers get out to inspect it. He could just make out some voices, and after a minute or so they seemed to have been beaten back by the intense heat as they returned to the truck, leaving a single soldier to guard the downed plane. To Barney's despair, the guard began a short routine, marching up and down a patch of road between himself and the wreckage. Any escape Barney might try would now surely be seen.

Finally, the German expanded his beat and wandered away. Gathering up his 'chute, Barney dashed forwards, stumbled through a fence and bolted into the pitch dark of the forest, half-running, half-staggering seemingly for an eternity, not daring to look back. At last, panting like a frightened animal, he sat down on a soft bed of pine needles, wrapped himself up in his silk parachute and vanished into a dreamless sleep.

•

Barney's eyes opened beneath a sky of cool, pale sunshine. Cocooned in his surprisingly warm bed of silk, he took in the tall spire of a pine tree, pointing away to the heavens, as if mockingly reminding him from where he had arrived some nine hours earlier. As his mind cleared, he recalled the last fix his navigator had given their pilot, mentioning to Wally the approaching Vosges mountains. In the nose, Barney had been following their progress on his own map. He knew that the Vosges ran roughly north–south through Alsace-Lorraine close to the German frontier, with Switzerland immediately to the south. How lovely, he thought, to spend the rest of the war in Switzerland. Where exactly he now was, however, in this jumbled corner of Europe, he could not be sure.

Then he remembered the little compass issued to all airmen cleverly secreted into one of the buttons of his flying tunic. Deciding to put as much distance between himself and the wreck (not to mention the frontier of Germany) as possible, he got up and began to head west. By 9 am, he again felt exhausted and ate some of the emergency rations stuffed in his pockets. In a small clearing, he stretched out in the sun and rested most of the day.

Late in the afternoon, he set off again, still taking advantage of thickly wooded country to conceal his trek west. It became bitterly cold. At one stage, he heard voices in the half-light, and two girls cycled close by on a rough country road. He felt a sudden urge to speak to them but remembered he spoke not a word of any other language but his own. Besides, he couldn't even be sure which language they were speaking. He hoped it was French.

The night came on again, and it began to snow. A clear moon helped him read the compass. Despite the cold, his feet were starting to burn. Flying boots were never made for walking, and his thin socks were starting to disintegrate. A short time later, he stumbled into a huge barrier of barbed wire stretched head-high in multiple rows. Away to his left, he saw a small wooden sentry box. He fell to the ground immediately, realising in horror that this could only be a national frontier, and, as he was heading west, he must therefore be in Germany.

No activity emanated from the sentry box, so he decided to approach. It was, as he suspected, deserted, but it straddled a road crossing the frontier, which Barney simply walked across. He silently chastised himself on the foolish sense of relief he felt entering France, knowing that he was not even remotely out of danger.

Barney walked on through the dark and bitter cold for another few hours, then again collapsed in sleep. This second night in the forest was not restful. The shock of having survived the crash beginning to subside, Barney now began to contemplate his future, and it did not look bright. Then it started to snow again.

At 7 am, Barney set off again, realising that his ability to survive in the French forest was severely limited. This day, he resolved, he would start to make a plan. Not far away, he came across the first sign of habitation he had seen since the crash – a rough barn on the edge of a wide paddock. He crept up cautiously, then noticed a small door, and before he knew what he was doing he was inside, his eyes trying to adjust to the dim light. As they did, he found himself standing almost beside a boy of about fifteen, who for some reason seemed not in the least surprised at his presence.

Awkwardly, Barney reached for that part of his escape kit that he had occasionally pictured himself using: his silk scarf with a map of Western Europe printed on one side and multiple phrases in various languages on the other. He pointed to the first: 'I am a British airman shot down and am in need of assistance.' The boy nodded and seemed to smile. Barney pointed to the second: 'Where am I?' Via sign language and a stick scraped on the dirt floor, Barney learned that he was indeed in the Vosges, about forty kilometres from Nancy. The boy also indicated with cutthroat motions that he had no love of the Germans and advised Barney to keep heading west. Barney thanked him but was glad to again be on his way. As useful as the boy was, Barney couldn't help but notice that he stank to high heaven.

As he was later to learn, Barney had landed near the small village of Lagarde in Moselle, a section of Alsace-Lorraine annexed to Germany after the French defeat in 1940, and which was earmarked to receive German-speaking inhabitants. His crossing of the frontier brought him from the annexed to the occupied zone of France.

Proceeding through more thick country, Barney now decided the condition of his feet was becoming intolerable and that, whatever his journey would be, he could not continue it without assistance. That afternoon, he emerged from the trees into the head of a small valley. Not far away ran a stream and a village consisting of a few cottages, adjacent to a road running parallel to what appeared to be a canal.

Returning to the cover of the forest, he took the risk of using his escape kit matches to light a small fire to dry his clothes. He ate the last of his emergency rations and waited until dusk, when, he resolved, he would approach one of those cottages and hope for the best.

A few hours later, his heart almost beating out of his chest, Barney Greatrex emerged from the cover of the forest and walked down the main street of the tiny village he had been quietly observing most of the day. With his dishevelled hair, three-day growth and filthy flying kit, he was well aware of just what a sight he must have made. Not that he needed to concern himself with the reaction of the locals, however, as there didn't seem to be any of them around.

Remembering the instructions drummed into him in training, as well as in the occasional escape and evasion lecture, he chose dusk to make his appearance and seek help. To further add to his discomfort, his feet and legs were now soaking, as he had misjudged the little stream he had crossed, which was nearly up to his waist. Approaching the first house in the street, he drew a breath and walked up to the front door to make the most important decision of his life. If these people were German sympathisers – and he was told France was riddled with them – he could be in the hands of the Gestapo within hours.

He paused. Thinking better of things, Barney went around to the back. He knocked twice, loudly, and waited. Nobody came to the door. He then tried the second house, which was also empty. Feeling his sails very much deflating, he began to wonder if the village was deserted, as no sign of life could be seen anywhere.

Only the very last house in the street revealed a chink of light from the back door, falling on the snow. This time, he didn't even knock and just pushed it open carefully. He found himself standing in an empty kitchen under an electric light. Feeling most unsure of what to do now, he banged several times with his hand on a heavy oak table. A door opened, and in walked a very sturdy, very French-looking middle-aged man wearing a waistcoat and a bushy moustache. He stopped, frozen, and looked him up and down as if seeing an apparition. Barney tried to glean the nature of the expression on the man's face. Quickly, he pulled out the scarf and began to point.

Suddenly, the Frenchman smiled broadly. Seconds later, however, he disappeared back behind the door and closed it. Barney heard voices. He later reflected, 'I knew that my fate, perhaps my life depended on what was going on behind that door.'

After a seemingly interminable period, during which Barney considered simply walking off and heading back to the forest, the door opened and in walked the Frenchman, now accompanied by a woman Barney assumed to be his wife. Then another, much older woman appeared, followed by another, and finally a grandfatherly figure with an identical moustache to Barney's host, but pure white. Barney wondered how many more individuals could be secreted in this tiny home. They each examined him in open-mouthed silence. Finally, one of the old women approached him, put her arms around his neck and kissed him on both cheeks. This apparently broke the ice, and all of them came to hug him or shake his hand. From somewhere, bread appeared, along with cheese, coffee and wine. Barney sat down to eat with gusto. It was unquestionably the best meal of his life.

Barney's gamble, he thought, just might pay off.

14

BECOMING FRENCH

The moment that Barney passed the threshold of that last house in the village of Mouacourt set an adventure in motion that would up-end every experience of his life, and in the crucible of adversity form comradeships that would endure forever. Today, even more than seventy years since the events took place, new generations on both sides of the globe have kept alive the story of the young man from the other side of the world who dropped from the sky to bear witness to one of the darkest chapters of France's traumatic four-year occupation by the Nazis. To many in tiny ancient settlements in this remote and beautiful part of France, Barney Greatrex was, indeed still is, 'The Miracle of Lagarde'. Initially, though, nobody knew who on earth he was.

Marguerite Christment, the wife of Auguste, the Frenchman into whose kitchen Barney stumbled, remembered vividly the moment for the rest of her life:

With my husband, Auguste, we lived in the last house in the village. It was night and we were just going to sit down at the table for our supper when someone walked in our back door. It was a man in strange clothing whose language I didn't understand, but who somehow managed to explain that he was an aviator. We showed him in and gave him something to eat. We had heard about the plane which had fallen near Lagarde the preceding days. What were we going to do with him? Our neighbour opposite knew a little bit of English. Barney told him his story and of his miraculous survival.

After the very welcome reception and supper, Barney was shown to an upstairs room. On being left alone in there, he tore off every stitch of clothing and collapsed into a bed, which had even been pre-warmed with a heating brick. After sleeping like a dead man for many hours, he was awakened by his 'hostess', Marguerite, bringing him breakfast of coffee and bread the next morning. In just twenty-four hours, Barney reflected, his life had most dramatically changed, and for some time he could not shake the feeling that he was trapped in some ghastly dream.

By sheltering Barney, his saviours, the Christments, had already committed an act that – they were well aware – would almost certainly result in them being sent to a concentration camp, or even shot, by the Gestapo. However, with the Rubicon of taking Barney in well and truly crossed, the Christments could do little but see it through. As it transpired, the older woman who had greeted him first with a kiss on both cheeks had two sons fighting for the Free French in Italy. Besides, she and her entire family utterly detested the Germans.

The Christments had had little to do with the Resistance movement so far during the war, but they suspected that their neighbour might have connections in that area. Barney remembers meeting him that morning, 'a young man of very striking appearance', who, as it turned out, even spoke a little English. Paul Bodot had in fact been a pilot in the French Air Force in 1938, but he was forced to give it up due to deteriorating eyesight. He was now in charge of a lock on the canal that Barney had noticed running through the village. Paul came immediately to visit Barney in his room, told him he indeed had connections and promised to alert the local Resistance HQ in Nancy to his presence. Meanwhile, he urged Barney to remain here with the Christments and keep his head well and truly down.

'Oh,' he asked as he was leaving, 'what name do you want to be known by?'

Barney thought for a moment and then remembered his mother's French origins in Normandy. 'Clapin,' he said. 'Jacques Clapin.'

Paul thought the name sounded excellent, nodded, turned and left.

The next day, Paul returned with what looked like a superbly forged French identity card, complete with the small passport-size picture of Barney taken in civilian clothes that the RAF cleverly included in every airman's escape kit for precisely this purpose. Barney Greatrex was now Jacques Clapin, and he knew that if he was to survive, he would have to play the part very well indeed.

As instructed, Barney remained in the cottage for the best part of a week, leaving his room but once, at night, to retrieve the silk parachute he had concealed in the nearby forest. Silk, he was assured by his hosts, was highly valued in these days of wartime austerity and would be put to a variety of uses, particularly ladies' underwear, as Auguste at one stage confessed slyly. Barney's uniform was burned and a replacement – a somewhat dowdy and ill-fitting set of clothes – was procured. This, however, fitted the part Barney would need to assume, as his new identity card described him as a deaf and dumb mechanic. With what level of proficiency a 'deaf mechanic' was supposed to perform was presumably left to the imagination.

In a week, Barney's life had transitioned from the terror of surviving an operational tour in bombers to the terror of surviving on the ground and on the run. At some stage, he had been informed that some locals had visited the crash site and had indeed found the remains of his crew. This realisation hit Barney hard. To make matters worse, it was reported that some of his companions apparently did manage to bail out, but too late for their parachutes to deploy, so they tragically just fell beside the aircraft. Faint scratch marks, it was reported, were observed in the dirt under their fingers. According to the locals, the Germans had buried them outside the perimeter of the local French military cemetery at Lagarde, deeming them unworthy of consecrated ground.

Left alone with his thoughts for the first time in months, Barney's mood darkened upon realising his family in Sydney would by now have received the telegram reporting him 'missing', and he tortured himself endlessly with the image of his mother opening it. He desperately needed to be busy once more. The only way to occupy himself was with a battered volume of the history of France in the last war, which he used to piece together some rudiments of the French language.

Suddenly, late on a Friday night, Paul reappeared, accompanied by his father. It was time for Barney to go. In his ill-fitting suit, and even a beret, which made him feel faintly ridiculous, Barney did his best to thank Marguerite and Auguste, but his gratitude was beyond any language. The risks they had taken for him, a perfect stranger, were immeasurable. They wished him well, but Barney sensed, too, their quiet relief at his departure.

For a long time, the Christments believed that they had kept the secret of their Australian airman to themselves. It was only after the war that Marguerite realised otherwise. 'For a long long time,' she recalled, 'we thought that he had gone totally unnoticed but after the liberation we discovered that several of the young people were aware of his presence. They had seen him out of the house several times to use the toilet!'

Paul's family, the Bodots, lived in a former cafe by the canal bridge. Here, Barney spent a cold night but was up early to catch the first bus into Nancy, about fifty kilometres distant, accompanied this time by Paul's father, who spoke not a word of English. Posing as *oncle* and nephew, they were the only passengers. As the small, charcoal-burning bus lurched into the early morning, Barney reflected that not a vestige of his former identity now remained. He was now 'Jacques', and he would do his best to think as, and believe himself to be, 'Jacques'. Then he glanced at the time on his air force–issue watch, still strapped to his wrist, underneath which was engraved his real name and RAAF service number, 413758. Shocked initially into preparing to throw it out of the bus window, Barney – for a reason he was never fully able to explain – decided to take the extraordinary risk of keeping it. It remained with him, undiscovered, throughout his entire time in France.

After a while, the bus pulled into a small town, and the few passengers they had collected alighted. Barney's *'oncle'* managed to indicate that he stay put – an instruction he obeyed. Suddenly alone in the bus, Barney felt terrified. If he was challenged, he knew he would give the game away in a heartbeat. To make matters worse, a German corporal joined the passengers and chose to sit directly in front of him. Barney felt that the pounding of his heart alone would give him away. Later, when describing this incident, some local maquisards informed him that the German was probably in the town in connection with his crashed Lancaster. Barney was glad he did not know that at the time.

On reaching the outskirts of Nancy, Barney and Paul's father alighted and walked in pouring rain to the centre of the city. On the way, Barney did his best to avoid eye contact with several more uniformed Germans. Near the central square, he was alarmed to see one particular building surrounded by myriad German sentries and decked out with many red, white and black swastika flags. More alarming, this was the building to which it appeared he was being led. The panic that he had been lured into a trap was extinguished only when they continued and entered the next building along. Now, Barney found himself in what looked like a solicitor's office, in front of a striking-looking man of middle age. His job done, and with palpable relief, Barney's *oncle* departed.

Starting to feel like a parcel in a game, Barney was now introduced to another man, who entered the room like an actor responding to a cue. This time, however, a French–English dictionary was produced and a rudimentary communication was established. To impress upon Barney the danger of his situation, the solicitor led both men to the window over-looking the heavily German-occupied building next door, which turned out to be the town's Hotel de Ville. Barney needed no such reminder, but it occurred to him as slightly bizarre that he, an RAAF airman, and two active members of the Resistance were here calmly taking in the local German military and Nazi headquarters, just a few yards away.

Issued with a better fitting pair of trousers and, finally, a warm overcoat, Barney now was told he was to undertake a trip by train to a safer area. There were so many questions he felt he needed answers to, but he knew now was not the time to ask. He took his leave from the solicitor and with his new 'handler' passed an astonishing number of German military on their way to the railway ticket office.

Every carriage bar one was reserved for the Germans, so Barney stood in the corridor, looking down as several men in Wehrmacht field grey brushed by. At Épinal, they needed to wait until the evening for a connecting train to what Barney was told was their destination, the spa town of Gérardmer in the more southern part of the Vosges mountains. Meanwhile, Barney was cold and hungry. The relief he felt, however, at being led by his guide into a warm and well-appointed restaurant was tempered by the presence of a very large number of German officers, who seemed to significantly outnumber the locals. When his guide got up from the table, having seen someone outside he knew, and told Barney to sit still and stay calm, Barney felt even worse.

Two Luftwaffe officers sat down at a table just a few feet away. Then, with horror, Barney watched the waitress make a beeline for him, with her notepad ready. She looked harassed. *'Puis-je prendre votre commande, monsieur?'* she asked Barney without looking up. Barney felt himself flush but could only open his mouth like a goldfish. *'Votre commande, monsieur?'* the girl said again, more impatiently. Barney eyed the Germans, who were well within earshot. The girl made a slight hissing noise and was about to say something else when Barney's handler reappeared at his side to take control of the situation, and not a moment too soon. Barney's appetite had suddenly evaporated.

The stress of lunch was alleviated a little by the two men passing time in a cinema watching a musical, dotted with the ubiquitous German newsreels, which exasperated Barney's guide but which he himself found rather impressive. Still with time to kill, the two walked across the Moselle River and opened the dictionary. Barney now began to ask what kind of future was being planned for him, but his handler remained elusive. Whenever Barney tried to construct a scenario around his being spirited back to England via neutral Spain, his companion laughed a little and changed the subject.

An hour or so later, drinking a beer at a large railway cafe surrounded by what looked to be hundreds of German troops, Barney was more than happy to find a seat in a compartment with two young French couples who had no interest in anything but each other. A quick transfer at Gérardmer took him to another bus, which wound its way uneasily up into the mountains. An hour later, he arrived at La Bresse, high up in a valley on the Alsace frontier. With a population of about 6000, this pretty mountain village was chosen for its remote location. It was a place away from the eyes of the Germans, and which the war had so far barely touched.

15

JOINING THE MAQUIS

The little hotel looked abandoned. Barney was amazed that there could even be a hotel this far up the mountain, pondering who built it, how and most of all why. But as they approached it in the moonlight after several kilometres trudging up a steep and narrow rocky mountain valley, there it unmistakeably was. 'Not far' were the only words his guide had uttered for the last hour since leaving the little station at Gérardmer behind them, before they proceeded to walk right past what appeared to Barney to be a perfectly acceptable and rather cosy village. 'Not far' continued to be his standard answer whenever asked how far there was to go. In the end, Barney stopped asking. Finally, panting at its doorway, hungry and exhausted by the stress of the travel but at least no longer cold, Barney anticipated lying down on some floor of this cold, dark and abandoned hotel and finding some rest. His surprise upon going inside, therefore, could barely be measured.

A Monsieur Remy furtively answered the prearranged knock. To Barney, he looked to be another typical middle-aged French peasant in a waistcoat. A few muffled words were exchanged in the darkened stoop, and then Remy beckoned Barney and his guide to follow. Passing through a second door, it was as if Barney had walked into an expertly concealed surprise party. 'I was actually dazzled by the lights,' he recalled later.

Barney found himself in a room with twenty or so others in front of a warm and raging fire. A glass of wine was placed in his hand. Then there were slaps on the back and laughter at his efforts to express his gratitude, not to mention his surprise, in French. Then a meal – a good one, of steak and potatoes – appeared, followed by more wine. 'If this had been my own native village,' Barney later wrote, 'I could not have been more affectionately greeted.' More amazingly, people were even addressing him by his name – his real name – and seemed to know his history as a downed Australian aviator. Here, it seemed, in these mountains apparently out of reach of the tentacles of Nazi control and where every inhabitant appeared to be with the Resistance, Barney could finally relax. He felt the intensity of the previous few days begin to thaw off his weary body. At 2.30 in the morning, thoroughly worse for wear, he staggered upstairs and collapsed into a bed. This, he thought as he lapsed into sleep, was becoming a very strange way to fight a war.

Although no one had quite managed to explain it in so many words, it now became apparent to Barney that he was being passed from one Resistance handler to another, but to what ends he had no idea. In the beginning, he had simply assumed that he was being put through the complex ratline network of the French Resistance, to be eventually spirited back to Britain via Spain, or in one of the Lysander spy planes making increasingly regular incursions into France. As time went on, however, he was less and less sure.

The next two days were spent in the starkly beautiful mountain setting of La Bresse, being introduced to a large number of Resistance fighters, one of whom ran the local bicycle shop and was in possession of a wireless set – an offence punishable by death if discovered by the Germans. This enabled Barney to listen to the BBC. Try as he might, however, he could gain no overview of what – if any – plans had been laid for his immediate future. He was told that, for his own good, he could not know too much of the bigger picture in case of capture, so he came to accept that, every few days, he would simply be instructed to gather his things and be prepared to move within the hour. Slowly, he began to understand that he would not be returning to England any time soon, and that he would be spending a great deal of time with some of the brave men of France's multifaceted shadow army, the Maquis.

Popular culture has transformed France's 'La Résistance' into a uniform image of an entire country of beautiful women in berets delivering secret messages on bicycles, and strong-jawed men in leather jackets clutching Sten guns, striking the hated Boche at will before melting effortlessly away into the glorious French countryside. In reality, particularly before 1943, France's organised resistance to the Germans was a minority phenomenon, with estimates of no more than two per cent of the French population being actively involved in subversive activities, from publishing underground newspapers to intelligence gathering and sabotage. Another eight per cent could be classed as passive resisters, willing to read such publications and quietly providing moral support to the growing resistance networks, but by far the bulk of the population simply kept their heads down and accepted what they thought to be the inevitable.

Stunned by an unexpected – and wholly avoidable – defeat in 1940, the French masses initially gave their shoulders a pragmatic shrug and did their best to find some normality in their lives. After all, they reasoned, how bad could their occupiers from the land of Schiller and Beethoven possibly be? Shock and disillusionment came quickly, as the victorious Germans morphed into utterly unacceptable tyrants bent on bleeding the country economically, materially and spiritually – aided and abetted by a French puppet government based in the spa town of Vichy. The first signs of defiance soon began to emerge. Initially, resistance confined itself to a propaganda war, with illegal printing presses running off anti-German pamphlets in basements in the dead of night, distributed away from the gaze of the dreaded Gestapo. Even from these early stages, the punishment for such activity was transportation to a concentration camp, or death. Nevertheless, as the regime tightened its stranglehold over the population – particularly as the French began to witness the treatment of the Jews and their own government's collusion in what would become the Holocaust – people became slowly more emboldened.

France, however, had been deeply fractured by a tedious carousel of endlessly changing governments throughout the 1930s and by an unstable society bitterly divided along complex social and political lines. Despite the universal revulsion as the true nature of the German occupation revealed itself, mutual trust and cooperation proved difficult. France's enormous communist party, for example – banned outright since 1939 – refused to have anything to do with organised resistance, regarding the entire war as a purely intra-capitalist conflict. In July 1941, though, after the German invasion of the USSR, it put its well-honed skills in clandestine organisation to good use, and in eighteen months its paramilitary Francs-Tireurs et Partisans (FTP) had become the most dedicated and brutal of all resistance organisations. Nor were their members exclusively French, with a disproportionate make-up of Polish Jews and Eastern European communists, as well as Spanish fighters from the lost Republican cause still eager to take up the fight against European fascism.

But the Resistance was not the exclusive domain of the left. As early as 1940, conservative resistance organisations had begun to emerge, such as the Organisation Civile et Militaire (OCM), founded by members of the bourgeoise, industry and the senior ranks of the civil service. This seminal resistance body went on to work closely with Britain's cloak-and-dagger spy service, the Special Operations Executive (SOE). Later, in 1942, the Organisation de Résistance de l'Armée (ORA) was formed by former members of the French Army, rallying behind the anti-German General Henri Giraud, whom they recognised as the legitimate ruler of France. This however put them in conflict with the great bastion of French conservatism, General de Gaulle, who had claimed the same title for himself from London.

A nation with a seemingly unshakeable love of bureaucracy, France arranged its resistance along similar lines.

On the left, besides the FTP, there was the fabulously named Armée Secrète and Combat, which later morphed into the Ceux de la Résistance (CDLR). Then there was Front Nationale, Liberation-Nord and Liberation-Sud, and myriad smaller organisations that came and went, often overlapping in both ideology and structure. Although nominally united against a common enemy, the alliances between the many facets of the Resistance were often fragile and, indeed, temporary.

Not all who joined, it should be noted, did so out of hardened political or patriotic convictions. For some, it was an adventure, for others a chance for romance (there were a good deal of women involved) and for others still, there being no sign of any imminent liberation at the hands of the struggling Allied armies, it was the only way they could think of to hit back at their Nazi occupiers and atone for the shame of 1940.

The greatest influx into the ranks of the Resistance came at the beginning of 1943, when Hitler's forced labour minister

Fritz Sauckel decreed that all able-bodied Frenchmen be called up and deported to work for the German war effort in what became known – and dreaded – as the *Service du travail obligatoire*, or STO. The attractive pay and conditions offered by the STO were quickly revealed as a ruse to lure a vast slave army into the factories and the mines of Germany's war industry.

Suddenly, desperate to avoid the STO's long reach, Frenchmen who had never considered opposing the Germans vanished from their homes and jobs overnight and headed to the hills of the French countryside to join growing guerrilla bands of the Resistance's secret army, known everywhere as the Maquis. The STO, more than any other single factor, historians agree, drove the young men of France into the arms of the Resistance. Otto Abetz, Hitler's ambassador to Vichy France, once commented that the Maquis should erect a statue to Sauckel, describing him as their 'number one recruitment agent'.

Taking advantage of this surge, from London General de Gaulle directed his agent in France, the brilliant and resourceful Jean Moulin, to bring the disparate elements of the Resistance together via the Conseil Nationale de la Résistance (CNR). Thus, in May 1943, in a small apartment on the second floor of 48 Rue du Four in Paris, barely a kilometre from Notre-Dame, the leaders of the various resistance movements as well as representatives from France's main political parties and pre-war trade unions met under the noses of the

Germans to be told in no uncertain terms to stop fighting each other and unite.

To that end, Moulin explained, the Allies were prepared to invest significant resources in the Resistance movement in terms of weapons, training and organisation – in effect, helping to train and equip a Resistance army to assist the Allied powers in the liberation of France. The caveat, however, was unity, and Moulin presented the disparate Resistance heads with an ultimatum: unite under one overarching organisation or play little or no part in the country's liberation. So – just in time, according to some historians – France's fractured Resistance agreed to coalesce around the lightning rod of General de Gaulle's Forces Françaises de l'Intérieur (FFI).

And just to allay suspicions that de Gaulle would not take such an organisation seriously, he placed in charge of the new FFI an already highly respected French general, Marie-Pierre Koenig, currently distinguishing himself in Africa. The Resistance leaders had no choice but to accept.

In fact, Britain's SOE had already been delivering small amounts of weapons, cash, equipment and other essentials via lone Lysander and Stirling aircraft, whose superb pilots, in the dead of night over enemy territory, had managed to pick out a particular paddock in a particular corner of French countryside aided by nothing but expert navigation and a prearranged signal from a flashlight on the ground.

Now, in the lead-up to D-Day, the effort would be greatly increased. Supply drops would be ramped up, and three-man 'Jedburgh' teams (one of which Barney was to encounter) would be dropped to instruct on the use of modern small arms, sabotage techniques, guerrilla tactics and hand-to-hand fighting. However, the Maquis would complain that they were never being given enough.

The war was slow to come to the Vosges mountains in France's north-east, and until 1943 both occupation and resistance were not particularly active. This began to change at the beginning of 1944 as the start of the inevitable Allied campaign to liberate the country drew nearer.

In the region where Barney Greatrex found himself, four major groupings of the Maquis had by late 1943 begun to organise themselves along basic military lines. Barney belonged to the fourth group, although, by the time he joined them, they had subdivided into nearly forty individual units, each with distinctive names linked to their part of the country. There were, for example, the Maquis de Châtenois, Maquis St-Jacques de Gérardmer and the Maquis du Séchenat, or the unit to which Barney belonged, the Maquis Piquante Pierre, named for a prominent high area near La Bresse, the mountain village which Barney had spent two nights in, and which he would come to know very well. As a Maquis base, the Piquante Pierre was a natural choice: its landscape was both partially clear and partially wooded, and dotted with farmhouses for cover; it overlooked the main road used by the Germans in the area, and was situated close to Alsace and then, further east, Germany. It also provided a good sized area for use as a parachute drop zone.

The Maquis was organised in small groups: a *sizaine* of six men, a *trentaine* of thirty-plus men, and a *centaine* representing four *trentaines* and their commanders. The commander of Barney's *centaine* was local man Jean-Paul Vitu, but known to all as 'Bébert'. After D-Day, when the liberation of France seemed imminent, the trickle of men joining the Maquis became a flood.

The crucible of each territory assigned to the various Maquis units was a specially marked out field suitable for night parachute drops or even landings by small aircraft. Each drop zone was given its own code. Piquante Pierre's, for example, on a plateau above La Bresse, was codenamed 'Coupole', and the signal to alert the fighters to an impending delivery – read in clear, clipped tones by the BBC Overseas Service newsreader at 1 pm and then confirmed at 7 pm – was the somewhat romantic *'J'espère vous revoir, chérie'*.

Food and supplies would come from sympathetic patriots in the villages and the general community, and, if Barney's experience was anything to go by, the men lived relatively well. Always, though, was the spectre of being uncovered by the Germans, either through carelessness or via a collaborator or German sympathiser, of which France had no shortage whatsoever. By far the greatest cause of Resistance cells being discovered and eliminated was Frenchmen turning on other Frenchmen, seeking to ingratiate themselves with their occupiers. The wrath vented by the Germans on the Resistance when they could find them was savage. Seeing them as no more than a terrorist hangover of a country whose government had legally surrendered several years earlier, they reserved a particular hatred for the Maquis and showed them not a shred of mercy. All maquisards knew full well their fate upon capture would usually be torture, and always death.

This grisly prospect seems not to have been in any way foremost in Barney's mind. However, over several weeks towards the end of the winter of 1944, he was rotated through a series of farms and forest hideouts designed to protect him and his new Maquis companions. In the brief journal he kept of the period, Barney recalls a seemingly never-ending journey from one safe house to the next. After farewelling the hospitality of the Remy family, he was escorted three and a half hours on skis (he had never worn them in his life prior to that morning) to an abandoned and dilapidated farmhouse higher up in the mountains. Barney stared with disbelief when his guides – who spoke almost no English – arrived outside its peeling walls. As he entered, he was surprised to realise it was full of people – his first close-up look, in fact, at a unit of fully fledged maquisards. 'They looked like pirates,' he remarked, 'but there was no doubting the warmth of their welcome to me.'

Inside was a kitchen and living room – in fact, the only rooms of which the place consisted – which had apparently seen much better days. Some old packing cases seemed to be the only furniture, but the first thing Barney noticed was the smell. An old wood stove – the sole source of warmth – leaked badly, and the winter gloom was lifted only by one or two oily hurricane lamps. This, combined with more than a dozen men of the French countryside living rough, made for a challenging atmosphere.

Although only there for a week, it was at this remote location that Barney learned, officially, that he was to become a fully fledged member of the Maquis. What enquiries he had made regarding being returned to England had been met only with shrugs of the shoulders and vague assurances that he would be put in contact with those people whose job it was to smuggle downed airmen such as himself back to safety, but after a while he began to realise nothing would come of it.

On the other hand, his reception by the Vosges resistance seemed never anything less than celebratory. Despite his lack of experience, as an Allied airman his addition to their ranks was apparently regarded as some kind of coup. Besides, Barney had in fact spent several years with his school cadets before the war gaining experience in camping, drilling and weapon training, all of which he had enjoyed immensely, and he seemed quite unfazed by the harsh conditions of camping.

If, he reasoned, he was unable to resume dropping bombs on the Germans, he could – at least in the meantime – fight them as an apparently highly regarded member of the famous French Maquis. Duly, it was at the run-down farmhouse somewhere in the hills above La Bresse that Barney – as Jacques Clapin – put his name to a document, was issued a service number and became an underground soldier of the Resistance. He was even given a salary of 900 French francs, paid in cash on the sixteenth of every month. Where this money came from was at first a mystery, until Barney learned that it, too, was supplied by London. How exactly he was supposed to spend it was another matter entirely.

Resigning himself to having to spend at least the remainder of the winter in the farmhouse, Barney settled into a routine of occasional training, cleaning weapons of various vintage, organising meals and awaiting the daily contact from the villager who came up from La Bresse with the latest news from the BBC. It was a simple, indeed spartan life for Barney, his daily rations consisting of ersatz coffee, bread and cheese for breakfast, soup or stew for dinner and tea. His small unit was always at the ready to receive orders from higher up the chain of command, although they seemed to Barney to be waiting in vain.

After a week or two, rumours began to circulate that the Gestapo were making fresh forays into the vicinity. A brief conference – which Barney found he could now follow surprisingly well – determined they should split up and disperse. Late on a Saturday night, in the middle of a blinding snowstorm, Barney set out with four others, whom he knew strictly on a first-name-only basis: André, Antoine, Louis and their leader, Bébert. All were locals who had spent their lives in nearby industries and farms, tough young men who knew the terrain of the Vosges intimately.

Trudging up and down an endless series of hills, Bébert confessed to Barney with considerable annoyance that the actual reason for their hasty departure was somewhat pedestrian. A local Maquis leader had been courting a La Bresse girl who, obviously dazzled by the young man's outlaw status with the Maquis, had boasted about it to a dangerous number of people. Their conversation in the snowstorm, as well as Bébert's candidness in revealing his frustration at not having been given very much to do by the higher Maquis organisation, began a bond between the two men that would last their entire lives. He assured Barney that soon there would be a great deal of work to do in purging their country of the hated enemy, as the talk and the rumours were now centring on the impending Allied invasion. Having originally expected it a year earlier, many in the Maquis had virtually despaired of the day ever arriving, but whenever and wherever it happened, said Bébert, they would be ready to emerge from the shadows and, in the words of Winston Churchill, 'set Europe ablaze'. For now, though, there would be more waiting.

Eventually, the small party arrived at another farmhouse, where they spent the night under the care of a family by the name of Perrin, who were sympathetic to the cause. In the morning, they were directed several hours away to yet another refuge, a small, log-built woodcutter's hut in a clearing deep in the forest, which reminded Barney for all the world of the little house in *Snow White*. 'We had to dig into a snow drift about four feet high just to get into the place,' he wrote. Here, he would spend the next five weeks, where the tedium and isolation would test him.

16

SURVIVING THE CHILL

Milk, cheese and potatoes would become Barney's staple during his time in the Maquis. The rations would arrive daily care of the Perrins, so the group to which Barney now belonged were at least well provided for. But, snowbound, usually cold and with little to do but wait for the thaw while staying out of the orbit of the Gestapo's net of contacts and informers, Barney found the boredom unbearable.

Arguments among the group increased, often centred around the Allied invasion of the Continent – if and when it would happen – and what their role would be. André, a dedicated communist from Nancy, disagreed bitterly with many of the directives of the Vosges resistance and debated endlessly with the others about the vision of France post-war. With the small group unable to venture out safely in daylight, Bébert struggled to keep them together. It proved too much for André, and he eventually decided enough was enough and went home. This, naturally, was utterly frowned upon, as the danger such a man could pose to his colleagues if captured was serious. Bébert, however, was powerless to stop him.

Nor did Bébert trust another member of the unit: Louis. Having been a regular soldier in the French Army in 1939, Louis nurtured his own views on proper military practice and was often contemptuous of the Maquis' amateurish methods. He bristled too against Bébert's seniority and, as an avowed Gaullist, was considerably to the right of much of the prevailing ideology of the Maquis. Louis had in fact attempted to escape to England via Spain and join de Gaulle's Free French Forces but had been captured by the Germans. Given the choice of ten years' prison or joining the loathed Légion des Volontaires Français to fight alongside the Germans in Russia, Louis chose his own option: escape. He knew well that his fate would be a particularly cruel one if captured again.

For reasons Barney could never quite grasp, Bébert nevertheless distrusted Louis, even refusing to allow him to carry either a pistol or a Sten, which Louis found particularly galling. The bitterness and ill will between them only intensified as the period of incarceration dragged on. Their ranks were gradually swelled with the addition of several other maquisards, such as a man Barney only knew as Joe. From Alsace, he had been an interpreter for the Germans at one stage, which made him potentially useful, but again the increasingly brooding Bébert regarded him with suspicion. Barney understood the need for caution. The Germans were adept at 'turning' Frenchmen against each other with threats and promises, or in many cases simply appealing to their natural disposition as Nazi sympathisers. The admission of such a person into their ranks would, every member of Bébert's section knew, see them wiped out to a man soon after.

Every fortnight, the hut received a visit – on skis – from the *chef* of their sector, whom Barney knew only as Le Bouk. He understood him to be a respected manager of a textile mill in nearby Cornimont. This was confirmed when Le Bouk handed over a much-needed supply of socks and underwear, which he had apparently spirited from his own factory. It was from him that Barney received his pay as well as news of the war. Le Bouk did his best to alleviate their terrible sense of isolation; their time would soon come, he assured them. The winter was receding now, and the invasion was expected within weeks, at which time they, and much of the dormant army of the Maquis, would mobilise into action. The hour of France's liberation, he promised, was at hand. Many of the men remained sceptical.

On another visit, Barney – still regarded as something of a celebrity – was handed an ancient French–German–English travellers' guidebook printed in 1896. Apologising that to be seen purchasing a more recent one would attract suspicion, Le Bouk hoped Barney could find some use for it.

Written very much with the well-to-do Continental tourist in mind, the book provided much amusement to the group when Barney read out the French phrases to them, many of which he could recall years afterwards:

We have a motor carriage.

It is very modern.

It has two-wheel brakes.

Are you enjoying yourself?

I hope you are not sick.

Bang! Bang!

(Madame) 'What is that?'

(Chauffeur) 'We are broken down! Now I will change the tyre. You see we have a spare one especially for that.'

(Madame) 'Well really my horse carriage is much nicer.'

Given their current circumstances, the section dealing with eating in fine European hotels was a source of particular amusement.

Aware of the deteriorating condition his men faced under continued confinement, as well as to alleviate the boredom, Le Bouk one day suggested to Bébert that he take Barney along with him on the supply run into La Bresse, where he could be checked over by La Bresse's only physician, Lapierre. The doctor spoke good English and was a trusted friend of the Resistance. If only to relieve the monotony, Barney jumped at the suggestion. The following evening, however, as he trudged up 150 metres to the crest of the mountain, Barney suddenly felt the toll of weeks of confinement. While Bébert seemed almost able to ski uphill, Barney found the one-in-three slope virtually impossible to negotiate.

Eventually, he stood, sweating and exhausted and with boots full of snow, above La Bresse. The view in the moonlight was spectacular, with the pretty mountain town ringed by a vertiginous mantle of white, fading to green and black shadows as the houses and streets began at the fringes of the valley below. With the announcement that it was a 'perfect night for skiing', Bébert pushed off confidently down the slope, Barney following warily behind. 'My method of braking is not to be recommended,' he later reflected.

Wet and bedraggled by the time he reached the bottom, Barney hid his skis with Bébert's behind a stone wall, and they proceeded the rest of the way on foot. At least Barney's designated role as a simple country bumpkin would be enhanced, he thought, by his present appearance. Their plan was for Bébert to spend a couple of hours making his nocturnal rounds to gather supplies while Barney was checked over by the doctor. Barney would need to remain there until he was collected. Although there were friends that could be counted on in La Bresse, there were also enemies. Vigilance, stressed Bébert with his characteristic finger drawn to his lips and a whispered *'Attention'*, must be maintained. But when the doctor's door was answered by an unfamiliar woman who explained he was currently absent on a house call, the two men did their best not to appear flummoxed. No matter, said Bébert calmly, we'll come back later.

Barney and Bébert began wandering the town together late at night – precisely the scenario Bébert had wanted to avoid. Calling at a local inn, the leader took a risk with the bar manager, a woman he half-knew, asking if she could conceal Barney for a couple of hours. The woman looked panicked and flicked her eyes towards some of her customers who were already eyeing the pair – particularly Barney – with curiosity. Taking the hint, Bébert and Barney offered a hasty *bon soir* and left.

The safety of the Resistance networks relied upon complete secrecy, where no member was supplied with any more knowledge about the organisation than was absolutely necessary. Bébert knew that taking Barney with him exposed both himself and the contacts he would meet to danger. But, on this night, there was no choice. Once again impressing upon Barney *'Attention'*, he drew him to the back door of a small shop and knocked three times in a prearranged sequence. *'Entrez, messieurs,'* sounded a quiet voice within, and the two men were quickly ushered into a closed grocer's shop. The proprietor was another typically French-looking middle-aged man, who eyed Barney with deep suspicion. In a moment, though, the tension evaporated, as Bébert introduced him – a little proudly, thought Barney – as the famous *'aviateur Australien'* who had come from the other side of the world and then dropped from the skies to help rid France of the detested Boche. The man's face lit up with recognition of the story, and Barney began to blush at what he suspected to be Bébert's outrageous amplifying of his exploits. Soon, however, the grocer had gathered his wife, several children and various other relations who seemed to inhabit the small dwelling to – in Barney's words – 'take a squiz at me'.

The grocer's wife was particularly taken with Barney. She immediately produced a decent bottle of wine, which, despite a half-hearted protest from Bébert, all agreed to share. A cake then appeared, while Bébert purchased the necessary provisions with what Barney saw to be an astonishingly large wad of cash. Bread, spaghetti, salt and vinegar were all stuffed into a large duffle bag while Barney enjoyed the cake and wine, the fact only slowly dawning on him that he and Bébert were going to have to carry it all back up the mountain – and on skis.

At one stage, a quick, furtive discussion took place, then from inside a cleverly disguised vegetable box a small radio was produced. *'Ici Londres,'* said the voice broadcasting from the BBC Overseas Service studio at 200 Oxford Street in far-off London – Broadcasting House had been bombed earlier in the war. They listened to both the French and English news broadcasts, while Barney, hearing his native tongue spoken properly for the first time in several months, suffered an acute pang of homesickness. The newsreader told of a large RAF attack on Nuremberg. Barney wondered whether any of his former 61 Squadron colleagues had taken part. Little did he know that this infamous attack was Bomber Command's most disastrous of the war, in which ninety-five bombers were destroyed.

Following the news, all present listened silently to the words 'and now here are some messages from our friends in occupied countries', and a series of cryptic lines was read out, coded messages signalling individual Resistance groups all over France. 'John is growing a long beard this week' might mean a supply drop for that night is confirmed. 'The Trojan

War will not take place' could mean the delivery of an SOE agent in the dead of night. The odd list of random lines of poetry and fragments of nursery rhymes or songs went on, as the small group listened. This night, the messages were not for them. Soon, however, that would change.

Once outside, the bonhomie was tempered as, with a deadly serious look, Bébert again implored *'attention'*. Meat was then purchased from a friendly butcher, and then, to Barney's alarm, a twelve-pound (5.4-kilogram) lump of sugar was bought from somewhere and stuffed into a small haversack that Barney then had to carry.

Finally, a return to the home of Doctor Lapierre found him to be in and receptive to the men's visit. Apologising for his absence due to an unexpected call-out, he warned both of them in perfect English that the Gestapo had indeed become more active of late, that rumours of a German military build-up in the area were rife, and that extreme caution was necessary. Barney was enormously impressed by the doctor's bearing, exuding as he did an air of courage and nobility. As Lapierre checked Barney over, finding him in reasonable health considering his circumstances, Bébert sought his wisdom about ways to alleviate the harshness of his men's living conditions. Barney sensed the high regard in which the tough Bébert also held the man. Though sympathetic, Doctor Lapierre could offer little, insisting on the importance of staying put. Soon, he assured them, things would change.

Their foray complete, Barney shook the doctor's hand emphatically, and he and Bébert once more tackled the mountain. After an hour or so, Barney announced he could go no further. By chance, they were close to the farm of their former hosts, the Perrins, and despite the hour were warmly welcomed. *'Je suis très fatigué,'* announced a breathless Barney to everyone's amusement. At 1 am, they arrived back at the hut, Barney a wreck, Bébert appearing not the slightest bit worse for wear.

A few days later, they discovered just how prescient the words of the doctor had been. A German deserter, they heard, had been recaptured by the Gestapo, working at a local sawmill. Under torture, both he and the mill owner had revealed Doctor Lapierre's role in the local Resistance. Forty-seven-year-old Albert Lapierre, it transpired, had lived and worked for twenty years in La Bresse, and had been a loyal and active member of the Resistance since the defeat of 1940, risking his life countless times by handling the passage of French prisoners escaping from the Germans, providing them with food and shelter, and organising identity cards. Later, he had established a parachute zone for the Maquis and a depot for clandestine supplies, and he had never ceased giving his medical services, free of charge, to the members of the Resistance and others in need.

After his arrest, he was taken by the Gestapo first to a prison in nearby Épinal, then to Dachau, and finally to Mauthausen concentration camp, where he was tortured for information about the Maquis but told the Germans nothing. Continuing even to treat prisoners as best he could from inside the camp, he died of exhaustion on 15 April 1945, less than three weeks before it was liberated by the Americans.

After the war, Albert Lapierre was posthumously awarded the Medal of the French Resistance, the Legion of Honour and the War Cross with palm. Today, La Bresse boasts a street named in his honour: 'Rue du Docteur Lapierre'.

Making the news even harder to bear, Barney was told that the doctor was arrested at 9 am on the very morning after his and Bébert's visit. For decades after the war, Barney would harbour a terrible, nagging suspicion that the two events were connected, oblivious as he was to Lapierre's wider connections. He need not have concerned himself. Resistance historians believe that other events were already underway to tragically seal the doctor's fate, and that the timing of the visit was quite coincidental. What cannot be disputed, though, is that Barney had met one of the truly great, but quiet, heroes of France on the last night of his freedom. He would never forget it.

There would, however, be no more visits to the village.

17

C'EST LA GUERRE

The routine of the hut went on. With little to do but take shifts in chopping the wood – which at least was in abundance – to feed the little stove, the party of Maquis, now five-strong, lived as best they could to await the spring. During the frequent snowstorms, when not a soul could come or go, Barney sensed acutely their complete isolation from the outside world. Conversation, such as it was, dropped to almost nothing, as every man, like a prisoner, vanished into the realm of his own thoughts. The only consolation, thought Barney, as he looked out at the snow, was that at least they were well hidden from the enemy. It was with mixed feelings, therefore, that he at last began to observe what he felt might never come: the spring thaw.

At first, the snow needed to be cleared from their door less frequently, then not at all, before gradually beginning to recede, revealing the first mosses and green shoots that

Barney had seen in months. Almost immediately, to everyone's delight, the birds returned, their morning song lifting everyone's spirits. A few days later, however, all woke suddenly to a sound no one welcomed: that of axes hitting timber. The local woodsmen had returned. The noise of their work was distant at first, but after a few days it crept closer, to what appeared to be just a few hundred yards away through the forest.

A quick conference, and Bébert decreed that, this close to La Bresse, they could not take the risk of their cell being exposed to the wrong eyes, so he arranged to move to a less accessible spot. In the second week of April, therefore, the party left their winter camp and found yet another lodge, several kilometres distant. This one being far better constructed than the former, Barney could not help wondering why they had not chosen it earlier.

No sooner had the party resettled than, to their considerable discomfort, two woodcutters appeared and began operations just a stone's throw from the new hideout. Unsure of what exactly to do with this unwelcome company, but also not eager to draw too much attention to themselves, Bébert made enquiries about them in the town. One of them proved to be an Italian, which may have assuaged Bébert's concern somewhat, knowing that the only people to detest the Germans as much as the French were the Nazis' erstwhile – but now savagely persecuted – ally, the Italians. His sources in town finding no reason to distrust the two strangers, Bébert gradually welcomed them into his confidence, conscious also perhaps of the boost that new and friendly faces may have on his men's battered morale.

It was a gamble that paid off. The maquisards, desperate for something useful to do, soon befriended the men – the Italian proved to have excellent skills in the kitchen – and even assisted them in their work of cutting down and preparing the pine logs for transportation in sleds down the hill. In turn, the men would warn Bébert when, as frequently occurred, German officers on leave took to pheasant shooting in the forest nearby. At such times, fires were strictly prohibited. One misty morning, the men froze in their cots as the sound of a shotgun was heard just a couple of hundred metres away. According to Barney, they were saved from discovery simply because of the mist, and the fact that the pheasants ran in the opposite direction. However, to the groaning resignation of the men, Bébert announced that, once again, it was time to move on.

Discovering yet another retreat deeper into the now fast-thawing forest, the men under Bébert's command were finally able to make some creature comforts for themselves in the form of straw beds and bunks. Befriending more wood-cutters – though always after discovering as much information about them as possible – Barney learned that one of them had possession of a wireless set at his home, just a few kilo-metres away. Bébert thought it was worth the risk to hear news direct from the outside world, and a small party made the nocturnal journey. After being given a meal, the wood-cutter warmed up the set. This time, the reported RAF air raids were centred on the French coastal defences. The build-up to the long-anticipated invasion, it seemed, was at last underway. Walking back that evening through the silent forest, Barney noted that almost all the farms he passed were deserted. Their owners and workers, as it was explained to him, were more than likely swept up in the STO and toiling in misery somewhere in Germany. Suddenly, the months of his confinement seemed a little less arduous.

One afternoon, one of the trusted woodcutters came to their door in a state of quiet agitation. A short time earlier, he had encountered a stranger in the forest – an oddity in itself – who was asking a series of pointed questions about a supposed Maquis camp in the area, which he claimed he wanted to join. The woodcutter gave nothing away and was immediately suspicious. There was something about this man, he told them, that he did not trust. After a detailed description, he left them with an urge to 'be on your guard'.

Sure enough, two days later, a stranger fitting the description approached the camp. He greeted Bébert and the group warmly, stating his desire to join them in their upcoming fight against the Germans. The image of his face etched its way into Barney's memory forever. He was about thirty-five, with swarthy and hard-lined features. He spoke with a French accent, but not a local one. His story was that he had been a prisoner of the Germans in Nancy, where he was tortured, and he showed a series of recently healed scars on his arms to prove it. The group gathered around him, observing him closely while Bébert did the talking. Barney stood back a little. This, somehow, seemed a strictly French affair. The man went on to explain that he was staying on a farm a few kilometres away and had heard rumours of Maquis in the area and, quite naturally, was keen to get at *le Boche*.

From where had he heard such rumours, Bébert asked. The man's answers were imprecise. Nevertheless, Bébert asked him into the hut, but not before insisting he remove his shoes, to prevent a quick escape. To be on the safe side, he was also made to surrender his wallet and identity card. The stranger was happy to do so, even drawing their attention to two letters from his girlfriend in Nancy contained therein.

Bébert relaxed a little, and after a while seemed convinced by the man's story. They could certainly do with more men, he reasoned. After an hour or so, he told the man he would most likely be able to join but he would like a couple of days to think about it. He strongly suggested he return to his farm, go nowhere else, and then return in two days' time. The man seemed grateful to the point of servility, shook everyone's hand and departed.

That night, Bébert made an unscheduled trip into La Bresse, which was now some distance from their new camp. One of his contacts, a policeman, agreed to make some enquiries about the stranger. He also called on Le Bouk, who was somewhat alarmed to be visited without notice by his subordinate in the field. This was a matter, however, of the highest importance. If the man proved to be truthful, he could be a valuable new member of the unit. If not, he had already seen enough to have them all liquidated. Bébert handed him the card and wallet. Le Bouk nodded, assessing the situation. Directing him back up the mountain, he would make enquiries and visit late in the morning.

True to his word, Le Bouk appeared the next day, pale and agitated. Nothing was known about the man, he said, nothing whatsoever. The address on the letters, moreover, was in fact that of Nancy's most notorious brothel. The men then waited for the report from their contact in the police. An anxious night was spent, the men posting extra lookouts for any sign of an approach from strangers. Early the next morning, Monsieur Perrin arrived with the police report. Their contact confirmed that the man was indeed an active member of the Milice (a Vichy paramilitary organisation formed to combat the Resistance) on a special assignment for the Germans. He was due to return the following day.

That afternoon, Bébert, Perrin, Le Bouk and another local Maquis commander held a conference in the hut in the forest. The atmosphere was grim. Barney sat at the back of the room and, as best he could, listened. The talk went on for two hours. Finally, speaking in low and unsmiling tones, the men departed.

The next day, the stranger returned. Bébert greeted him warmly. Barney never forgot the look in his eye, a strange blend of fear and hope. The previous evening, the plan had been laid out. Barney had been urged to act as normal as possible. Nothing was to give the game away. The man seemed intrigued at Barney being an *Australien*, almost congratulating him on it and shaking his hand vigorously. Barney maintained the ruse brilliantly. He could smell the stranger's sweat as well as his fear. Flying in Lancaster bombers with six other men, he had become familiar with the smell of fear.

Coffee was prepared. The entire group sat with the man. An atmosphere of bonhomie – so convincing that Barney almost believed it himself – seemed to warm the room. Bébert spoke long about his love of France, and his hatred of the Germans and those traitors who, even now, assisted every day with their tyrannical occupation of his country. He laid out the responsibilities of the Maquis, their reliance on one another, each man's absolute and unwavering trust of the one beside him. The stranger nodded in agreement. Soon, said Bébert, their time would come and maquisards all over France, just like these men sitting around this room, would receive the order to rise and lend their weight to the great Allied invasion that would hurl these fascists from their country. Until that day, however, when that cryptic prearranged command was heard over the airwaves from their friends poised in London, they would harness their resources. Rising up against the Germans now, and alone, would be suicide. The man agreed, even proposing a toast to that glorious day.

For Barney, it was all too much. 'I felt disgusted at what I considered was the levity and duplicity of these Frenchmen,' he later wrote. Scraping his chair against the wooden floor, he offered an *excusez* and left the room.

Bébert, he sensed, was not happy with him. Now was not the time to give any indication of his feelings, nor give the game away to the enemy. He could almost hear Bébert remonstrate with him. *'C'est la guerre!'* he would spit at him afterwards. 'This is war!' Barney, of course, knew it, knew that there could be no ending other than that which had been agreed upon the previous evening, but as he picked up his axe to split wood, just a few metres from the door behind which the stranger was having the last conversation of his life, he still prayed for a different outcome.

Hours later, in the moonlight, digging the grave for the man whose expression he would never expel from his mind, Barney could only remind himself, over and over, *C'est la guerre, c'est la guerre, c'est la guerre* . . .

18

THE THAW

Not a word was mentioned about the execution of the traitor. It was as if the incident was simply expunged from everyone's memory as soon as it had occurred. Nor did anyone besides Barney seem in any way troubled by it, and after a short while, to his own uneasy surprise, he found he was untroubled by it also.

Once or twice, on a night raid, as Barney had lain there in the Lancaster's nose, bomb release in his hand, he could, by craning his neck backwards through the perspex, some-times catch the briefest glimpse of the bombs as they fell from the aircraft, outlined against the flames of some burning city: tumbling black slugs of TNT and RDX that seemed to travel with the aircraft for a moment before plummeting into the cauldron of chaos below. Only occasionally had Barney allowed himself to wonder just what, or who, those bombs would hit. The target, of course, was always the priority, but what about the nights when there was no real target – merely an expanse of roofs and streets and houses and lives that, by the mere pressing of his thumb, he was set to obliterate? How many complete strangers' lives had he thus destroyed from high up in his aeroplane, where nothing could be seen? Hundreds? Thousands? This stranger gushing blood at his feet was simply one more. To dwell too much on his fate, when that of so many others hardly darkened his brow, would seem somehow hollow, even absurd.

After such an incident, however, it was deemed essential that the group break up. With the loss of their agent, the Gestapo would be alerted and looking. The small band of maquisards shook hands outside the hut that had sheltered them from both the elements and the enemy, and then, pledging to see each other during or after the Liberation, they departed.

At the last minute, a host family had been found for Barney: that of Eugene and Marie Mougel, a relatively well off family of La Bresse. The Mougels owned a number of properties, one of them being a farm with a stone cottage nestled under the rocks that outcropped just below the highest peak in the district, La Grosse Pierre. Known as the *maison d'enhaut*, or 'house up high', this spot above the town was where the Mougels would traditionally spend the warmer months of May to September.

The mountain consisted of high-quality granite – hard and of good colour – the mining of which had proved profitable for the Mougels in supplying tombstones and monuments across France. For reasons unknown, this remained one of the few enterprises untaxed by the Germans. The Mougels were well known in the district, and their four children – Emma, twenty-four, sons Gaby, twenty-two, and René, seventeen, and youngest daughter, Bernadette, fourteen – were close. Despite the terrible risks, they took in Barney as if he was one of their own.

In typical French rural style, the large main living room of the *maison d'enhaut* also served as the kitchen. In one corner sat a large wood-burning stove; in another, a table and two benches rested under a window giving a superb view down the village and its environs, the perfect vantage point from which to spot trouble, or the approach of unwelcome visitors from the village.

Barney's quarters – in which he lived and slept most of the day – was a small bedroom off the living room, containing nothing but a straw bed, a crucifix, a very tattered print entitled *La Sauveur du Monde* and a 1927 calendar, which was in fact somewhat useful, as it divulged postal and telegraphic information for the area. At the foot of the bed was a trapdoor leading down to an unventilated cellar, to which Barney would make daily forays to retrieve the best potatoes for the main midday meal. On one wall was another small door, through which he had to stoop, leading outside to a small yard with a fowl house, now occupied by three goats, and beyond that an outside toilet. Barney dreaded having to visit this in wet weather as it became ankle deep in mud.

Being virtually the same age, Barney and the eldest son, Gaby, soon formed a friendship, despite the language barrier – which in any case Barney was overcoming at a rate that surprised even himself. Gaby too was in hiding, to avoid being taken into the STO, so – as much to relieve the boredom as to provide an extra escape route – the two lads decided to construct another secret exit. Finding saws and other tools from Monsieur Mougel's workshop, they removed one of the wall panels and made a partially lined passage that led under a store of hay and then to the outside of the house, just big enough for one person to crawl through at a time. They then reattached the panel to conceal the entrance. After consideration, it was decided that one more layer of security was needed to foil any Gestapo agent who might decide to test the wall panels, so what appeared to be a simple cupboard was installed in front of it.

At the back of the cupboard, another false panel was built, which concealed the entrance to the secret passage. The family were all impressed with the construction, save Madame Mougel, who, stony faced, contemplated the gravity of its use, and prayed openly that that day would never come. As proud of their handiwork as they were, Barney and Gaby wholeheartedly concurred.

This respite from the monotony did not last long, and Barney, with too much time on his hands, cooped up in an albeit friendly prison at the beginning of summer, felt his morale, and even his sanity, slipping. Gaby supplied a small telescope, which they would point towards the town below, discussing in broken French, with the aid of Barney's phrase-book, the story of each house and each person they could see. 'If we saw a man on the road a mile away, Gaby would tell me his life history,' remembered Barney. 'We could see something like twenty farms from our window and I knew exactly to what degree the family in each could be trusted.'

As the weather warmed, Barney found an opportunity for distraction in assisting Gaby in one particularly profitable side-line of the German occupation of France: the manufacture of honey. In a nation deprived of almost all importations, sugar became very scarce, and, as a substitute, honey could fetch extremely high prices. 'My friends the Mougels,' said Barney, 'estimated that they cleared the equivalent of 75 pounds profit per annum from 18 hives. M. Mougel suggested that if we moved down to the lower farm, we could occupy ourselves by making some new hives.'

Both Gaby and Barney were enthusiastic about the idea, but Bébert, when he found out, was aghast, believing it to expose Barney to the danger of being discovered. Barney felt that the risks were worthwhile, not only because the living conditions would be so much better but also because he longed for some useful work to do. 'It would also perhaps,' he said, 'go some small way in repaying the Mougels for the hospitality which they were giving me so ungrudgingly, and, never let it be forgotten at such terrible risk to themselves.' It was with relief, therefore, that the two young men left the mountaintop one night bound for the larger farm below.

Finally feeling a sense of purpose, Barney and Gaby set to work in the ancient farm workshop, with tools fashioned decades earlier by Gaby's grandfather. They lost themselves in the ancient art of beehive-making, eventually creating sixteen of them.

Having never had the experience of rural living at home, Barney was fascinated by the rituals of the apiary, and how every member of the family had their allotted task in the honey-farming process: assembling the combs four at a time into a barrel, which was then swung horizontally between two supports; taking turns to rotate the barrel by a handle of antique appearance, pushing the viscous golden liquid with centrifugal force to the outer sides of the barrel, where it magically drained, golden and cloudy, into pots.

The various members of the family would arrive and, in the traditional method, suck the combs, spitting the precious wax into a receptacle for a hundred later uses. Then the honey was heated, and the water and wax drained off and evaporated, leaving a precious sweet confection.

'At about four o'clock every afternoon we used to assemble in the kitchen and have steamed potatoes, cheese and honey,' Barney recalled. 'If Madame went out for a moment, Gaby would rush over to the crock and seize an extra slice of bread on which to spread honey.'

Occasionally, visitors from the many neighbouring farms would call in to oversee or advise the ritual. 'When visitors came,' said Barney, 'I remained hidden in the store room behind the kitchen. On these occasions I found the honey pot quite a solace.'

All but adopted by the family, Barney's presence in the homestead was known to only one outsider: Robert, the beau of the eldest Mougel girl, Emma. Robert had been in the French Army before being captured early in the 1940 campaign, and he had recently been released after years as a prisoner of the Germans in Danzig to tend his widowed mother on her small farm. Barney remembers him as solemn and slow of speech, and always greeting him with an intense '*Comment ça va?*' and a strong handshake. He hoped he could trust him.

The memories of those last few weeks spent hiding in the upper slopes of the Vosges mountains stayed with Barney forever. Never daring to step out of the house in daylight, he became accustomed to the sounds of dozens and dozens of gently clanking cowbells as the animals were brought up from the farms to the community pastures that surrounded the little cottage. On an adjacent summit just three kilometres away, the peaceful rural tableau was, however, interrupted by a German observation post, which Barney could see clearly through Gaby's telescope. Every evening, he watched the three German soldiers make their way up the mountain track to take their place in the nightly vigil watching for Allied aircraft.

Again and again, Barney was amazed to the point of bewilderment as to why this family of strangers were risking everything – literally everything – to assist him. The consequences – for him as well as them – of being caught were simply too terrible to contemplate. Yet, day after day, this simple but honourable French family – just as the Christments had done in the weeks after being shot down – fed and protected Barney at their own expense and without a breath of complaint.

One evening, when he tried to glean from Gaby some sense of what motivated his family to take such risks, Gaby smiled and said simply, 'Barney, when your country has been invaded, occupied and defiled by people such as these, then, my friend, you will understand.' Later that night, the sky was filled for nearly an hour with the sound of aircraft engines passing overhead on their way towards a German city somewhere to the east. Barney suspected it was Stuttgart. On the horizon, the glow of red burned all through the night. He knew just how it would look from his 'office' in the Lancaster's nose, but the memories of him directing his pilot onto the target with his emphatic calls of 'left, left a bit . . . steady' and so on felt part of another life, and long long ago. Suddenly, Barney was itching to once more get at the enemy. He would not have long to wait.

19

JE MARCHERAI AVEC VOUS

'People of Western Europe. A landing was made this morning on the coast of France by troops of the Allied Expeditionary Force . . .' The words coming over the small and primitive radio set froze Barney where he stood, peeling potatoes for the midday meal. It was 8.30 am on 6 June 1944, D-Day. Ironically, Barney was the only one to hear General Eisenhower's extraordinary words that morning, the Mougels being outside, engaged in their various summer chores. But the realisation that the great day had at last come caused Barney to hurl caution aside, bolt out and tell Madame and Monsieur, Gaby, René, Bernadette and Emma in almost gushing terms that the moment for which they, and almost the entire French nation, had yearned for for four years was finally at hand.

It was what Eisenhower said next, however, that would pertain to Barney Greatrex's immediate future, perhaps even to his fate: 'All patriots, men and women, young and old have a part to play in the achievement of final victory. To members of resistance movements, whether led by nationals or by outside leaders, I say: follow the instructions you have received.' Finally, the dormant resistance armies, crouched for months in secret cells, in cities and in forests across France, would come to life. For some, though, the price would be terrible.

The broadcast over, Barney returned to the potatoes, his hands now shaking. He remembers the rest of that day spent in almost unendurable anticipation. From whisper to whisper, the news travelled fast. At about 3 pm, a neighbouring farmer rushed in, breathless, to inform the Mougels. He was slightly crestfallen to discover they already knew. He nevertheless had also heard the local Maquis had been ordered this very night to assemble at a certain farm in the mountains at midnight. The farmer left, and several hours passed. Would word also come for Barney to join the ranks of his comrades, or had he been forgotten? Despite what he knew would be the risks, the notion of being excluded from the great test now seemed unbearable. The evening wore on, and still no word. Madame Mougel decided there would never be a more appropriate time to open some of their precious rationed wine. '*À Liberation!*' sounded the toast, but despite it being their finest bottle, Barney could taste nothing.

Almost on cue, a deep knock sounded on the door. In the dusk light stood Bébert. He was tired but excited, having walked many kilometres rounding up the scattered members of the unit. He apologised for the hour but confirmed what the excited farmer had heard. Orders had come to mobilise, and now was the time. Turning to Barney, he looked at him squarely with his dark and powerful eyes. 'Will you stay here, or will you march to victory?'

Shaking, but without a moment's hesitation, Barney placed his hand solemnly on his heart. '*Je marcherai avec vous.*' Another toast was called for and the precious bottle was emptied. This time, remembered Barney, it tasted magnificent.

•

Despite the long and brutal years of their occupation, Barney never ceased to be amazed at the unquenchable optimism of the French people. Never for a moment had they lost their absolute certainty, he noted, that the day of victory would come and that the Germans would be forced out of their wounded but beloved country. During the long months of hiding, there were times when Barney himself was not nearly so optimistic. Living on speculation and rumour, he believed the fabric of the Resistance could not have lasted another three months before starting to unravel. Already, the inevitable tensions had started to reveal themselves, and, as far as Barney could observe, D-Day had arrived just in time.

Three hours after Bébert's appearance at the Mougels' *maison d'enhaut*, he and Barney were trudging in heavy rain up the mountain. Nothing, however, could dampen their spirits. They were speculating on the great Allied armies even now sweeping in great swathes across the French countryside towards them. Surely, they would arrive at their little Vosges valley in no time at all!

At a small farm, they joined several more Maquis enjoying a fine supper and being waited on by two pretty farm girls whom Barney happened to remember wore lipstick for the occasion. The morale of these men was now sky high. After a brief rest, they were on the road again, to meet up with the main body of the Maquis, which Bébert estimated would be in the several hundreds. When arriving at the midnight rendezvous point, however, all were slightly deflated to be met by precisely four equally disappointed Resistance fighters.

Don't worry, one of them said, a mile or two away was a party of twelve escaped Russians who would be willing to swell their ranks. A farm boy was sent over to give them the message. A short time later, he returned. The Russians, it seemed, were quite comfortable where they were, but would 'probably' join them the next day. After a brief discussion, the men decided they would push on without them.

Resuming the journey, Barney felt the months of confinement on his woefully unfit body. His boots were also too big and his socks inadequate. The rain came down again. They decided to shelter under some bushes, which afforded little protection from the weather. Barney caught some muffled conversation suggesting their guide, a young farm boy, was probably lost. 'Where are we heading?' he ventured to Bébert. 'Belfort,' came the answer, a little uncertainly. Barney's feet were already blistered. Belfort, wherever it was, could not be close enough.

After pushing on through the damp night, Barney, his feet now in agony, announced he could go no further. The others, far from chastising him, seemed almost relieved and, throwing themselves down on the driest piece of ground they could find, quickly went to sleep. Bébert said he knew of a farmhouse nearby and headed off. Just before dawn, he returned with not only some fresh bread and cheese but also a decent pair of socks. Barney's gratitude was beyond measure.

Totally contrary to the plan and everything they had been taught about basic military manoeuvres, the little party was now proceeding to a main Maquis rendezvous point in broad daylight, led by a guide who appeared less than sure he knew where he was going. With no choice but to take him at his word, the men silently fought their exhaustion and trudged on. At one point, they came to the main Le Thillot–Belfort highway. Every rule they had learned about concealment told them not to cross it, but they were too tired to care. Luckily, no Germans were to be seen.

Another hour's walk brought the men to a farm on a plateau above Le Thillot, where, from nowhere, they were confronted by several men armed with Sten guns. After a tense few moments during which Bébert established his identity, they were allowed to proceed to what had been hastily set up as a local Maquis headquarters. Around sixty men – some in uniform, others in civilian clothing, but all armed with various weaponry and being addressed and drilled in groups both large and small – gave Barney a streak of reassurance. Finally, he thought, he had arrived at something that resembled an army. Over here was a pile of ammunition, which he presumed to have been dropped to them during the night. Next to it was a large stack of meat, bread and wine. Most of the faces around him, Barney sensed correctly, were from neighbouring farms. Most seemed to know each other. As for the command structure, that was still unclear.

To his embarrassment, Barney was announced to all as an RAF airman, which created a sensation among those curious to know the story of his escape. Retiring exhausted, he spent his first night feeling that, finally, he was a genuine member of this strange, ragtag army, the Maquis.

Next morning, Barney was presented with a brand new pair of boots, part of a stash purloined from a local Vichy warehouse. To his relief, they fitted perfectly. Soon after, the elusive Russians turned up, as well as a Hindu soldier wearing British battledress. His story was equally remarkable as Barney's, having been taken prisoner by the Afrika Korps in Libya in 1940 and choosing his moment to escape when his POW camp was accidentally bombed by the RAF. That was several months earlier, and how he had managed to remain concealed Barney could only guess at. To his great joy, Barney also encountered a French Merchant Marine officer who had been parachuted in a few nights before and whose English was fluent. After nearly four months on the run, this was the first time that Barney had been able to speak to someone in his own language at length, and the relief was immense.

This officer brought Barney most of the war news he had been desperate to hear. Bomber Command, he was told, had lately concentrated its efforts on smaller, tactical targets in the run-up to the invasion, and often in daylight. This idea Barney found particularly astonishing. Bombing was dangerous enough at night, but he could only wonder at the casualties entailed in revealing yourself to the enemy in broad daylight. The French officer (whose name Barney could never remember) put the young Australian to good use, helping train the men to use some of the weapons delivered by the RAF, the instructions, amazingly, all being in English. Barney's speciality became the bazooka. After poring over the thick, green-backed booklet, he conveyed what he could of this formidable weapon to his comrade students. His instructional repertoire did not, however, extend to live firing, as they had only been provided with thirty-one projectiles.

Such complaints about the paucity of weapons received quickly became a chorus. 'How are we expected to fight with so little?' was a question that would be asked time and again over the coming months.

Barney now began Maquis duties proper, starting with long stints as a guard and as part of reconnaissance parties.

The Germans, it was understood, were now alerted and in time would attempt to crush the rise of the Maquis if the Allied armies did not reach them first. As the weeks following D-Day came and went with no sign of the Allies, and rumours began to spread about the entire Anglo-American offensive being bogged down in the difficult 'bocage' country 600 kilometres to the west in Normandy, uniting with them gradually became a forlorn hope. Men unused to camping in the open, and having expected to do so for only a few days, became bitter and depressed. Supplies began to run out. At one stage, Barney was forced to shelter with thirteen other Maquis in a farmhouse as a three-day mountain storm rolled in. Their only sustenance was plain boiled macaroni.

From time to time, the unit was visited by the local Maquis chief, who would stay for inspections and talks, but Barney suspected he knew little more of the bigger picture than his men. Supplies continued to dwindle, rumours took hold, and morale once again plummeted. Barney at this point considered asking his commander if he could be spirited into nearby Switzerland, it having been earlier suggested to him as a possibility. Barney's Hindu soldier friend had formerly decided that the poor organisation of the Maquis was unsustainable and had himself attempted to make for the Swiss border. Barney never discovered whether he succeeded.

Just on midnight one night, Barney heard an alarm signalling that the Gestapo had discovered the camp and, with elements of the German Army, would be there by dawn. The news could not be ignored. Quickly breaking up into small groups, the men struck camp and headed off into the night, Barney being led once again by Bébert, who had decided to return to the familiar territory around La Bresse. Barney became part of a multinational if motley crew of twenty-one, comprising nine Frenchmen and two French women whose husbands were in the hands of the Gestapo, six of the Russians, two Alsatians, another former soldier from the Indian Army, and one lone Australian, himself.

Barney found the Russians to be particularly interesting characters: warm, brave and tough but never lacking in humour. There was Nicholav, a young blond lad from Minsk who, after having been captured during one of the great battles in the east, had been taken to work as a slave at a tobacco factory in Strasbourg, from which he had escaped. Then there was a constantly laughing peasant from Rostov who had an enormous appetite and would devour everything in sight. One boy from Smolensk had been captured at the tender age of thirteen in 1941 and was now desperately homesick. Their leader, and the strongest character in the group, was Vladimir, an officer who had graduated from the Moscow Military Academy. He worshipped Stalin and was a committed communist. According to Barney, he was 'a most likeable fellow'. He spoke French and also a little German, and had already had an extraordinary war, being captured near Leningrad during the great German offensive in 1941. In the depth of winter, he had been part of a death march from Tallinn in Estonia to Halle in Germany. Of the 43,000 men who had set out, Vladimir was one of only 2000 to have survived. Although shocked, Barney believed every word of it. He forever remembered the story as one of his first inklings of the true nature of the enemy he was fighting.

From Vladimir, Barney learned more than he could ever imagine about life in Russia, a country that had seldom, if ever, entered into his thoughts. He told Vladimir of his father's engineering business, which he would one day like to run. The concept was so alien to Vladimir that he found it amusing and dubbed Barney 'the little capitalist'. He longed to go back to his beloved Soviet Union, but little did he know that, having spent time in the west, even against his will, his status upon returning to Stalin's Russia would be precarious indeed.

20

BACK TO LA BRESSE

Within a day or two of striking camp, Bébert's party had whittled down to only ten or so Maquis, with the others having dispersed to various hiding points in the mountains. Those remaining included Barney, and the Russians, who refused under any circumstances to be separated.

With nothing but a military map of indeterminate vintage to guide them, at one point all of them strayed over the border into Germany, and were saved only by Vladimir's military training and quick thinking. With relief, at around 4 am, they finally approached one of the more dilapidated farm-houses above La Bresse, which Barney had in fact spent some time in earlier, only for Bébert to announce that his wallet, containing some £300 in cash and several hundred more in bread coupons – which were no less valuable for having been forged – was missing. For the next several hours, the exhausted little party retraced their steps and, sometimes on hands and knees, searched for it in the slush. Miraculously, it was discovered before being too water-damaged. In stony silence, it was handed back to a severely chagrined Bébert.

As the group approached the farmhouse once more, two men were observed walking up the road towards them who did not seem to carry the bearing of the Maquis. Fearing them to be Gestapo, Bébert's group sheltered in the woods until they passed, before proceeding to the cold and unwelcoming refuge of the farmhouse. It was still as miserable as Barney had remembered it.

Later that afternoon, a visit from a local Maquis leader confirmed that the Germans were being reinforced and were likely to make a stand in the Vosges over the coming weeks. As a preliminary to this, said the leader, the Gestapo had become very active, determined to root out any resistance before the Allies approached. The two men they had seen in the night, he assured them, would in all likelihood have indeed been Gestapo on the lookout for signs of the Maquis.

This was not news some of the party wanted to hear, and three of them immediately dumped their gear and headed off for home. Bébert remonstrated but could do nothing. This left Barney and the Russians in a particularly vulnerable situation. Bébert, however, vowed to find the Russians a safer refuge for the moment, and suggested Barney return to the Mougels until new orders were received. Bidding farewell to his curious new friends from the east, Barney turned down the hill and, after hiding in the forest until dusk, knocked once more upon the familiar door of the Mougels' *maison d'enhaut* above La Bresse.

Eleven days after leaving the bosom of the Mougels, an exhausted and dishevelled Barney staggered back into their cottage. As he would write many years later, 'So much for my second venture with the Maquis.'

•

It was not until mid-August, just as the joint American and British armies were finally struggling free of fierce German defences around Normandy and breaking out towards Paris, that Bébert once again arrived at the Mougels' door to summon Barney to battle. The Resistance, he assured him, had evolved since their initial explosion into life immediately following D-Day and was now far better supplied and organised. A new camp was now set up, and Bébert still wanted Barney to be a part of it. Without hesitation, Barney once more accepted.

The Mougels had again taken Barney in without question, and at a time even more fraught with risk. The Germans were now alert and rising in numbers, determined to crush this growing secret army that they feared would cripple their ability to meet the Allied armies when they arrived. The time of inactivity was coming to an end.

Bébert was true to his word, and Barney was indeed impressed by the site of the new camp, set up in a proper defensive position on a high plain in the forest about fifteen kilometres from La Bresse. The unit of nineteen men comprised almost all locals from the nearby town of Gérardmer.

They camped in military-style bivouac tents set up to merge as best they could into the trees. The area was also dotted with farmhouses, almost all of which had been abandoned and quickly requisitioned by the Maquis. Guards were placed to monitor the two well-concealed tracks that led into the place. They were well supplied, almost to the point of embarrassment. Every day, a load of fresh food came up from Gérardmer, and Barney could not remember when his rations had been this good. 'We actually had steak for dinner every night,' he recalled, amazed. It was obvious that the Maquis had been receiving much-needed help, both locally and from further afield, care of the RAF. They were, in Barney's words, 'a very happy band', but still they lacked orders.

One Frenchman Barney befriended was Henri Oiseau, a former jockey who had spent a year or two racing on the British circuit and spoke good English. Returning to defend his country at the beginning of the war, he had been captured during the collapse of 1940 but had managed to escape from his POW camp near Stuttgart amid the chaos of an air raid, in which Barney himself had participated seven months previously. He thanked Barney sincerely for his efforts that night.

The camp grew quickly, with dozens of new Maquis seeming to arrive daily. Soon it reached one hundred, then 200 strong. Instructions from England on what exactly they were supposed to do, however, were few and far between. Every day, the wireless set was monitored, ears listening intently for the mention of the prearranged words that would signal their unit. Meanwhile, matters closer to home needed to be dealt with.

Quietly one afternoon, Bébert informed Barney that a Gestapo informer had been identified in Gérardmer and needed to be dealt with before he could cause too much damage. The unit would head into Gérardmer that evening. Before Barney could volunteer, Bébert announced that he was to stay behind and mind the camp, and that the decision was final. With the memory of how the last such traitor was 'dealt with' still fresh, Barney silently thanked him for the unspoken favour.

Later that evening, with the camp all but dead, Barney kept a lonely vigil. Soon after the party had left on its grim mission, however, a breathless courier arrived from the local Maquis headquarters. The BBC had given their coded signal and a drop was scheduled for the designated parachute zone further up the mountain that very night. Without a second to waste, Barney rounded up a local farm boy and ordered him to catch up with the men, now well on their way the ten kilometres to Gérardmer, and deliver the message. With a sigh of relief, Barney witnessed their return an hour before midnight.

A further hour's march through the forest now with Barney they emerged into a well-concealed clearing, about 275 metres wide and half as long. Three heaps of dried logs were prepared, forming the points of a triangle. Settling into the long grass nearby, the men sat and waited. In hushed conversation, the nature of the drop was anticipated. Would it be small arms, perhaps? Ammunition? Explosives for use on the train networks to foil the movement of German soldiers? The hours passed. The aircraft failed to appear. Then, more disappointment as the first brushstrokes of pale touched the horizon. The men lay back in the grass, resigned in dismay. There would be no drop tonight.

There was also no drop the next night, nor the one after that. Had the courier made a mistake? Rumour and misinformation, after all, thrived in the Resistance. For four nights, the Maquis waited, hoping that bad weather had perhaps delayed the much-anticipated arms drop. Their ears strained for the sounds of engines in the dark skies, but none was to be heard.

On the fifth day since the signal, while in a Maquis farmhouse, Barney listened with others to the BBC 1 pm broadcast. As the cryptic messages 'for friends in occupied countries' were read out, a commander next to him let out an excited, '*Voila!*' and bolted out the door. Again, the signal. The drop was on once more.

This time, the men were not disappointed. At exactly 12.45 am, the drone of aircraft engines could be heard approaching from the west. In the darkness, a voice rang out, and the three bonfires, primed to burn quickly, pierced the darkness. At about 500 feet, the matt undersides of two Halifax bombers, which had taken off from the most secret aerodrome in Britain, RAF Tempsford, passed overhead in a roar, leaving a string of white parachutes in their wake. In a moment, there was silence again, interrupted only by the jubilation of the men. Barney remembered the 'plop' of thirty-two containers hitting the ground all around him. The fires were immediately extinguished, and mule wagons were brought up to take the booty to the Maquis' secret cache.

Having waited so long for some attention from England, Barney's unit now received it in spades. For several nights in a row, the SOE Halifaxes returned, each time dispensing a full load, which fluttered down and was collected in the strictest silence possible. Sometimes, the uncooperative breeze would carry the parachutes into the forest, where they would lodge in the tops of pine trees. Being colour coded, they were all too visible by daylight, and there was often no alternative but to cut down the tree. There being no known way to quietly cut down a hundred-foot pine tree, Barney forever wondered how the Nazis, who surely were already alerted by the sound of low-flying aircraft, did not catch them red-handed at the outset.

Other containers came down in a swamp that bordered the forest, forcing the men to spend hours retrieving them, while trying not to drown amid the almost impenetrable mud and reeds. On one occasion, Barney had to shelter under a pine tree as the containers landed all around him. One, laden with hand grenades, burst open on impact, setting one of them off. Barney hit the ground. There was another explosion, then the whole lot went up, creating a boom that must have been heard for miles. The fellow Maquis cursed their bad luck. Hand grenades were a particularly prized weapon, and those would now never be thrown at the Germans.

As the Maquis slowly became better armed and equipped, Barney noticed – and quietly despaired at – the growing jealousy between the various units, who seemed eager to swell their ranks simply to outdo their neighbour. More and more men began to appear, eager to join despite appearing to Barney to be boys or old men, full of enthusiasm but of doubtful ability. In a short time, the group had swelled to over 400 recruits, but there was still only enough equipment to arm about 140. 'London will send more guns' was the curt reply whenever Barney queried the group's ability to absorb so many new faces. It now seemed inconceivable to Barney that the Germans could not be aware of this burgeoning and unwieldy camp in the mountains.

From their eyrie, the Maquis looked down on the roads winding through the valleys and passes of the Vosges, crammed with columns of Germans heading west from Germany. Sooner or later, they reasoned, some of them would peel off and head up the mountain to meet them.

One afternoon, the overall chief of the Vosges Maquis, a Monsieur Gonand, informed his men that the RAF would again that evening be making an appearance. Tonight's delivery, however, would be special indeed.

That night, 250 men again crouched in the field and lit the signal fires at the sound of approaching aircraft. This time, it was a sole American Liberator that passed low overhead. Some of the parachutes came down with the usual thud of containers, but others, Barney could just see, were larger and more silent. Somewhere in the darkness in front of him, a rustle was heard.

Suddenly, a tall and unfamiliar figure in flying gear emerged into the light of one of the fires. 'Good evening,' said the man in an American accent. 'Major John Rees, US Army.'

Taking his extended hand, Barney forgot his cover of 'Jacques' and spluttered out his real name in reply. The maquisards stood, jaws agape. Soon, three more men emerged from the gloom – Frenchmen, in British battledress. The maquisards came from everywhere to catch a glimpse of these warriors dropped from the sky. Rees began handing out packets of cigarettes and chewing gum from voluminous pockets on his overalls. 'He spoke French like a Parisian,' recalled Barney. 'It was 2 am before we all turned in for the night, but I think most of us were too excited to get much sleep.' Finally, the Maquis were going to be shown how to take the battle to the Germans.

The dreaded government telegram, as received by Barney's parents a few days after his failure to return from the mission to Augsburg. It would be months before they knew of his fate. *Courtesy of Barney Greatrex*

61 Squadron Commanding Officer's letter to Barney's father, Basil, regarding Barney's fateful twentieth mission, incorrectly noted as his nineteenth. The letter pays tribute to Barney and holds out hope of his return. *Courtesy of Barney Greatrex*

LISTS OF PHRASES

FRENCH
DUTCH
GERMAN
SPANISH

FRENCH

ENGLISH	FRENCH	ENGLISH	FRENCH
One	Un	Twenty	Vingt
Two	Deux	Thirty	Trente
Three	Trois	Forty	Quarante
Four	Quatre	Fifty	Cinquante
Five	Cinq	Sixty	Soixante
Six	Six	Seventy	Soixante-dix
Seven	Sept	Eighty	Quatre-vingts
Eight	Huit	Ninety	Quatre-vingt-dix
Nine	Neuf	Hundred	Cent
Ten	Dix	Five Hundred	Cinq cents
Eleven	Onze	Thousand	Mille
Twelve	Douze		
Thirteen	Treize	Monday	Lundi
Fourteen	Quatorze	Tuesday	Mardi
Fifteen	Quinze	Wednesday	Mercredi
Sixteen	Seize	Thursday	Jeudi
Seventeen	Dix-Sept	Friday	Vendredi
Eighteen	Dix-huit	Saturday	Samedi
Nineteen	Dix-neuf	Sunday	Dimanche
Minutes	Minutes	Week	Semaine
Hours	Heures	Fortnight	Quinzaine
Day	Jour	Month	Mois
Night	Nuit	O'clock	heures

ENGLISH	FRENCH
I am (we are)	Je suis (nous sommes)
British (American)	Anglais; (Américain)
Where am I?	Où est-ce que je suis?
I am hungry; thirsty	J'ai faim. J'ai soif
Can you hide me?	Pouvez-vous me cacher?
I need civilian clothes	J'ai besoin de vêtements
How much do I owe you?	Combien vous dois-je?
Are the enemy nearby?	L'ennemi est-il près?
Where is the frontier?	Où est la frontière
BELGIAN	Belge
SWISS; SPANISH:	Suisse, Espagnole
Where are the nearest British (American) troops?	Où sont les forces angl (américaines) les plus proches?
Where can I cross this river?	Ouest-ce que je peux trave cette rivière?
Is this a safe way?	Est-ce que ce chemin n'es dangéreux?
Will you please get me a third class ticket to . . .	Voulez-vous me prendre billet de troisième c pour . . . s'il vous plaît.
Is this the train (bus) for . . ?	Est-ce que c'est le train (a bus) (car) pour . . .?
Do I change (i.e. trains)?	Dois-je changer de train?
At what time does the train (bus) leave for . . . .?	A quelle heure est-ce qu train (autobus) part pour
Right; left; straight on	A droite; à gauche; tout
Turn back; stop	Revenez en arrière; ar vous
Thank you; please	Merci; s'il vous plaît
Yes; No	Oui; Non
Good morning; afternoon	Bonjour
Good evening; Night	Bonsoir
Consulate	Consulat
Out of bounds; Forbidden	Défense de pénétrer; défendu

Having survived bailing out over France, Barney needed to learn the language quickly. His annotations are still visible on a list of local phrases provided as part of his escape kit. *Courtesy of Barney Greatrex*

One of Barney's local Resistance unit, Paul Bodot. Without Paul's help, Barney's time in France would have lasted a matter of days.
Courtesy of Barney Greatrex

The Mougel family – who took incredible risks hiding Barney from the Germans, a debt he felt he could never repay – Gaby, Bernadette, Robert (Emma's fiancé), Emma, Eugene, Marie and René (from left to right). *Courtesy of Barney Greatrex*

Barney's Resistance unit commander, Jean-Paul Vitu, aka Bébert, adopting a suitably Gallic pose. *Courtesy of Christiane Gilbert*

Lieutenant Colonel Guy Prendergast (right) of the Special Operations Executive and commander of the Jedburgh mission 'Pavot', pictured here earlier in the war while serving in the Long Range Desert Group.

The ruined Vosges village of La Bresse as the Germans left it in late 1944. Barney has marked the *maison d'enhaut* where he stayed for a time with the Mougels. *Courtesy of Barney Greatrex*

Barney's letter of recognition from the US Third Infantry Division, which left an impression on Air Chief Marshal Harris himself. *Courtesy of Barney Greatrex*

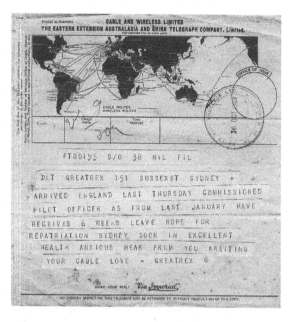

CABLE AND WIRELESS LIMITED
THE EASTERN EXTENSION AUSTRALASIA AND CHINA TELEGRAPH COMPANY, Limited.

FTB0195 S/O 38 NIL FIL

DLT GREATREX 151 SUSSEXST SYDNEY =

ARRIVED ENGLAND LAST THURSDAY COMMISSIONED
PILOT OFFICER AS FROM LAST JANUARY HAVE
RECEIVED 6 WEEKS LEAVE HOPE FOR
REPATRIATION SYDNEY SOON IN EXCELLENT
HEALTH ANXIOUS HEAR FROM YOU AWAITING
YOUR CABLE LOVE = GREATREX

MARK YOUR REPLY "Via Imperial"

The best news Barney's mother could wish for: the telegram informing her that he was safe and well, and hopefully coming home soon. *Courtesy of Barney Greatrex*

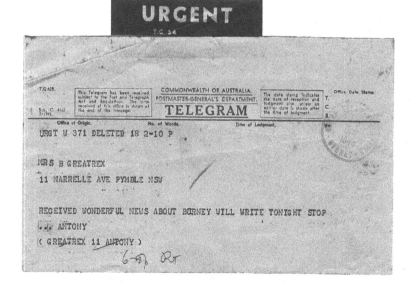

Antony's telegram to Elsie Greatrex upon hearing of Barney's rescue. *Courtesy of Barney Greatrex*

Respected British war artist Eric Kennington's portrait of Barney Greatrex. He believed it to be one of his best. *Courtesy of Alex Lloyd*

Back in Australia in early 1945, Barney shows off his newly issued RAAF tropical kit uniform with his officer's stripe finally on his shoulder. *Courtesy of Barney Greatrex*

A post-war procession in La Bresse to remember those who perished during the destruction. *Courtesy of Barney Greatrex*

Back home, Barney's parents coaxed him into dressing up in his erstwhile role as a Maquisard, with his sister Pleasance as a nurse, and brother Antony in his RAAF uniform. Barney himself looks less than impressed. *Courtesy of Barney Greatrex*

Barney at Choloy War Cemetery in 2013 on his final visit to France, standing by the headstones of his crewmates Einarson and Worth. *Courtesy of Charlie Mort*

Seventy-two years after the event, Barney, along with four other airmen, receive the French Legion of Honour in Sydney, June 2016. *Courtesy of Richard Mort*

PART THREE

21

THE JEDBURGHS – A NEW TYPE OF WAR

Several months earlier, at precisely 11 pm on the night before D-Day, a single black Handley Page Halifax aircraft rose into the night sky above SOE's clandestine aerodrome at Tempsford in Bedfordshire and turned south. Far below in the dark, the 5000-strong fleet of ships that, in a few hours, would open the 'Second Front' by landing men along the beaches of Normandy jostled for their allotted place in the great armada and prepared to sail.

The big bomber soaring above them, however, carried no bombs. Its cargo was a trio of figures sitting quietly near the rear exit door, doubtless lost in their own thoughts. They were three extraordinarily fit, extraordinarily skilled men – one Englishman, two French – who, after months of punishing training in the United States and then Britain, were as expert as one can be in the arts of guerrilla warfare, sabotage and hand-to-hand combat, both armed and unarmed. Collectively, they were given the codename 'Hugh', and they may or may not have realised that they were that night making history.

Not only were they virtually the first uniformed Allied soldiers to land in France (more or less splitting the honour with the men of the Oxford and Buckinghamshire Light Infantry who were at the same moment preparing to daringly take Pegasus Bridge behind Sword Beach) but they were also the first of many similarly composed 'Jedburgh' teams dropped into France to help train and coordinate the French Resistance. The operation's name – which it shared with the Scottish Borders town of Jedburgh – had been randomly assigned from a Ministry of Defence codebook.

Apart from the ad hoc exploits of T. E. Lawrence in the Arabian deserts thirty years earlier, this was the first concerted attempt in the history of warfare to organise an insurgency in support of a military campaign. From the outset, so as to distance themselves from spies, the 'Jeds' always insisted on operating in uniform. Such boldness, it was also assumed, would encourage the Maquis as well as give the Jeds the sense of authority they would need to train and lead inexperienced men on missions of sabotage and hit-and-run attack.

In fact, the Jedburgh teams could have dropped much earlier, but politics intervened. Although the self-appointed leader of the Free French, General de Gaulle, believed himself to be the very embodiment of France, destined to both lead and shape it after the war, not everyone shared his conviction, least of all his major allies, the British and the Americans. If Churchill could barely tolerate de Gaulle, both Eisenhower and Roosevelt detested him, were deeply mistrustful of his long-term ambitions, and felt under no obligation whatsoever to facilitate his apparently God-ordained right to become ruler of France as soon as the fighting had stopped. Hence, and to de Gaulle's eternal fury, the precise timing of D-Day was kept a secret from him until the very last minute. One of the consequences of this policy, however, was that many covert operations such as the Jedburghs were held back until D-Day itself, when their services could have been put to much greater use considerably earlier.

It was agreed initially that each Jedburgh team would comprise one officer from either the British SOE or its American equivalent, the Office of Strategic Services (OSS), a second and sometimes third officer who would be a native of the country in which they were operating – in this case, France – and a radio operator who could be any of the three nationalities. Even arriving at this had been a long and diffi-cult road. The British SOE had for years held the Americans at arm's length when it came to special forces involvement, somewhat patronisingly asserting that they had been in the secret war business for a lot longer than them. Besides, they added, even those American officers who could manage reasonable French did so with such an atrocious accent that they would stand out a mile. As the war progressed, though, and the United States became by far the heavier lifter in bringing the war to Western Europe, SOE bowed to the inevitable and began to treat the Americans as something like equal partners.

All this would have been the last thing on the minds of Captain William Crawshay – the leader of that first Jedburgh mission – and his small team as they watched the aircraft's jump light turn from red to green and proceeded to leap through the Halifax's open door into a black sky and God only knew what lay below.

Between D-Day and the end of 1944, there would be just short of one hundred such Jedburgh operations carried out across Western Europe, every element of which was protected by a series of complex and often bizarre codenames. Captain Crawshay himself was given the code 'Crown' (appropriately, perhaps, as he was eventually knighted), with his two French companions given the cover names of not only 'Louis Legrand' and 'René Mersiol' but also, to confuse things further, 'Franc' and 'Yonne'. Other Jed names were taken from French and German place names, the periodic table, and even pharmaceutical drugs such as 'Chloroform' and 'Novocain'. Some missions were given almost comical titles, such as 'Bunny', 'Cedric' and 'Cinnamon'.

There was nothing light-hearted about the Jedburghs' objectives, however. After arming the Maquis and giving them the basics of demolition and guerrilla warfare, the Jedburgh teams were directed to put them in touch with the invading Allied armies, so they could prepare the ground for their advance. Hence, the Jed teams always jumped with at least one highly trained wireless operator, whose precious weapon was a small, specially manufactured battery-powered radio set.

In this way, it was hoped that the disparate elements of the Maquis – which in the weeks after D-Day were estimated to be approaching 100,000 strong – could be harnessed into carrying out coordinated guerrilla operations in the path of the advancing Allies in accordance with Eisenhower's overall plan for the liberation of France. It would prove to be a very tall order.

Initially, at least, some Jedburgh teams found their Maquis far less capable – and sometimes far less willing – to fight than they had been led to believe, and although each team commander carried a letter of introduction personally signed by de Gaulle, many of the great general's compatriots had almost as little time for him as they did for the enemy. Many Jed officers were dropped with no idea of the complex rivalries and divisions existing across the various Resistance organisations, and they found trying to lead them akin to herding cats. Their accompanying French officers could also fall foul of the local commanders, who suddenly felt their position threatened, or who sometimes came from wildly opposing social or political classes.

Most Maquis were of course more than willing to fight, but they often lacked even the most basic skills of fieldcraft and tactical training, as one of the most famous Jed commanders, Major Tommy McPherson, had found out in June. Attempting to instil confidence in the Maquis unit he had come to train, McPherson planned and led an attack on a German armoured column in the Dordogne. The attack succeeded, but twenty out of twenty-seven of his guerrilla fighters were killed, almost

entirely through a lack of understanding of the simplest principles of crossing ground under fire.

Barney Greatrex and his Piquante Pierre Maquis knew
nothing of this, of course, but were simply relieved that their
unit's call to action had, after the weeks of almost unbearable
waiting, finally been made. A couple of nights later, another
aircraft despatched another officer, who Barney soon learned
was Major Rees's commander and a true luminary in the
world of special operations, Lieutenant Colonel Guy Lenox
Prendergast, DSO (Distinguished Service Order).

At forty-three, and still with film-star good looks, Guy
Prendergast in an earlier life had been a Sahara Desert
explorer based in Egypt. When the war came, he gained
a commission in the Royal Tank Regiment and was hence
the perfect man to help form and lead one of the first true
'behind the lines' units in history, the Long Range Desert
Group (LRDG). For two years during the see-sawing Western
Desert campaign, Prendergast and his small, hand-picked
band of men roamed the open spaces of Egypt and Libya in
a motley assortment of jeeps, lorries and half-tracks, prodding,
reconnoitring and generally annoying the Germans behind
their lines, having an impact far in excess of their modest
numbers. Working with men who were well trained in desert
warfare was one thing, but now trying to coordinate people
in France who were basically civilians clutching weapons
was quite another.

Having had some wireless training, knowing the local
area and being an English-speaker, Barney immediately

approached Major Rees to put himself forward to assist. He liked the idea of working closely with these professionals from England. Besides, the more he observed of the Maquis, the less confident he felt about them.

22

JED 'PAVOT'

In the early hours of 12 September, taking his now familiar place in the fuselage of a Liberator bomber, Lieutenant Colonel Prendergast silently contemplated the somewhat unedifying reality that he was now three days late for the mission he was supposed to be commanding and which had started without him. He was cold and uncomfortable, and felt slightly ridiculous, weighed down with a .45-calibre pistol, a short-barrel rifle or carbine, ammunition, binoculars, money belt, escape kit, flashlight, tobacco and map case, over which he wore a body-length camouflaged smock. He was also, of course, strapped to a parachute. Bound up like a mummy and barely able to move, he had needed to be helped out of the truck and up the ladder of the aircraft, which he could only approach in short, jerky steps, much to the amusement of the watching Liberator's crew.

Seventy-two hours earlier, Jedburgh 'Pavot' had had a rocky start. As Prendergast wrote in an extensive and lively report after the mission, his team and their equipment had taken off from RAF Harrington, eighty kilometres north of London, in four black-painted American B-24 Liberator bombers on the evening of 8 September. Given the codename 'Pavot', but (to complicate matters) part of a larger mission called 'Orgeat', Prendergast's team consisted of six men under his command, with Major Rees as his second-in-command. They were joined by four FFI officers: a Captain Casset, and Lieutenants Florent, Fauveau and Thome. It was all for naught. 'All aircraft failed to find the target and we returned in a semi-frozen state to the aerodrome after a 6 or 7 hour flight,' wrote Prendergast.

The next night, they tried again, but at the last minute Prendergast's pilot became ill. The remaining three Liberators nevertheless pressed on, but only one was able to find the correct rendezvous, dropping Major Rees and Lieutenants Fauveau and Thome, the latter coming down in a tree and burning his hands sliding down his parachute rigging. On 10 September, Prendergast (his pilot now presumably recovered) tried again, and once more all aircraft failed to locate the target. 'By this time,' he wrote in exasperation, 'we were all heartily sick of spending each night trussed up in parachute harness in a bitterly cold Liberator. The only bright spot in an otherwise miserable existence was the excellent breakfast laid on by the US Air Force each morning when we returned.'

Prendergast's original orders had been to liaise with senior Maquis leaders (all of whom had their own confusing sets of codenames and aliases) directing Resistance activities across a wide area of France. However, the rapid advancement of the US 3rd Army after finally having broken out of Normandy, as well as the US 7th Army advancing from southern France, rendered the scale of the operation redundant, as many of those areas were now already liberated. Prendergast would therefore confine his efforts to the central south-east Vosges region, still very much in German hands, and where it was suspected, correctly, that the Germans were intending to make a winter stand. Here, he would attempt to organise the various elements of the Vosges Maquis, spread as he knew them to be throughout the mountains, coordinating them with the needs of the advancing American forces. His primary contact was the Maquis *chef regional* of several *départements*, forty-year-old Gilbert Hirsch-Oldendorf, otherwise known as Colonel Grandval and given the SOE codename 'Planète'.

First, though, he had to get there, and it was not until his fourth attempt that, at 0124 hours on 12 September, Prendergast was able to observe, 'this time our crew appeared to be well trained in navigation, as to our great joy we arrived exactly at the correct place and found the lights without difficulty'. His pilot, Lieutenant Cunningham, however, records it in fact as a much closer call. In his own separate report of the flight (which had been given the curious codename 'BOB 188'), Cunningham complains of the Maquis' skill on the Morse lamp: 'Very poor code letter. Very long dits and dashes making it very difficult to interpret.' Nor was he happy with the weather forecast he had been given: 'wind opposite from briefing. Overcast 7000–8000 feet. Visibility poor. Everything landed approx 30 yards to left of center light.' Nevertheless, the target was found and Jedburgh Pavot was finally underway.

Jumping after the canisters of weapons and equipment, Prendergast nearly came to grief when the unpredicted wind noticed by his pilot blew him across the landing ground and into the forest. 'The dropping ground was situated on the summit of a hill,' he stated, 'and for parachuting men, left much to be desired.' A French demolitions instructor – code-named 'Passage' – who had been included at the last minute broke his leg coming down on a stone wall. Prendergast, however, was intact, but, gathering his chute in the darkness, was now forced to listen, despairingly, to his two accompanying Liberators – full of much of his equipment – circling overhead as they struggled to find the drop zone. Eventually, they gave up, turned and headed back to England, their motors fading away to the west.

Along with Pavot's commander, twelve containers of arms had at least been dropped (Cunningham noted one whose chute failed to open). These were eagerly gathered up by the Maquis throughout the remainder of the night. Prendergast was met by the local Maquis leaders, including the leader of the 4th Vosges Maquis group, Monsieur Gonand alias 'Lucien'. Feeling well flattered by the presence of a real live British colonel, Lucien escorted Prendergast to a farmhouse, where he met up again with Major Rees. Apart from enquiring what had taken him so long to arrive, Rees informed him that the Germans were rumoured to be preparing for an attack on the camp any time soon, and that the men of the Maquis were woefully ill-equipped to deal with it.

At a conference the next morning, Lucien gave Prendergast and Rees something of a reality check by informing them that the idea of coordinating the various mountain groups of the Maquis was quite impossible. They were essentially cut off from each other by the deep valleys between the mountains, at the bottom of which ran the main roads, which were constantly in use and patrolled by the Germans. Also, there was almost no communication except by runners, and movement was extremely difficult. However, Lucien assured Prendergast that the Vosges Maquis were totally committed and extremely brave, and that they could soon be numbered somewhere close to 5000 men.

Prendergast was quietly sceptical about this, but he was nonetheless impressed by an eager young bomb aimer from Australia, whose extraordinary story of survival since bailing out of his Lancaster bomber the previous February had fascinated the Jedburgh Pavot commanders. Rees and Prendergast agreed that the young Australian could indeed be of some use to them. For his part, Barney was more than happy to oblige.

23

TROUBLES WITH THE MAQUIS

Far from the arrival of Jed Pavot having a unifying effect on the local Maquis, Barney records that it seemed to mark the beginning of their disintegration, as the various factions were now finally presented with the resources over which they could squabble. The more effort that went into trying to forge the Maquis into a disciplined military unit, the more they fragmented into two separate camps, centred around the personalities of two low-level commanders who detested each other. This extended to the now regular air drops, when the two sides would race to secure the lion's share of guns, ammunition and supplies for themselves, at the expense of the other. 'It was this division of effort and failure to unite under one leader,' wrote Barney, 'which contributed to our undoing.'

Nevertheless, knowledge and training continued to be dispensed, as Rees, Prendergast and the FFI officers taught large, open-air classes in sabotage, weapons training and demolition – covering such details as the correct points at which to secure explosives to a road or rail bridge to ensure it came down. Hand-to-hand combat was taught, with information given on how to kill a man silently, or from behind with the use of a wire garrotte.

Every day, however, the Jedburgh professionals were forced to reassess the Maquis' understanding of military matters. Making regular tours of the camp's defensive positions, Prendergast stated that he 'was not unduly impressed with the way in which these positions had been sited . . . Bren guns were located in such a manner as often to have only 100 yards of open ground covered, when a slight move would open up a whole mountainside to fire'. It also emerged that the earlier estimations of the Maquis' strength in the area were:

> quite imaginary, and that in fact there were about 400 armed Maquis, all located in the local mountain mass . . . we always found it difficult to tie Monsieur Gonand down to an accurate statement of his effectifs, as he was full of enthusiasm, and invariably looked on any man who carried even one grenade as an armed man. This was statistically correct, but was not an adequate armament for beating off a determined German attack.

False alarms regarding such attacks seemed also to try Prendergast's patience:

> Jumpiness is inevitable when one is dealing with uneducated peasant folk who are quite untrained to report what they

see. Rumours flew like wildfire throughout our stronghold, and when a Maquis saw a few Germans marching along one of the roads overlooked by our positions, a runner was immediately sent to say that we were being attacked.

A problem of communication with the American Army also began to emerge. For the Pavot mission to be of any use to the advancing Allies, Prendergast had been instructed to make contact with the US 3rd Army to verify their exact position. On a daily basis, he had been requesting, as well as providing, such information, but so far he had received no reply.

Alarmingly, London then informed him by radio that the US 3rd Army was in fact advancing slower towards the Vosges than had been originally believed, and that they were not likely to meet up with them as soon as had been hoped. Prendergast recorded his disappointment in his report. He had been prepared for his Jed mission to be jumping into any kind of action – even catastrophe – the moment his boots hit French soil, but inactivity had not been anticipated. 'We liked to think of an American army stirring itself on our behalf,' he confessed. Instead, he sent the curt message to London: 'send more arms and ammunition, and quickly'. Later that same night, another drop delivered weapons to equip another hundred men.

Despite Prendergast's concerns, the Pavot Maquis reported some early successes. On the night of 14 September, he reports:

a small party of Maquis had successfully derailed a train in a tunnel between Bruyères and Saint-Dié. The operation was very well planned, and the men deserve great credit for the operation, as they had to pass through country thick with Germans to reach the railway line and return again.

Nevertheless, the camp did what it had been threatening to do for some time: split in two, with a smaller group of men relocating several kilometres away towards La Bresse. As an exasperated Rees and Prendergast pointed out, such division of forces ran counter to all military logic, but they discovered themselves to be increasingly powerless in matters of internal Maquis politics.

It was a fatal decision. A few days later, word came through that the Germans, albeit in small numbers, had made a dawn raid on the smaller of the camps, achieving partial surprise but luckily failing to exploit their initial gains. A fierce skirmish had ensued, and, to Prendergast's and Rees's encouragement, it was reported that German casualties had been heavy. The Maquis had themselves lost eleven men killed and five wounded, and the remainder were ordered to stay put and take up new defensive positions. Perhaps the most serious aspect of the engagement was that the commander on the spot had panicked, blowing up his own reserve of ammunition when it appeared likely he would be overrun, reducing their already inadequate stock.

Compounding Prendergast's woes, he now began to receive urgent enquiries from the advancing US 7th Army as to the state of the Maquis as well as German defences in the Vosges, information he had in fact been instructed to provide to the

US 3rd Army, who had not thought to pass it on. In tones that barely hid his anguish, he lamented to Barney that had they but done so, he would at least have felt that his mission had achieved some purpose. 'It was most unfortunate that we did not receive these messages sooner,' he penned dryly in his report. Nevertheless, he transmitted what he could to the Americans, running the constant risk of being picked up by the German radio direction finding [D/F] equipment. 'I was rather worried about the chance of being D/F'd, but one could not do anything about it,' he said. Not that his reports were of much use to the Americans, in any event. 'I replied giving the latest dispositions and explaining that as a fighting force, the Maquis in our area were virtually non-existent.'

Prendergast now came to the important decision that, in the increasingly likely event of a serious German attack on their stronghold, the Jedburgh mission, if overrun and dispersed, must carry on, if only to send intelligence back to London. As for the men of the Maquis, it was learned that General Tassigny's French First Army was also advancing (albeit slowly) towards the Vosges, along with the Americans, and that any displaced Maquis fighters would be able to join them, providing of course they could reach them.

Prendergast also, in his words, 'Decided to test out the Maquis statement that movement on foot is virtually impossible . . . and to find out at firsthand how the experts move and what conditions were like.' Hence, on 19 September, he despatched Major Rees on an expedition accompanied by '3 of the best guides in the Maquis and with No. 413758 W/O

GREATREX B, an Australian airman who had baled out on 25 Feb. in the VOSGES and who had been living with the Maquis ever since'.

Barney had offered Prendergast his assistance on this expedition early, but was warned by him bluntly that the journey would likely take them into the path of the columns of both retreating and regrouping Germans they had been observing below. Considering his safety to be compromised wherever he now stood, Barney accepted the proposal as an honour. Two days later, at 10 am, the party of five – Major Rees, brothers Henri and Maurice Odile, René Lacompte and Barney Greatrex, who was now cradling one of the precious carbines – slipped quietly out of the camp.

Down through the winding valleys and forest gorges of the mountain they descended. The three Frenchmen politely suggested that perhaps Rees should exchange his uniform for the anonymity of civilian clothes such as they wore, but – not for the first time – Rees refused. Despite being behind enemy lines, he was not a spy but an American soldier, and he would always appear as such. These principles, though admirable, believed the Frenchmen, would make them stand out like sore thumbs to any German patrol. Their watch for any signs of the enemy remained constant.

Barney's fitness, at least, had gradually improved, and he pondered how just a few weeks previously, after his winter confinement, he would have found such going impossible. Rees, whose own report on the mission also survives, decided to aim for a flattish plain that would most likely afford an excellent view of all approaches. From there, his instructions were to make his way towards Gérardmer 'to find out firsthand information and also to see how the experts moved around'. First, however, a series of main roads had to be crossed, all crammed with the retreating elements of the Wehrmacht heading east towards the Reich through the mountain passes.

It was the closest Barney had come to the enemy. For several hours, the five men waited behind a hedge as the rumble of vehicles and the march of men passed by, so close Barney could make out individual voices. The clatter of half-tracks and the stench of diesel became incessant. Turning on his elbow, Barney occasionally lifted a wary eye above his green parapet to watch the passing procession. Like soldiers everywhere, he thought, they looked young – some just boys, much younger than himself. Some were laughing; others silent and grim. All looked exhausted, but, to Barney, not defeated. Not yet. Sometimes, a horse team would pass, giving off a smell of grass and leather, a curious element to such a modern and supposedly invincible army.

Drifting into a half-sleep, Barney was brought to attention by the shove of Major Rees. 'Get ready,' he whispered. 'Looks like there's a break in the traffic.' Indeed, the sound of the procession had waned. Rees coolly raised his head. 'Now. Go,' he said. Barney's leg had gone to sleep, and he struggled to maintain the swift pace of the leader. Suddenly, all of them were across the highway and into the cover of the forest, not a German to be seen.

Now the men put on the pace, desperate to make up more ground before dark. Rees was thankful for the help of his local guides. 'From there on,' he said in his report, 'it was comparatively easy due to the fact that my guides knew all the back roads and we were under cover of the woods at all times.' Luckily, the days were still long.

In another hour or so, the men had put a thousand feet (300 metres) of mountain behind them, making their way up steep tracks that seemed to disappear up ahead, but that always managed to open out again as one approached. At the end of the day, they had arrived at the little plateau Prendergast had spied from the camp four or five kilometres distant across the valley. They were, however, behind their schedule. 'One thing I did not realize,' wrote Rees, 'was the length of time it would take to reach an observation point overlooking Gérardmer, because instead of arriving there around 15:00 hours, we did not get there until approximately 18:00 hours.'

The plateau was small, with a handful of farmhouses dotted around, and, like an eyrie, gave a commanding view of all approaches. 'From this observation point we had a wonderful view of the Town of Gérardmer itself,' Rees wrote, 'and also the roads leading in and out of it. One could see a great deal of German activity, especially ill-equipped and unorganized groups of Germans who had retreated from other parts of France and were on their way back.'

Barney surveyed the scene, casting his eye over the hills, valleys and towns that had now become familiar to him. There was the town of Gérardmer, and beyond a spur to the left he knew there was La Bresse and the Mougel family, which he still felt a part of. He thought of Madame Mougel, whom he had never once addressed by her name, Marie, the girls and his friends, brothers Gaby and René, overwhelmed still by the gratitude he would always owe them.

Rees and Barney studied the countryside and took notes. Rees made some rudimentary maps of the area. 'We remained in observation until approximately 20:00 hours and then decided to spend the night with a farmer that my guides knew very well and who they were sure of and then start back early the next morning,' he wrote.

When the men bedded down in relative comfort on a generous pile of hay, Rees attempted to contact the main camp on one of the portable radio sets, without success. At around five the next morning, they set off under a grey sky to observe more of the country around Gérardmer, but at approximately 8 am a series of explosions and gunshots boomed out. All stood staring into the otherwise quiet morning. Across the valley, at the camp they had left twenty-four hours earlier, they could see that another German attack was underway, this time in force.

The five men stood in utter helplessness as tracer and heavy machine-gun rounds lit up distant tree trunks. Then came the flash of a hand grenade, followed seconds later by its distant boom. Shaking his head, Barney could only reflect once again on the weird good fortune that seemed to accompany him like a shadow. Had he declined the invitation from Prendergast, he could well have been caught up in the dreadful maelstrom now taking place across the valley. His thoughts went to his Maquis colleagues and particularly to his new CO, Colonel Guy Prendergast.

•

Prendergast had indeed managed to survive the attack, later reporting that a column of Germans had been spotted approaching from La Bresse in the hour before dawn. The camp in fact was not taken by surprise, and it put up a reasonable fight that impressed even him. 'The battle grew in intensity,' he later reported, 'with mortars, machine guns and grenades being used freely. It appeared that an attack in strength was taking place and that the Maquis was likely to have to move elsewhere, even should the Germans withdraw, which was unlikely.'

Pulling back with little more than the wireless equipment, Prendergast and a small party of fifteen were dispersed into the woods, and then guided over some steep and rough terrain to safety. As soon as he was able, Prendergast sent a message to London stating they were under attack. 'The going was very bad as our guide led us by the most difficult route to avoid meeting a German patrol . . . the Maquis was obviously being thoroughly beaten up and dispersed.'

•

Across the valley, after the firing had desisted, Rees and Barney's party decided to try to make their way back to the camp to ascertain what had happened and report on Colonel

Prendergast's situation, not to mention that of Jedburgh Pavot itself. Descending once more, they found that things had changed overnight. 'All along the road leading through the valley were German sentinels posted every twenty yards,' observed Rees. 'We immediately thought that a major attack was being carried out by the Germans and decided to try and reach our Maquis again by sneaking through the sentinels.'

At one point, the party came under fire from a German MG34 machine gun, its distinctive fast staccato passing close over their heads. Withdrawing, Rees decided to seek cover until nightfall. At 9 pm, they set out again, but they made such noise in the thick and rocky undergrowth that they again received fire from the edgy Germans, who were now shooting at any sound in the dark. In a hoarse but emphatic whisper, Maurice Odile – one of the guides – decided that perhaps it would be best if they found another barn to retire to. All thought this to be an excellent idea.

The next morning, after another night in the hay, Rees despatched René Lacompte and Henri Odile to bring back food and information respectively. Both were successful. René returned with cheese and potatoes (seemingly the staple of those in hiding in wartime France), while Henri stated that he had run into a maquisard who informed him that the camp had dispersed and that Prendergast and a small command party were safe. More worryingly, he reported that the Gestapo were said to be on the lookout for an American major who had been parachuted in to help the Maquis. Rees took the news quietly. 'At that point,' he says, 'we had to move very fast and we went by devious back roads, crawling along hedges in the direction of a farm called Les Charmes, which was on one of the prearranged withdrawal routes that the Maquis would take if attacked.'

Cold and wet, and with no food or way of making a fire, they pressed on, but a quiet conversation with the Odile brothers convinced Rees that turning up at a Maquis farm this night was simply too dangerous, as the Gestapo were likely to be watching everyone in the area. They were better off where they were. 'The result,' says Rees, 'was that we had to remain in the forest which made living very hard due to the fact that it was raining and it was very foggy, wet and cold: also that we had no food or equipment with us.'

After a night of misery, they set off again and soon approached the outline of a small farmhouse. No one seemed to be around, and in any case they were all too miserable to care. They nevertheless approached with caution. To their surprise, a front door was thrown open and Rees was embraced by each member of a family who seemed thrilled to be in the presence of an American major. An excellent meal was prepared in their honour, after which the party of five retired to a barn in which an illegal wireless was kept. As everyone huddled round, their spirits were buoyed by the startling news that the American Army had that day taken the town of Épinal, just fifty kilometres away. The Germans, however, knew it too, and were determined to prevent them getting any closer.

24

FUGITIVES

The next day, the party of five did not have to go far before meeting further scattered remnants of the Maquis army. They described a ferocious German attack, followed by the occupation or destruction of all the farmhouses in the area to deny them a base. The men Barney and his party encountered were in no mood to recontest the situation and were bent on doing nothing but finding their way home as quickly as possible. He could hardly blame them.

The miserable weather now turned worse, as a series of wet and foggy fronts moved in. With the Americans now close, Rees decided that the direction in which they would head was towards them. The little party, displaced once more by the fog of war, set off west on foot. Barney was continually amazed at the cool demeanour of Major Rees, who never gave off any impression other than conviction that everything would in the end turn to their favour. His knowledge of warfare, superbly trained as he was by the American OSS, was astonishing. One of the tricks Barney learned was that by wrapping a wet cloth around the end of a Sten gun – a somewhat light weapon that was really little more than a machine pistol – it gave off a deeper, more raucous sound when fired, potentially fooling any enemy into believing it to be far heavier.

Travelling by a printed silk map issued to all Jedburgh teams, they followed a rough line of paddocks, gathering behind hedges for cover whenever they could. In the distance, often through the fog, they could hear a constant rumble of men and vehicles. Knowing them to be German, they were suddenly grateful for the dismal weather.

Nearing the town of Gérardmer, rumoured to be something of a local German stronghold for the coming battle, Rees reluctantly agreed that a farmhouse should be sought out in which to shelter for a short time before getting away before dawn. Barney remarked that every single such farm they had passed seemed to have been abandoned, some seemingly at short notice. Rees chose what Barney thought to be the most miserable-looking tumble-down he had seen. The small group exercised their usual caution in approach: from three sides, weapons at the ready. It was just as grim on the inside, and almost no food was there to be scrounged. Besides, thought Rees, it was too exposed. They decided to search for another.

The next establishment was far more inviting, as several other dispersed soldiers had already discovered for them-selves. Standing in the doorway to the place, Rees, Barney and particularly the Frenchmen were amazed to be facing three Indian soldiers wearing British khaki battledress. The Indians, however, saluted the American major confidently. Their leader, a sergeant, explained that, following years in captivity after being taken in the desert in 1941, they were being marched back towards Germany from a French POW camp at Épinal, which had come under threat from the Allied advance. In the confusion, they had taken their chance and escaped, and were now making their way towards, hopefully, Switzerland. (Recalling the first such Indian warrior he had met recently at the Maquis camp, Barney was similarly bewildered at how these men, in British uniforms, travelling through German-occupied France, were supposed to conceal themselves!)

The Indians freely confessed to being just about spent, the last straw being that the German attack on the Maquis camp had cut the north–south road they had intended to use. A farmer had that day given them a decent piece of pork, but even in their desperate hunger they would not touch it. Having no such scruples, the major accepted the gift on behalf of his own party. A decent meal of pork and fried potatoes was enjoyed that night, their first in several days.

The next morning, the party – now joined by three lost soldiers from His Majesty's Indian Army who had been convinced that walking to Switzerland over a German-occupied mountain range was probably beyond them – set off. At this point, Barney began to notice the increasing sounds of Allied fighter and fighter-bomber aircraft, high above, searching for a break in the cloud. When they found one, he prayed they would not be tempted to strafe them in mistake for the enemy.

After walking for another full day, though in fact covering little distance owing to their need to remain concealed, the party found themselves in a particularly gloomy part of a dark and damp pine forest. The environment was starting to sap the last traces of energy from each man. Major Rees, constantly checking his map against a small compass, alone seemed none the worse for wear, and he suddenly announced that there was some sort of farmhouse up ahead.

Barney was never quite sure how he had actually seen it, but he was as good as his word. After another kilometre or so trudging up the cloying path, they stood a little back from a farm building that Barney described as 'being in a very ruinous state'. At first, no one was quite sure if it was even occupied. Barney noticed '1805' – the year after Napoleon became emperor – carved into a dark and ancient door frame. The major and Barney, still rather apprehensive about the whole business, arranged that one of the Indians should knock at the door and bring the farmer to meet them at a place a little way off. In plain terms, Major Rees made it clear that the other Indian gentlemen would remain with them, if not exactly as hostages, then as a guarantee of good faith.

The men retreated to the forest but a short time later were confronted with the slightly surreal sight of the Indian soldier returning with a Catholic curate wearing a full-length black clerical robe. They introduced themselves, but it was apparent, says Barney, 'that the man was almost inarticulate with fright'. Despite this, he produced some blankets, offered them a little food and indicated they could stay on the property in an ancient and voluminous barn at the back of the house. All the while, the man kept looking over his shoulder, as if expecting a German patrol to emerge at any moment, and he was desperately anxious to get them off the forest path, no matter how out-of-the-way it seemed to be.

The next day, something of the curate's fear seemed to have rubbed off on the men, and all suddenly felt that this strange and bleak place should not be lingered in a moment more than necessary. Soon, they were headed once more into the forest, where several more scattered Maquis were encountered, one of whom had been taken prisoner during the battle but had managed to escape. He'd been badly treated by the Germans, with his face cut severely with a bayonet. He swore, however, that he had given away nothing and was in no doubt that his lucky escape had saved his life.

Another party of Maquis turned up, plainly relieved to encounter the major, for whom they'd been looking these past days. Colonel Prendergast, it transpired, was in a farmhouse just a few kilometres back and requested they make their way there forthwith. Rees did not have to be told twice.

It was a sober reunion. Prendergast looked a little pale through lack of sleep but was otherwise in good order. He too had spent the last few nights flitting across a series of barns in farms either abandoned or owned by people whose loyalties he had no choice but to trust. He informed Rees that the attack on 20 September had been made by a force of about 2000 German troops against the Maquis force of only 400 armed fighters. Twenty of those had been killed and another twenty wounded. In addition, somewhere between forty and a hundred were said to have been captured by the Germans and shot.

Then there was the tragedy of roughly forty young Alsatian boys who had escaped from an enforced German labour camp to the east, at Colmar, where they had been digging fortifications along the German frontier. Having only recently found their way back home, they immediately joined the Maquis in the mountains and had been put into a requisitioned farmhouse close to the parachute field. This had been one of the first places destroyed by the Germans when they attacked, and many had been killed.

Prendergast estimated that about half the Maquis fighters had managed to slip through the German cordon and presumably gone into hiding, or were attempting to make their way towards the American and French armies. A total of twenty-one farms – some being used by the Maquis and some not – had been burned to the ground.

Rumours – and they were rumours, stressed Prendergast – had the German casualties at several hundred killed and wounded, but in any event the Maquis fighters had fought well, taken full advantage of the natural defences of the camp and made the Germans pay dearly for their attack. Perhaps the weeks of instruction had not, after all, been in vain.

Prendergast also gave the sobering news that he was no longer in touch with any of the Maquis commanders and it seemed their fighters had now been dispersed and were either in hiding or attempting to reach the French Army via the American lines. The Maquis of the Vosges, it seemed, had fought their last major fight.

He added that his communication with London had been less than satisfactory, but at least the mystery of why the US 3rd Army had not been responding to his messages had been cleared up: he was speaking to the wrong army! As he later stated in his report:

> I had asked London as well as the 3rd US Army itself to supply this information daily, but had received no reply. The BBC seldom mentioned this front so it was only by listening carefully to gunfire that we were able to guess at their approximate front line. But as we had several German batteries near us, it was not always possible to differentiate between the departure of a German shell and the arrival of an American one!

Finally, a rather cursory message was received from 3rd Army HQ to the effect that they were nowhere near the Vosges – in fact, way to the north – and why were they bothering to communicate with them in any case? It transpires that it was not in fact General Patton's 3rd Army, which had come through Normandy, that Prendergast needed to talk to but the US 7th Army, which had in July landed on the beaches of Saint-Tropez and were now pushing up towards them from the south. With this army, however, Prendergast had had no communication whatsoever. The look of despair on his face was palpable.

A day later, he learned that the local Maquis under the command of a parachuted French officer had perhaps made their situation even more perilous by attacking, of all things, a party of seven German deserters, killing two but allowing the remainder to escape. 'This affair would not seem to improve our position,' he said. The following day's report seems to sum up their situation: 'Foggy again. We decided to remain in the barn.'

'At this point,' wrote Prendergast later, 'we began to think seriously of our future . . . It was unanimously decided that all of us, Maquis and [our] Mission, had better lie low until it should become possible to reach the Americans.'

25

MOUNTAIN FRONT LINE

By now, the war was coming closer to Barney Greatrex and the displaced warriors of Jedburgh Pavot. With the original purpose of the mission confounded, their new role – confirmed officially by radio from London – was to disperse and find their way to the advancing American forces. This, however, entailed entering a war zone.

Now, there were no Maquis safe houses to rely on. They would simply have to take their luck where it was offered. Towards dusk, in a spot Prendergast described as 'well off the beaten track', they approached an isolated house. Barney still clutched the carbine he had been issued back in the now scattered Maquis camp, but he had no real desire to use it. Major Rees, still an impressive figure despite the days spent on the run, startled a middle-aged French woman, a Madame Colnel, at her front door. Initially, she wanted nothing to do with this gang of dishevelled-looking Maquis led by a British and American officer with three extremely exotic-looking Indians in tow. In his excellent French, Rees calmed the woman, politely requesting she provide some shelter. Despite shaking with terror for her two sons, who were on the run from the STO, she agreed, but only for the night. Rees thanked her, saying that would be fine. They stayed for a fortnight.

As the battle for France moved closer, so did the number of German forces crowding through their corner of the Vosges. Now, it was simply too dangerous, they determined, to risk travel. Presuming the Germans must inevitably at some stage come to the house, the men would hide in the nearby forest by day, returning only in the evening. Unfortunately, the rain and cold refused to lift, making any time outdoors particularly miserable.

Apparently situated somewhere in the middle of a triangle of German field gun batteries, Barney's party became, in his words, 'the anxious spectators of exchanges between German and US artillery. The whine of the shells was plain. On occasions, the noise of gunfire was so loud that it would shake the whole house.' Whether to remain where they were and risk destruction – by either getting caught by the Germans or being blown to bits by artillery fire – or to break out and try to reach the forward elements of the American line became a constant and shifting debate. Then the American advance seemed to stall as the Germans held them off. Along the roads, reinforcements could clearly be seen heading towards their own front line somewhere to the west. The Wehrmacht, it appeared, was preparing to make their long-anticipated stand in the natural fortress of the Vosges mountains. 'For three days we rested here, hiding in the woods during the day. It was very wet and dismal,' records Barney. 'Once or twice the mist lifted and we could see about fifteen miles [twenty-four kilometres] down the valley.'

From a vantage point when the weather occasionally cleared, they could watch a US 155-millimetre gun concealed in a distant copse trying to root out a German battery. In the binoculars, the olive-green foliage seemed to shake momentarily like liquid, before spewing out a mute flash, followed by a wave of smoke. Seconds later, the soft, deep boom reached their ears. Sometimes, Barney almost thought he could see the travel of the shell hurtling towards them before crashing with another report some kilometres short of their position. Then the German batteries would reply with a far louder crack from various points, even to their rear. The duel continued, weather permitting, for about a week. Finally, one afternoon, a great flash was observed in the valley below, as the American gun found its mark and the German position, along with its complement of ammunition, went up in smoke.

The Indian soldiers seemed to be taking the stress worse than anyone, frequently panic-stricken by the proximity of the Germans as well as the artillery fire, and apparently at the end of their rope. It was feared that in their increasingly febrile state they would become a liability. Another refuge farther from the front, it was decided, should be found for them. Maurice said he knew of a friendly priest nearby who had in the past supplied the Maquis with milk and cheese, and who might take them in. Barney and Major Rees accompanied them as Maurice led the way, using the occasional road but keeping to cover at the first sign of any activity. 'The Major carried his .45 Colt, ready all the time,' said Barney, 'just to show that we would not stand any monkey tricks.' Occasionally on the journey of about five kilometres, a vehicle would be heard approaching, which the men knew could only be German. As they took cover to watch these vehicles pass, Barney noted that they were indeed German: ambulances with battered red crosses on the sides, heading quickly away from the direction of the front.

With the Indians safely, albeit reluctantly, delivered to their new keeper, the party returned to the farmhouse, where they seemed to have gradually allayed the initial fears of the female owner. Emboldened by the sounds of Allied guns to the west, she allowed herself to believe, finally, that the Germans were on the verge of expulsion from her part of France. The diet she could supply, however – again, cheese and potatoes – was becoming inadequate. Venturing carefully to a neighbouring farm, Prendergast peeled off some of the generous wad of francs he had been supplied with but had barely had a chance to use, and purchased a calf, which for a further sum the farmer was happy to butcher. Several more were purchased during their stay, the meat being given to their hosts and the several maquisards they encountered, similarly dispersed and seeking to avoid the Germans while searching for a way to link up the French and American forces.

American shells now began to land closer and closer, sometimes barely a kilometre or two away. Then, during the night, they tore up the road just below the barn, which Prendergast took to be a sign of the Americans' impending advance. Just as well, he records, as 'we were heartily sick of this inactive and boring life with nothing to do all day but wait for the next meal. Our tobacco supplies were by now exhausted which made life even more difficult.'

At this stage, Prendergast received an urgent message from a Maquis commander in the area codenamed 'Sapois' to the effect that two Frenchmen from the Milice, the detested Nazi puppet police force, had arrived at a farm a very short distance from their own and were openly stating that they had been sent there by the Germans to look for the Maquis. With the potential for this situation to end extremely badly, Prendergast despatched Henri Odile to investigate.

Three hours later, he returned, looking particularly alarmed. His reconnaissance had informed him that the described men were in the vicinity and indeed with the Milice, and that in all likelihood they had already observed Prendergast and his men. This, Prendergast decided, required urgent action. Argument ensued among the group as to what form that action should take. The Frenchmen were adamant that this was a solely French matter and that they should be given a free hand to deal with it in their own swift and inevitably brutal way. Prendergast insisted on a more cautious approach, and that his and Major Rees's involvement would go some way to assure a semblance of legal procedure. A plan was born to which the maquisards reluctantly agreed.

'This small bit of aggression,' said Prendergast later, 'after days of inaction put us all in good heart.' Just before departure, however, their enthusiasm was dampened when the already tense atmosphere of the house was electrified by the sound of a gunshot, followed by Madame Colnel's cries of '*Merde!*' and '*Nom de Dieu!*' Of late, Prendergast had observed, 'she had somewhat got over her fear of housing us and had resigned herself to having her farm burnt and her two sons shot if we were found by the Germans'. This, though, was the last straw, when one of the Maquis accidentally let off a round from his Sten in her kitchen, hitting her young cook in the leg and wounding another with stone fragments from the tiles.

'Madame came rushing in with a torrent of protests and lamentations,' recalled Barney. 'She said that even *Les Boches* were preferable to us.'

The careless shooter spluttered idiotically that he didn't realise his gun was loaded, and the injuries, fortunately, were slight. The strain for everyone in the house, however, ratcheted up even further. When all had calmed down, Barney assisted Major Rees in dressing the man's wound.

Wasting no more time, the party proceeded to the Milice house at dusk. The plan called for Prendergast and Rees, weapons drawn, to burst in and confront the men, accompanied by Lieutenants Florent and Fauveau. The remainder of the group would surround the farm in case the men attempted to make a break. 'We arrested the miserable *Miliciens*, disarmed them, tied their hands behind their backs, and handed them over to the Maquis for necessary action,' wrote Prendergast. 'I then ordered the members of the Mission back to our barn, as I considered that the trial and punishment of these men was not the affair of military personnel.'

Thus, for a pitifully short hour in 1944, the leaky barn of Madame Colnel's lonely farm in the Vosges became a makeshift courtroom, where the matter was, literally, life and death. The 'trial', such as it was, was brief: more an exchange of abusive accusations of treachery and treason, which the Milicien could hardly deny. There was no defence, even from the accused themselves, merely counter-abuse followed by a plea for mercy, which was always going to be denied.

The punishment was delivered swiftly by one of the more hardened of the Maquis, who took the first Milicien behind the barn and emptied half a Sten clip into him. What the poor Madame made of this is not recorded.

'Then, unfortunately,' Prendergast records, 'things went wrong.'

Transfixed by the shock of the execution, the Maquis, unused to the necessity of keeping a cool head in such situations, allowed their concentration to slip, and the remaining man, seizing his moment, bolted into the night. Prendergast records:

> the Maquis spent the night and following morning in searching for him, without result. We were therefore now in far greater danger than before as this man knew

exactly where we were hiding and had seen the Mission at close quarters.

Barney recalls a good deal of arguing and recrimination among the Maquis as to who exactly was at fault, but before things descended into complete farce Prendergast announced that, after a few hours' rest, the party would have to move on, much to the undoubted relief of the long-suffering Madame Colnel.

As for Prendergast's report of the following day, 5 October, one could be forgiven for detecting a slight tone of exasperation when he stated that 'as usual, Henri Odile had the situation completely under control. He decided to put us in an impenetrable forest for the day while he did a reconnaissance.'

Arriving just after sunrise, the men nestled down in the midst of a pine grove to await Odile's return. Barney remembers yet another tedious meal of cold potatoes and cheese, augmented at least by the discovery of some hazelnut trees, and a large jar of honey brought to them by a local school-teacher and friend of the Maquis, who also gave them the news that American shells were now falling on his school a kilometre or so away and that the Germans had cleared all civilians from the village. Through the forest ahead, the sound of small arms and machine-gun fire could be heard in the distance.

Late in the afternoon, Odile returned, saying that he had found a barn with a good deal of hay in a valley to the west. It was, however, right in the middle of several German positions. It was probably safer, he argued, to continue in the direction of the Americans and risk being discovered by German frontline troops, who would probably be too busy to deal with them anyway, rather than head east and be picked up by the Gestapo or the Milice, who were lurking behind the front lines for precisely that purpose. There was, of course, little chance of an American shell being able to distinguish between them and the Germans, but, as every decision at this point entailed no small degree of risk, all agreed that being shot or blown up was preferable to interrogation and torture.

'That night, we set off in single file,' recalled Barney. Climbing a ridge in complete silence, each man followed the vague shadow of the one in front of him and trusted that Odile could find his way in the dark, as the sounds of gunfire became louder with each step. Finally, they filed into a large barn behind a tumble-down farm and, without a word, lay down in the hay.

Barney was the first to wake and cast his eye around the place. It was large and had certainly seen better days, with many of the slats in the walls missing, enabling him to see clearly to the outside. 'No sooner had I got up from the hay on which I had been sleeping, than I heard the sound of guttural voices just outside,' he later wrote. His blood froze. He glanced around to see Major Rees standing tensely, Tommy gun at the ready, finger up to his mouth to urge silence. Through the gaps in the decaying timber, Barney could see the field-grey backs of around ten German soldiers leaning up against the walls, barely a few feet away. One of them carried a large machine gun over his shoulder, the butt of which knocked heavily with a thud. 'The thought flashed through my mind that this was the end,' he says.

Not daring to move, Barney took one glance at the still-sleeping Colonel Prendergast and another at his carbine, on the other side of the barn, which he was now cursing himself not to have picked up. Any movement, however, would surely draw attention. 'Except for the gallant major,' he says, 'the German patrol would have no opposition. They would just walk in and wipe us out.' Frozen where he stood, Barney heard Colonel Prendergast begin to stir behind him, and he spun around to urgently point outside and signal silence.

He was too late. Turning back, Barney saw the face of a German soldier, his helmet clearly visible, peering through the broken wall and spying Major Rees with astonishment. With a metallic sound, the German cocked his gun and took aim. A shout went up from somewhere, and then occurred what Barney would describe later as 'my last and most miraculous escape', as, with a loud crash, Major Rees disappeared.

Rees was a big man of six foot three and, says Barney, 'built in proportion'. As Rees took a step back, Barney in a flash anticipated the brief and one-sided firefight that was about to occur. Instead, Rees put his weight onto a patch of rotten boards under a hole in the roof that should have been repaired years earlier, and, with a loud splintering sound, he crashed through to a cellar no one knew about directly below them.

The retreating, battle-weary Germans, says Prendergast, were so alarmed by the noise that they 'gave a collective shout, took one look over their shoulders and beat it as hard as they could into the forest. We also departed into another forest.' Like a scene from a comedy, both sides bolted from the barn – the Maquis down the hill; the Germans up – as witnessed by two surprised sentries that Prendergast had placed some way off, and who had somehow completely missed the arrival of the German patrol.

Had they lingered long enough, the Germans would have found little resistance in Colonel Prendergast's poorly armed flotsam of fighters. As it was, the only casualty seems to have been the dignity of Major Rees, who turned out to be none the worse for wear, having fallen but a few feet to the floor below.

Some distance off, the men encountered their cook, who had spent the night at another farm and was returning with a bucket of fresh milk for breakfast. 'So, Germans or no Germans,' says Barney, 'we stopped and had some refreshments.' Prendergast, however, insisted they move into the deepest part of the forest, where they could take stock of their situation. They were obviously, he said, now deep inside the German front line, so the danger of being captured was acute. The notion of finding another safe house was out of the question, as the Germans were undoubtedly occupying all the houses in the area. They would instead have to spend at least the night right here. Prendergast ordered some men to begin preparing shelters made from ferns and branches, and sent Henri Odile out once again to try to round up some food. Meanwhile, he took Barney and a small party up a ridge to look out over the valley below.

To their relief, in the distance barely three kilometres away, they could clearly make out American jeeps and the unmistakeable outline of Sherman tanks. Barney's heart skipped several beats as he finally laid eyes on the liberation he and his comrades had anticipated for so long. It seemed so easy, thought Barney, to simply begin walking in their direction. Then Prendergast pointed out something else, immediately below them: farms with German vehicles parked outside. 'We could see them with the naked eye just pottering about outside their farms,' he recalled. 'It seemed that between us and the Americans were a valley full of Germans.' Both men knew that any attempt to reach safety would not get far.

At dusk, after some of the men had used their skills in making some surprisingly sturdy shelters and even mattresses from ferns and the local foliage, Henri Odile returned with pots of soup he had prepared at a nearby farm. Asked if he had seen any Germans, he laughed grimly, saying they were everywhere, including at the farm where he had just prepared these meals. The men ate in silence.

26

THE FINAL MARCH

The next morning, the small group of Maquis, now numbering around seventeen, endured an American artillery barrage that made Barney recall the stories he had heard as a child about the great battles of the Somme and Pozières. 'For two whole days and nights we lay hidden while shells whined over our heads,' he later recounted. Sensing that the great German retreat east was slowing, the Americans brought up the heavy weapons for a concentrated effort to deny them the chance to regroup in the mountains at the door to their frontier, with one of the unintended side effects being to nearly wipe out Barney Greatrex and co.

Every surrounding farmhouse and shed seemed to have been the target of the American 155-millimetre 'Long Tom' guns, which could hurl a shell twenty-three kilometres to a target. No such range was needed here, however, as Prendergast could easily observe through his binoculars the twelve-man

crew scurrying around the great green barrel just a few kilometres away, preparing it to fire. They heard the crack, then
the whine of the shell as it sailed towards them, finding its
mark behind or in front.

Crouched in among the fern shelter they had created for
themselves, the men could do nothing but wait, listen and pray.
The foliage could conceal, they knew, but not protect. 'The
things we liked least were airburst shells which searched the
valley periodically and were very noisy,' recalled Prendergast.
The barrage continued without let-up, day and night, sweeping
in great arcs across their valley, seeming to seek out the
German positions concealed in groves or farmhouses. Like
a violently disturbed ants' nest, the Germans too were now
everywhere. 'On one occasion,' says Barney, 'whilst hiding a
few yards from a path, a Jerry walked right past me and I
could read *Afrika Korps* on his arm.'

Trapped by friend and enemy alike, the men waited in
a stupor of stress and boredom, occasionally attempting a
joke before it was drowned out by the deep whining sound
overhead. In dread silence, they would count the barrages
falling closer and then receding. 'We were,' wrote Prendergast,
'continually expecting a heavy barrage put down on our wood.'

The next morning, those expectations were nearly realised
when a deafening roar of flame erupted barely fifty metres
from their position, shaking the earth in a percussive flash
that left ears ringing and men showered in stones and debris.
Nerves, already jangled, were stretched to breaking point.
At one point during the first night under fire, a Frenchman

crept up on all fours to the position where Barney, Rees and Prendergast were crouching. '*Mon Colonel*,' the young man whispered hoarsely with wild eyes, '*je pense que nous sommes encerclés pas les Boches!*' Prendergast tried his best to comfort the man by assuring him that if that was indeed true, *les Boches* were probably unaware of the fact, and that in any case they would soon be with the Americans. The man nodded and crept back to his position, but Prendergast knew that he, like the rest, was at the end of his tether.

After a sleepless night, the dawn was greeted by a mortar barrage that crept like a fiery carpet towards them, making a quicker, more cracking sound than the artillery. Prendergast called for every man to take cover as the mortar bombs landed and exploded around them.

As intense as this experience was, it was mild compared with the treatment being meted out to a pine-clad hill just a couple of kilometres away that had contained a German gun position. Even at that distance, the ground under the men shook as wave after wave of shells tore through it like a demented giant, hurling fully grown trees like matchsticks, and spewing smoke and flame. As the men watched in awed silence, they wondered how anything living could remain on that hill, and how easily they could have chosen that as their hiding place. Afterwards, the Americans told Prendergast that this had been the heaviest bombardment they had laid down since the height of the Italian campaign.

A short lull eventually allowed Barney to accept a midday meal of the tedious staple of cheese and potatoes, the effects of which had begun to add mild dysentery to the men's woes. 'I had a strong feeling that day that things were working up to a crisis,' he recounted. Sure enough, late on the second day, a young farmhand ran up to them, talking excitedly and indicating a hill to the right. *'Les Américains . . .'* he said breathlessly, informing them that he had spotted men in khaki uniforms just a couple of kilometres away over the hill, and that he could lead the way to them.

A conference was quickly called. The front, said Prendergast, was now extremely fluid and remained highly dangerous, with the Germans steadily falling back as the Americans began to break through onto the plateau. Any unannounced approach in their direction would in all likelihood be met with gunfire. He therefore proposed sending an envoy to warn the Americans of their plan, which would be enacted with the utmost care at dawn the next day. 'We talked it over and decided to send one of our party, Roger Herlory, to try and contact the Americans,' remembered Barney. Major Rees and Prendergast penned and signed a short but detailed message, alerting them that a party of Maquis would be approaching from the enemy side the next morning. They would, he assured them, be carrying a white flag.

Prendergast wished Herlory the best of luck and made sure he tucked the message deep into his boot. He also reminded him of the consequences of being caught by the Germans, whose lines he would be effectively passing through. Herlory assured him he knew the risks, and thanked Prendergast and Major Rees for the honour of serving with them in this dramatic hour for his beloved France. He shook their hands, as well as Barney's, and disappeared into the darkening forest. Wishing him all the luck in the world, Prendergast realised he would have no way of knowing whether Herlory had made it to the Americans.

Fearing they would not reach the crossing point by dawn, Prendergast suggested to Major Rees that the party take advantage of the lull in artillery fire to proceed closer to the front line. All agreed, with no one wishing to spend another moment in their miserable forest shelter.

So, for the last time, Barney packed up his meagre possessions, slung his carbine over his shoulder and walked into the night. Consulting the map, the French locals pointed to a cluster of farmhouses a few hundred metres from where Prendergast had told the Americans he would meet them. Making as little noise as they dared, the men filed along the forest track. There was no laughing or talking or singing now, and, as desperate for tobacco as they were, not a cigarette was lit. The Germans, they knew, were close, and at every step the burst of a Schmeisser or blistering 'rap' of a heavy machine gun was expected to erupt out of the night. To be killed this close to what many now considered the end of their war was simply too much to contemplate.

Eventually, after a couple of hours of follow-the-leader, a single whistle was heard at the front of the little column, and the men peeled off to a barn being indicated by Henri Odile. Fortunately, there was plenty of hay, and the men, damp, hungry and exhausted, flopped down in silence for a few hours' rest. Barney, however, records 'a very uncomfortable sleep'.

The next morning, 9 October, only Rees and Prendergast were awake before dawn. Both knew that this was perhaps the most dangerous moment of their entire ordeal since parachuting into the Vosges Maquis a month earlier. To cross over while still dark courted the considerable danger of being fired upon by the Americans. Dawn, however, brought both opposing armies to alert, and at the sight of a line of men heading west carrying a white flag, the Germans were likely to shoot without asking any questions. Besides, no one knew whether Herlory had even reached the American lines, nor whether they would be alerted to Prendergast and his party coming over to their side at the designated crossing point. It was also too dangerous to remain where they were once the sun came up, as the Germans were likely to be moving in numbers through the area. It was decided to once more send the redoubtable Henri Odile on a final reconnaissance to ascertain the lie of the land up ahead. Meanwhile, the party would retire once again to the cover of the woods.

Henri was the first to be roused. When his perilous mission was explained, he listened in his typically quiet way, his features inscrutable, nodded, and then agreed without a moment's hesitation. Ten minutes later, with wishes of good luck from Rees and Prendergast, he vanished into the darkness as the first glows of pale grey sky rose in the east.

All the men were now awake, and in a few minutes they too were on the move. As Barney remembers, 'At five AM, we all set out with high hopes that our existence as fugitives would soon be over.' Waiting huddled in the woods nearby, the party could hear the sounds of the Germans preparing their daily defences: the start of an engine, the shouting of an order in the distance. Overhead, an aircraft could be heard but not seen. Quietly, Prendergast and Rees kept an ear out in dread for the sound of a rifle crack or machine-gun burst from the direction in which they knew Henri Odile to have headed. One man dared to light a cigarette, but he was reprimanded harshly by Rees in his perfect French. Sullenly, the man stamped it out, watched enviously by his colleagues.

As Prendergast, tired and hungry as the rest, considered what kind of shelter could be made should they be in for a long wait, Henri Odile reappeared, barely an hour since his departure, breathless and as wild-eyed as anyone had ever seen him. 'Hurry,' he implored, glancing anxiously at the lightening sky, 'we must all hurry before it becomes too light. The Germans are everywhere.'

As the group set off from the forest, Odile explained to Prendergast in hushed tones how he had met a farmer who assured him that an American forward post was on the other side of his farm. But it was dangerous. A few days earlier, another Maquis group had attempted a junction under similar circumstances. In the ensuing confusion, a gun battle had erupted, with one man killed on each side.

Emerging from the protection of the forest, the group, led by Henri Odile, found themselves in precisely the situation they had sought so hard to avoid, revealed in full view to the enemy. As they approached a farm taking shape in the dawn light, Henri gave a muffled shout from the front of the column – more like a hiss – urging his comrades to hit the deck. Barney dared to look up. There, less than 200 metres away, a squad of a dozen or so armed German soldiers were preparing breakfast around a canteen. As unobtrusively as possible, the men shuffled behind the cover of a hedge and waited, all the while watching the day beginning above them. Someone up ahead passed the word down that the coast was clear, and they set off again.

'How far?' some of them would ask. The reply from Henri was always the same. 'Three hundred metres,' he would say impatiently, 'three hundred metres.' Barney remembers the almost unbearable tension of that flight from the forest. 'Dawn was breaking on the mist-enshrouded plateau and firing almost ahead of us caused me to keep very low down and have my carbine cocked.' From somewhere came a burst of machine-gun fire; from somewhere else a crack of three rifle shots. Who they were meant for was not clear, but the men kept their heads down and kept walking, feeling that whatever now happened, they were beyond the point of no return. 'By this time,' says Barney, 'I knew it was now or never.'

By now, Barney and the rest of the Maquis felt they had travelled 300 metres several times over. As they continued, one foot placed stubbornly in front of the other, they had the sense they were crossing some kind of no-man's-land. Sounds in the half-light felt close up, then deep in the distance. Each man trusted, literally with his life, the direction the leaders of the column were taking. A shell whistled, and the column stopped involuntarily. Then came the crump of it hitting the ground and exploding, to their relief, behind them. As the light grew, it threw a dewy film over everything, soaking already worn-out boots and shoes that were never meant for battle. At least the morning did its best to muzzle their footsteps in this vague and uncertain landscape.

Another farmhouse loomed up. It was small, and the friendly honking of geese and barking of dogs undercut the tension of the men. Suddenly, from inside, a middle-aged man emerged, followed by his wife and a gaggle of children. The men stopped. It was the first farmhouse still inhabited by its owners they had seen for days. The scene was somehow surreal. The family looked curiously at the Maquis but did not seem afraid. Henri Odile stepped up. '*Où est la ligne américaine?*' he asked directly.

The man appeared not to have understood, as if he was hearing a foreign language. There was a pause, and Henri began to ask the question again. '*Monsieur . . .*' he said, but he was cut off by the man, who replied quite calmly, '*Il y a un garde américain cent mètres à droite là,*' and pointed ahead. Barney, who eight months previously knew not a word of French, understood him utterly, but he could scarcely believe his ears. 'I could have kissed the whole family,' he wrote later.

Prendergast now stepped forward and, in his perfect British officer's French, asked the woman if she could possibly spare a white tablecloth. The woman dashed inside without a word and re-emerged with the still-folded cloth in her hand.

Rees immediately attached it to his rifle, and after offering their thanks the men began heading off in single file up the lightening track indicated by the farmer.

'I shall never forget the scene!' recalled Barney. 'The mist was rising in patches and desultory firing could be heard all round.' Barney was close to the front of the column, behind Prendergast and Rees carrying the white flag. Any German spotting them now would know exactly what was happening and open fire. Upon turning a bend, Barney's heart sank as, silhouetted in the mist, a figure in a steel helmet and greatcoat with an automatic weapon trained on them halted their progress. Instinctively, Barney ducked, and 'Merde!' was heard behind him as the realisation spread through the file that their long bid for freedom had fallen at the last hurdle.

Then, another rustle from the front as a word was passed down the line: 'Américain!' Barney looked up and saw, to his relief and astonishment, Colonel Prendergast with an outstretched arm walking towards the figure, who, Barney could now see, was wearing a US Army helmet.

It transpired that the American sentry had received no notice of their arrival, had no idea of the fate of Roger Herlory, and had been just about to shoot. Soon, however, the tension started to subside and Barney began to register that his ordeal was really over. He felt his body go limp. Laughter broke out among the men, and the lone, bewildered American soldier was soon surrounded by a gaggle of smiling, filthy, exhausted and unbelievably relieved Frenchmen.

The American urged them, however, to be quiet, saying the Germans were close. He seemed astounded at how they had managed to come through their lines undetected. With haste, he led them back towards his unit. At various points, they were challenged by more Americans, but a code word was uttered, and soon caution gave way to amazement at this band of home-made soldiers who had apparently escaped from the very maw of the enemy.

In a few hundred metres, the battalion headquarters appeared, and suddenly Americans were everywhere, shaking hands and asking questions. They were surprised beyond words at the sight of one of their own, Major Rees, still in his uniform, which he had stubbornly resisted divesting despite the most concerted pleas of the Maquis.

Rees held his own miniature press conference out in the field, taking questions from his admiring compatriots and answering as much as he felt he could. Barney found he too had an audience of enquiring Americans, who observed him with an almost tangible curiosity as he spoke. 'Gee, you speak pretty good English for a Frenchman,' one of them eventually felt moved to observe. 'I explained who I was,' says Barney, 'and then realised that, by force of habit, my speech was still 50 percent patois.'

Then, the food arrived. 'Our party numbered seventeen,' says Barney, 'and the Americans gave us sufficient rations for forty!' Having lived for so long on a diet of cheese and potatoes, the men fell on the largesse of the American Army catering, devouring everything in sight, particularly anything sweet. 'In between mouthfuls,' recalled Barney, 'we were interrogated, and were able to pass on some valuable information as to enemy artillery positions.' Then the American cigarettes were passed around to calm raging nicotine addictions, and maps of the region were produced. Combing their memory as best they could, the men marked known German dispositions and concentrations for the grateful US artillery officers, sensing for the first time in a long while that their experience was contributing to the war.

Such a shock was all this to the men's depleted constitutions that almost all of them, including Barney, were soon sick. It would take some time, he realised, to adjust to being back in the bosom of friends.

Another jeep ride, and Barney, Colonel Prendergast, Major Rees and the men of the Maquis arrived at the forward HQ of the US 3rd Army, currently at Remiremont. There, they were interrogated and given yet more food, and Barney, Prendergast and Rees were all fitted out in brand-new US Army uniforms. After so long in borrowed and now battered civilian clothes, Barney wore his with a particular pride.

As soon as was possible, the news of Barney's survival was transmitted to the RAF – where, after a few days, someone in an office in Bomber Command Headquarters in High Wycombe would remove his name from the long list of those marked 'Missing'. Then, a telegram was composed and sent to alert his next of kin in faraway Sydney that their son Barnaby Ryder Greatrex, missing presumed killed for eight months, was in fact safe and well.

Meanwhile, the Americans didn't quite know what to make of Barney. Several times, he told his ordeal to his interrogators, who took notes but mainly looked at him in stunned silence, mesmerised by the story of his adventure.

Finally, after eight months of living in shacks and farm-houses, through the bitter winter, surviving on luck and the unrepayable kindness of others, it was time for Barney to farewell his companions, as well as the magnificent mountains of the Vosges, which he had felt he had almost come to know as a second home. All the men of the Maquis shook his hand as they prepared to disperse back to those parts of their country that were now wrested from the Germans, or join the division of the Free French Army still very much in the fight to liberate *La Patrie*. '*Bonne chance*,' they said to Barney, shaking his hand. '*Merci, bonne chance*', '*Au revoir, à bientôt, j'espère*'. He stood with tears in his eyes, knowing that, for the most part, he would never see these brave faces again.

When it came to his farewells of Colonel Prendergast and Major Rees, the men saluted and then shook hands. 'Greatrex, if all Australian airmen are as sturdy as you . . .' Prendergast began to say but was somehow unable to finish the sentence. 'Good luck, Aussie,' said Major Rees, with his characteristic grin and confidence, neither of which had wavered for a moment since the night he was dropped. 'You'd make a fine officer, you know, Greatrex.' Barney laughed and thanked him. Little did he know, however, that the laugh was on them. As he was soon to discover, in the very week he was posted missing, his offer of a commission had come through, becoming effective in July. For the past eight months – at least nominally – he had been Flying Officer Greatrex.

'That night,' says Barney, 'lying in my tent, I did not sleep a wink. The events of the past eight months crowded through my mind.' Foremost, however, was the melancholy realisation that his rescue finally and irrefutably marked him the sole survivor of 61 Squadron Lancaster LL775 O for Orange. More acutely than at any time since coming down on that freezing February night that now seemed a decade in the past, Barney felt the tremendous loss of his six comrades, those six fine fellows whom he had trained with, lived with, and so nearly died with.

He was also now acutely aware of the further shock – albeit one of relief – that his family were now about to undergo. For eight months, they had believed him to be most likely dead. How now were his poor parents – uneasy at the best of times with emotional upheaval – to cope? Barney felt a helpless wave of guilt, and began to think of himself almost as a man returned unexpectedly from the dead.

In his tent, now well behind friendly lines with American guards outside, he listened most of the night to the distant crumps of the 155-millimetre guns firing, their flashes briefly illuminating the green canvas walls. For some time, he lay there, somehow unsure whether he was still up there in the mountains, where he knew those shells to be falling, sheltering in the moss and the pine glades with the brave men who had been his family these past months. 'My thoughts went back to those indomitable sturdy French peasants, by whose bravery and fortitude our band of Maquisards pulled through. I prayed that those who were still in the midst of battle would survive.'

Barney had lost count of the number of times he had dodged disaster and oblivion, but at each realisation that he was still on this earth, he had heard that nagging voice once again asking, 'Why me?' Still, he was not closer to an answer, and at that moment he felt that if the power was his to change places with any one of his crew, he would do so without a heartbeat's hesitation.

27

RETURN

Mission Pavot – one of the last of the nearly one hundred Jedburgh missions undertaken by SOE and its American counterpart, OSS, in France – was over, and its leader, Colonel Prendergast, was less than satisfied by the results. Upon his reception, he underwent the first of several debriefings – somewhat desultory affairs where he reported that, in his view, little of what he considered to be the original purpose of the mission had been achieved. At Remiremont, he did at least – like Barney – appreciate the excellent breakfast afforded by the OSS staff, and he enjoyed a reunion with many of the Maquis he had worked with in the field, including several of the leaders of the Vosges Maquis. Even the chief of the Remiremont police – who had for years been working secretly for the Maquis – called by to renew his acquaintance. They had previously met the night after his parachute drop a month earlier. At that time, his face had carried the tension of a man playing a deadly serious game with a ruthless enemy. Now, his town liberated, he was simply another hero of *La Résistance*.

For the final time, Prendergast was also reunited with many of the maquisards he had not seen since the German attack on their mountain position in September, and in his report he indicates the genuine affection in which he held them. 'After lunch we said goodbye to the Maquis . . . who were taken by truck to the French 3rd Div. We were very sorry to see the last of such faithful men.'

Upon returning to London, Prendergast submitted his 'Report on Mission PAVOT', marked 'TOP SECRET' and comprising over twenty closely typed foolscap pages. It was received by the OSS WE Section in October 1944. His conclusion, reproduced here in full, is redolent with Prendergast's disappointment at what he and his mission might have been able to achieve:

> It was most unfortunate that the Mission was not sent in much earlier. As it was we were at all times in country too thickly populated with Germans to be able to achieve much. The Maquis in the VOSGES was too newly formed and not well enough trained and armed to be able to hold its own against a determined German effort to disperse it. If it had had time to grow up in strength like other Maquis it would have been a formidable fighting force.
>
> Such members of the Maquis who know the country well could now be used as guides, for which work they would be invaluable. Of the remainder, with training they should

make good fighting troops, once they have got over the inferiority complex which years of German domination produces.

I cannot honestly say that the Mission achieved much, except to send a few scraps of intelligence, but we all had an interesting experience and learned a lot.

This somewhat melancholy conclusion is followed by a short addition by Major Rees, who seemed keen to assert that, as Mission Pavot's commander, Prendergast had absolutely nothing to be ashamed of:

I would like to add my commendations to those men already mentioned in Colonel Prendergast's report, also I have nothing but the greatest respect for Lieutenant Colonel Prendergast himself. This Officer already has a very good war record behind him and I certainly feel that he, through his calmness and his coolness and sound judgement throughout the trying times that the Mission endured, went a long way in bringing us all back to safety. At all times he set the highest example for his men to follow. He was tireless in this work and always was planning ways in which the Mission could be usefully employed, even though we were in hiding.

Prendergast finished his very eventful war as a brigadier in charge of the nascent Free French SAS, and he was awarded the DSO and even the Czechoslovakian Order of the White Lion, 3rd Class.

Barney had yet one more adventure to play out before his return to England. Being driven the 400-kilometre journey from the Vosges to Paris, he presented himself at RAF headquarters, which was located among the splendour of Versailles. Here, standing before several bewildered intelligence officers in his new American uniform, he observed that no one quite knew what to make of him. Most returning airmen fitted neatly under the category of POW, but Barney, having successfully dodged the Germans for eight extraordinary months, was now marked down as that rarest of birds, 'evader'. Further complicating matters was the fact that Barney's commission had come through in his absence, and that he was now to be dealt with not as a humble NCO (non-commissioned officer) but as Flying Officer Greatrex, B.R. 'Consequently,' he says, 'there was no special organisation for dealing with such a case as mine.'

After recounting his story – seemingly for the umpteenth time – Barney was the subject of several communications to London. Equally at a loss as to precisely which section of British military bureaucracy he should be pigeonholed, the War Office in London decided the best thing for all concerned was to pack him off back to Australia, via England, as quickly as possible. Barney thought the decision an excellent one.

Forty-eight hours later, Barney Greatrex found himself sitting at an aerodrome on the outskirts of Paris that had recently been used by the Luftwaffe as a night fighter base. At one end stood two sinister-looking Heinkel 219 'Owl' night fighters with their mottled grey livery, odd tricycle landing gear and VHF aerials poking out the nose, making them look like prowling grey ghosts. It was monsters such as these, he thought, so dreaded by himself and his fellow bomber crewmen in the night skies of his tour, that had accounted for so many of his comrades.

As he sat in the busy waiting area, aircraft and aircrew came and went. Barney cut a somewhat forlorn figure – skinny and exhausted, barely fitting the rough RAF blue uniform he had been obliged to exchange for his American khaki. Every few minutes, the roar of Spitfires and Dakotas added to the bustle of the active wartime airport. In his hand, Barney held an official letter written by an American major, outlining his status and allowing his passage back to England. Exactly which flight he was expected to be on, however, was something no one seemed to know or particularly care about.

After several hours of being thus ignored, his mind went back to the days with the Mougels, and he wondered exactly what they were doing at that moment, as he sat away from any danger – except perhaps of being bored to death by the inscrutable passage of RAF protocol. Suddenly, his reverie was interrupted by the arrival of three men with a great deal of gold braid on their hats, filled with purpose as they strode in Barney's direction towards the tarmac. Barney's military training suddenly compelled him to do something he had not done in a very long time: stand and salute. Getting to his feet, he raised his right hand to his temple as the men passed. The leading officer returned his salute, and then to Barney's surprise slowed down and came towards him.

'What are you doing here, Pilot Officer?' he asked.

As Barney began to answer, he was struck by the man's demeanour: stocky, in his fifties, perhaps, with a short, sandy-coloured moustache and without doubt the hardest pair of blue eyes he had ever seen. With a jolt, Barney realised he was standing in front of no less a figure than Air Chief Marshal Sir Arthur Travers 'Bomber' Harris, the head of Bomber Command itself, one of the most powerful figures of World War II and, in a very real sense, Barney's former boss.

'Ah, well, sir, I'm trying to get back to England, actually,' Barney managed to stammer out with relative coherency, and upon further questioning he gave a brief outline of where he had been for the last eight months since being shot down. Harris, adopting the slightly puzzled look that many who had listened to the story seemed to assume, asked to see his orders. 'Well . . .' he began as he glanced at the signature on the form, 'I can take you to Northolt if that'll help. Up to you. We leave in five minutes.'

So, on the morning of 13 October 1944, seven months and eighteen days since being shot down in a dark and freezing forest, Barney sat in the almost surreal surroundings of a specially fitted RAF Dakota next to one of the most powerful men of the war. The seat, he remembered, was unlike that of any aircraft he had ever sat in: soft and generous. The hour and a half flight was smooth and uneventful, and a waiter in a white jacket brought a drinks tray around. Harris had a gin and tonic. Barney politely refused. Not long into the flight, Harris pressed Barney for more details of his time in France, being particularly keen to know on precisely what trip he had been shot down, and the exact circumstances.

He seemed to Barney well acquainted with that mission to Augsburg, and quite unmoved by the fact that Barney had been the sole survivor of his Lancaster, preferring to hear his interpretation of operational matters. It was not until quite far into the conversation that the notion occurred to Barney that Harris had personally ordered the attack, as he had with almost all of Bomber Command's costly missions.

Soon, from his spacious chair, Barney watched the friendly green of England begin to roll beneath him, and a few minutes later he was on the ground, saluting Harris one final time and thanking him for the ride, doubting anyone to whom he told the story would believe it.

After a night in a London hotel in which he spoke to no one, Barney examined another chit of paper with which he had been issued, ordering him to a prearranged debrief in a gloomy RAF office in Whitehall. Two disinterested intelligence officers heard his account of his months with the Maquis, taking notes and asking questions alternately. Unlike everybody else who had been told the story, Barney detected little in these men besides officiousness, even boredom.

As they were about to conclude, however, one of the men looked back over his notes and fell silent. 'Please tell us again how you exited the aircraft,' he said after a pregnant pause. Barney recounted the attack by the fighter and his escape through his own bomb aimer's hatch in the aircraft's nose. 'You say the aircraft was in a *spin?*' asked one of the men pointedly. Barney concurred. 'A tail-spin, yes, sir,' he said. The man probed further: 'And you were able to open the nose escape hatch whilst the aircraft was in such a spin?' Again, Barney nodded his head, but slowly. The two men put down their pens and looked at each other. 'Please wait here,' they said, leaving the room, as if there was a possibility of Barney opting to leave.

A few minutes later, they returned with a middle-aged group captain, who pulled up a chair and looked at Barney carefully before examining his file. 'Warrant Officer Greatrex,' he began, using Barney's now incorrect rank, 'please explain the circumstances by which you were able to leave the aircraft.' Again, Barney told it to the now three stony faces in front of him, but he slowly got the uncomfortable sensation that he was not being believed. 'Can you please stand and demonstrate the method by which you opened the escape hatch?' asked the group captain. Perplexed, Barney did his best, explaining that he must have just caught the lip of the thing before prising it open with his prone body as the aircraft spun. It was, in fact, difficult for him to remember. Copious notes were now being taken.

'Warrant Officer Greatrex,' the group captain resumed, 'are you absolutely sure you are telling this board the complete truth as to how you exited Lancaster LL775 O-Orange after it was attacked?' Barney gave them a convincing assurance that he was telling the complete truth, and their expressions gave way to surprise. 'Warrant Officer Greatrex,' said the officer, 'what you are telling us is something we believe to be not physically possible.' Barney was speechless. 'We have conducted extensive tests and concluded that there is no way that a man of average strength such as yourself can overcome the enormous centrifugal forces generated by a spinning aircraft and operate the inwards-opening nose hatch of a Lancaster. What you are telling us Greatrex is quite extraordinary.' The three of them looked at Barney now in silence, but at least, he could see, they believed him.

'I guess,' he added, 'I was just very lucky.'

•

After a month in a Personnel Holding Unit, Barney in November found himself back where his time in England had started, in Bournemouth at No. 11 Personnel Despatch and Reception Centre, billeted in the same slightly battered seaside hotel in which he had spent a month or so in early 1943, waiting to get into action. Now, he was the old hand, in a new crop of eager young men. With each one who asked him excitedly about life on operations, he was vague, but he advised them to curb their enthusiasm, they would get into it soon enough, and the going would be tough. His answers, he could see, were neither what they expected nor wanted to hear. Of his time with the Maquis, he told no one.

Barney's parents, having been given their son back, now resumed their letter-writing. Only one letter and a handful of telegrams survive from the period following Barney's return to England. In the letter, he talks of doing little but sleeping and spending time with some of his father's English business associates. He revels in the gossip from home, seeming to enjoy immensely the everyday minutiae of ordinary lives. Only once does he indicate his true feelings when, having spent an enjoyable New Year's Eve in the country, he remarks, 'the only thing that mattered was the constant stream of bombers going overhead night and day, without a stop. Too many memories for me.'

As the war was reaching its climax in Europe, Barney turned his back on it all, and boarded a ship that would take him home via the warm waters of the Mediterranean and the Suez Canal. On 22 February 1945, nearly a year to the day since being shot down, his ship rounded South Head and steamed into Sydney Harbour, where his parents, Basil and Elsie, were waiting at Woolloomooloo, right where they had seen him off in September 1942. In the two years and five months Barney had been away, he appeared to his parents to have aged a decade.

•

It was not until eight months later, during his difficult adjustment back to civilian life, that Barney, after much effort in trying to track down or at least discover some news about his friends still in France, received a letter from his erstwhile protector and friend Gaby Mougel. Barney's written French, always far from perfect, was now fading fast. He took the thick envelope into a far corner of the garden, away from any distraction, to decipher it. It was a gloriously sunny Sydney day.

With a pounding heart, opening the envelope carefully, Barney could see that Gaby had handwritten on lined pages. In mounting shock, Barney began to read the terrible story of the ordeal of his beloved Mougel family and the pretty mountain village he had known so well.

28

GABY'S LETTER AND THE TRAGEDY OF LA BRESSE

'Dear Camarade Jacques,' begins Gaby Mougel, still using the name Barney adopted soon after his arrival in France. Writing three months after the end of the war in Europe, Gaby's tone is at first playful and familiar, an old friend happy to toss around affections. Gaby misses his friend Barney and wonders whether he resumed flying after his arrival back in England and even now is preparing to fight the Japanese. In fact, the war in the Pacific had ended over a month prior to Barney receiving the letter, but Gaby expressed no doubt that if Barney had been involved, he would have made the finest account of himself, as usual. He asks if he has found a 'little wife' for himself back home, and for himself says that he'd prefer to remain free, just for a little longer.

Then, Gaby's tone changes:

I am still in the best of health, as is all my family, but alas, we no longer live in La Bresse village. Since the Boches burnt our two houses we have sought refuge in a small farm at Cornimont. Oh yes! The dirty Boches – they burnt La Bresse completely in three days and three nights . . .

Gaby then proceeds to give Barney his eyewitness account of the tragic destruction of his pretty mountain home in November 1944.

•

The Vosges were by no means the only mountains in France to become a home to the Maquis. Other well-organised groups operated from the hills of the Savoy and Aveyron to the south, the Corrèze to the west, the Jura and the Cantal, to name a few. All of them were dedicated to their cause of assisting the advancing Allies in the liberation of their country. The Vosges, however, would always be a particularly tough nut for any army to crack. Its vertiginous slopes, winding tracks and endless gullies represented the perfect natural defensive fortress – standing as a bulwark at the gate of southern Germany and the Rhine river beyond. Despite any assistance the men of the Maquis may be able to lend, the Americans and their allies looked with dread upon its capture.

For the Germans, too, the Vosges were vitally important. As with much of the province of Alsace-Lorraine, with its long history of changing hands and being fought over for centuries

– most recently being taken again by Germany in 1940 – it was regarded as *Heimat*, the Reich's most western province, and would be defended as ferociously as any other piece of German soil. By late 1944, it was also one of the few places in France still to be in their hands, and so, despite the war having moved on and Paris having been liberated the previous August, Germany decreed that a stand would be made from the high slopes of the Vosges.

The Germans also sensed that fortune was swinging in their favour. By September 1944, the Allied advance had slowed considerably since their long plunges into France from north and east, with men and equipment becoming tired just as winter was approaching. Some American divisions had in fact moved so quickly from the south of France, they were still in light summer uniforms and were now overextended. The Vosges was also one of the few areas in the current battle for Western Europe where the forces of Germany and the Allies were relatively evenly matched. The Maquis, they believed, could be dealt with, and for this reason: Heinrich Himmler, the leader of the SS, was appointed personally by Hitler to oversee the security of the Vosges, knowing he would be particularly savage in rooting out and destroying the hated Maquis.

At the German Army's disposal were reinforcements of no less than seven infantry divisions, a mountain division and a Panzer brigade. These were some of the defences noted all too well by the Piquante Pierre Maquis, as well as Barney and co. when in hiding. Already ideal defensive territory, the

Vosges were reinforced further by thousands of pillboxes, vast stretches of barbed wire and mines, roadblocks and other obstacles numbering into the hundreds. Despite this, for the average German soldier the gloomy crags and foggy gullies of the Vosges were dreaded as a death zone where, behind every rock and hidden in every shadow, an enemy with a knife or a Sten gun lurked.

Thus, in October 1944, the stage was set for one of the most savage and now least remembered campaigns of World War II, fought in the bitterest European winter in nearly half a century, and which dragged on well into the following year, consuming tens of thousands of civilian and military lives in an ultimately pointless campaign, the end result of which was never seriously in doubt. And one of its first victims was the quiet little mountain town of La Bresse, which would suffer terribly at the hands of both the Germans and the Allies.

•

Despite the inadequacies observed by Barney, Prendergast and Major Rees, the Germans held a particular loathing for the Maquis, as they did for the local resistance organisations in all the countries under their brutal occupation. The only concentration camp on French soil, Natzweiler-Struthof, was even built in the Vosges, dedicated to punishing those who dared actively question Nazi rule. From its construction in 1941, until its inmates were forcibly marched to Dachau as the Allies approached in 1944, it was estimated that the SS killed 22,000 of its 52,000 prisoners from all parts of Europe.

The overall impact of the Maquis on the Germans as a whole has been debated virtually non-stop since even before the war ended, and their efficiency varied from region to region, but it is indisputable that the Germans came to regard them as a real threat, particularly approaching, then following, D-Day. It was at this point that the scale of Special Operations Missions from England in support of French Resistance organisations – such as Jedburghs – rose dramatically. In the last three months of 1943, for example, some 105 Special Ops sorties were flown to France, but by mid-1944 that number had jumped to 1665.

From 1943 onwards, sabotage of the railroad system increased rapidly, and the Germans reported 534 sabotage actions for September that year, up from a monthly average of 130 recorded just a few months earlier.

After the war, General Eisenhower paid the Maquis perhaps one of their greatest tributes, stating:

> I consider that the disruption of enemy rail communications, the harassing of German road moves and the continual and increasing strain placed upon the German war economy and internal security services throughout Occupied Europe by the organised forces of Resistance, played a very considerable part in our complete and final victory.

Even his nemesis, German Field Marshal von Rundstedt, concurred, referring to the situation in France in late 1943:

The organised supply of arms from England to France became greater every month ... it was already impossible to dispatch single members of the Wehrmacht, ambulances, couriers, or supply columns without army protection to the I or IX Army in the south of France.

Thus, as late as September 1944, with vast swathes of France already wrested from the Nazis, Himmler paid a visit to the Vosges town of Gérardmer, to outline his plan for the systematic deportation of the French male population from ages fifteen to sixty-five along a 250-kilometre line down the western slopes of the Vosges mountains. It was believed this would not only neutralise any further Maquis 'terrorist' activity but also prevent a link-up between the Maquis and the advancing Americans – a scenario the Germans dreaded.

It was understood that this order involved showing the men of the Maquis – whether on the battlefield or captured thereafter – not a scrap of mercy. The brutes of the Gestapo and the SS would carry this out to the letter. In the subsequent operation, a total of 4746 Frenchmen would be deported from the Vosges, most being required to march, mainly on foot, to dig ditches and defences along the German frontier, or be used as slave labour for the industries such as the German V1 and V2 rocket program. At least half would never return. This was the scenario facing Gaby Mougel, his family and his compatriots in the Vosges in late 1944.

•

Barney had last seen Gaby the morning he left the Piquante Pierre camp in the reconnaissance expedition on 19 September with Major Rees. Both had thought it would be a short absence, but just a day later the Germans attacked.

In the dispersal of the Piquante Pierre Maquis following the battle, Gaby found himself alongside his and Barney's section commander, Bébert. Like most of the men after the attack, they believed – for the time being, at least – that the game was up, that the Germans were intent on destroying them, and that it would be unwise to give them the chance. The most prudent direction in which to head, therefore, was towards the Americans, providing they could be found.

Finding an old house in the middle of the gloomy forest, Gaby and Bébert held up there for two days and nights. They were thankful beyond words for the ever-present blanket of thick fog, which concealed them from the Germans who could be heard all around them, and in ever-increasing numbers. The longer they delayed, they reasoned, the harder it would be to pass unnoticed through the German lines.

After two days, the wait became intolerable. Making their way out into the forest in the pre-dawn, they progressed carefully for several kilometres, trying to remain within the cloaking green cover as much as possible. As Barney and Prendergast had also discovered, however, the further west they proceeded, the greater the German presence was felt. Several times, when approaching a road, the way was barred by sentries, seemingly – to Gaby and Bébert – on the lookout for them and them alone.

At one stage, shots were fired nearby and some shouting erupted from the other side of an embankment. Not waiting around long enough to discover whether the disturbance was on account of them, the two men retreated east to the protection of the damp green woods. 'Bébert thought it would be best that we should separate,' wrote Gaby, 'so he hid on a farm whilst I went to the house of my cousin Marguerite at Rochesson.' From here, slightly further to the west, Gaby intended to make another attempt to cross the German lines alone. Marguerite presented as innocent and charming, and no one – particularly the Germans – would have suspected her of quietly aiding the local Maquis, or that her cousin Gaby was an active member. It was with some confidence, therefore, that Gaby walked along the network of winding and intricate forest tracks – well known only to locals like himself – to Marguerite's and her family's small house on the outskirts of the little Vosges town of Rochesson.

Emerging from the forest late in the afternoon, he stood back a little to check the house for anything that appeared untoward, then strode through the front door, which opened onto a living room. 'Ah, mon frère!' said Marguerite brightly. She was standing near a fire, looking at him with a fixed smile. Gaby froze, as sitting around the small room were four German soldiers. Instantaneously, he snapped into the part of 'brother'. 'Bonsoir, messieurs,' he greeted the men, noticing an array of Mauser rifles and helmets stacked neatly along one wall. A couple of them grunted and looked him up and down coldly, but they seemed otherwise uninterested.

Two days earlier, eight German soldiers had decided to billet themselves at the house. Gaby now had to play his cards extremely carefully. Feigning the character of an affable but dimwitted youth, he chatted blandly with those few Germans who had a few words of French, doing his best to appear nonplussed but in fact concealing the fury and revulsion he felt to his very core at their presence. It was not until the next day that he and Marguerite had a chance to speak in private. Gaby told her of his plans to leave immediately, to which she instantly protested. To leave so soon would arouse suspicion, particularly in light of the recent battle with the Maquis in the mountains. He must stay at least another day and appear relaxed at all times.

In the end, Gaby spent four nights under his cousin's roof with her uninvited German house guests, who came and went day and night. As some consolation, they seemed to Gaby gloomy, fearful and despondent, speaking of little else than their inevitable defeat. The war, they knew, was lost, and it was now a question of how they could survive this final, suicidal stand their generals had decided they must make.

The interlude gave Gaby time to reflect on his own family in La Bresse, and whether his home was likewise ringing to the thump of German boots. Besides, one or two of the soldiers had begun to ask pointed questions about how he had managed to avoid the call-up of the STO. His mumbled excuse about having been given 'special family exemptions', he could sense, rang hollow.

On the fourth evening, still playing it as cool as he dared, he casually announced he was returning to his parents in La Bresse. He wished his 'sister' and her companions a good evening and turned to go into the night. They again grunted but seemed otherwise unsuspicious. Walking back towards the forest, Gaby felt the tension of the previous few days drain away. He had just carried off the acting role of his life.

His path home took him back across the field where the battle had taken place nearly a week earlier. Having dispersed the Maquis, the Germans did not have the manpower to hold it and had themselves now departed. It was all now eerily quiet. As he made his way across the plateau, he heard a whistle, and responded with one in kind. A handful of figures in black stepped onto the path in front of him, and then relaxed as they recognised one of their own. One of the local Maquis chiefs, whom Gaby knew as 'Campazzi', stepped forward. 'He was hiding in the forest with a dozen boys who had escaped from the battle of the Maquis,' writes Gaby. A couple of them he knew. One of them said that he had been captured by the Germans after the attack but escaped certain death by hiding in a stack of hay for nearly a week. Another spoke of fifty rifles that had been taken from the SS and were now concealed somewhere in La Bresse.

'I gave them all the news and some food,' says Gaby, informing them that he was heading home to La Bresse. The others looked at each other and advised him to exercise extreme caution. The Germans, he was told, were now actively attempting to wipe out the Maquis and, having lost a good deal of men and equipment during the fight, were particularly savage. Anyone male seen walking or travelling would automatically be suspected of being with the Maquis. They could not vouch for what he might find at his village.

The next day, Gaby arrived at La Bresse, which looked all but deserted. He did not dare go to his family's main house in the town, choosing instead their *maison d'enhaut* a kilometre or two above it. It was deserted. A young village girl was bribed to get the message to his family that he was back, hiding above them in the hills, and that he was hungry.

The next day, Gaby's sister Emma and brother, René, turned up with a cow and a goat, grateful beyond joy to see their brother alive, having had no news of him since the battle. They told him that the village was virtually under siege by the Germans, who were watching everything and everyone.

'Then,' writes Gaby, 'the German Kommandantur issued a deportation order: "All men between the ages of 16 and 65 to go immediately to Germany," and if the Germans found any man who had not gone, he would be immediately shot.' A reign of terror now descended upon the peaceful mountain village. Those men in La Bresse who did not get out fast enough were rounded up by the Germans. In the *maison d'enhaut*, Gaby and Emma were joined by their father, and brother, René. 'Each of us had a revolver,' he says. Many of their neighbours were also in hiding, but not as carefully as they. By day, the Germans watched, and at night the horror began. Usually between 10 pm and midnight, recounts Gaby, groups of Gestapo systematically searched every house in the village, breaking into cellars and ceilings, where a father or a brother could be concealed. 'They found many of our companions. Some were sent to concentration camps, but many were killed. Three of my cousins were shot, including the fiancé of my cousin Angèle.'

Terrified for the rest of his family, Monsieur Mougel travelled back to his home to be with his wife, and daughter Bernadette. The two boys, meanwhile, hollowed out a space in the hay, and hid. Then, the shelling started.

As the cold began to bite, the order was given for the conquest of the Haut du Faing, a strategic height between La Bresse and the town of Cornimont five kilometres to the south. Fighting alongside the Americans of the US 6th Army Group were Frenchmen of General Jean de Lattre de Tassigny's newly reconstituted French First Army, given the important role of fighting on their own soil. Included in the initial assault were French colonial troops of the 3rd Algerian and 2nd Moroccan Infantry Division, many of whom had fought the bitter Italian campaign of Monte Cassino earlier in the year and were well experienced in mountain warfare. Particularly, they understood the importance of artillery, and at 9 pm on 7 October strategically placed La Bresse felt the full force of a massive preliminary bombardment, which did not let up for a hellish six weeks.

From their elevated position, brothers Gaby and René watched the shells pour down onto the town. The weather, which had been miserable for weeks, now deteriorated sharply. The temperature dropped, and the snow began to fall. In a couple of days, seven shells had struck parts of the Mougels' large house and property, soon rendering them uninhabitable.

Nearby, the battle had commenced for the slopes of the Haut du Faing, which would last twelve days. The shelling and the gunfire could be heard day and night, and would be some of the bloodiest in the entire campaign to liberate France. The 3rd Algerian Division suffered terribly, losing 1200 men killed and nearly 5000 wounded. The Germans, however, suffered worse, losing 3000 killed and an unknown number wounded.

In the entire La Bresse commune, which covered several larger towns including Gérardmer, it is estimated that 146,000 shells of all sizes were expended. For Gaby and René, the noise was terrible and unceasing. Down in the town, it was even worse, with entire families who had not managed to escape being reduced to living in their cellars as their homes disintegrated above. Cheese and potatoes became the staple, the milk running out early as those cows that had not fled in panic were either killed by the shelling or, deprived of pasture, ceased to produce. Families would dash from house to house either seeking or distributing what sustenance they could afford to keep their neighbours alive.

One resident who lived through the siege of La Bresse as a small child remembers it as 'six weeks during which we lived terrorised in the cellars, every day bringing destruction and death to the town's civilians'. Up to forty people, he recalled, were crowded into some cellars. At one stage, his mother gave birth with the help of the village midwife, by candlelight, as the sound of shells careened overhead. He recalled not only the shelling but also the rain, which for an entire week was unrelenting, cruelly seeking out the many holes in the roofs and walls of houses to further torment the miserable inhabitants trapped within. 'On the 18th,' he wrote, 'it was my 4th birthday. It rained all night. In the village, the wounded German soldiers descended from the Haut du Faing to regroup or be evacuated . . .'

At night, foraging parties ventured out into the fields to scratch up the potatoes, which became harder to find as the snow settled and the ground hardened. In the lulls between shelling, the Germans rounded up what people they could to force them to dig trenches below the town for the defensive line to which they knew they would eventually fall back.

'After several weeks,' recalled the boy, 'the candles begin to run out.' Ingeniously, someone in his family rigged up a dynamo attached to a bicycle, which people took turns in pedalling to produce some rudimentary lighting. 'It is like a bike race where people ride not to win, but to produce the most clarity of light.'

Despite their trials, the inhabitants of La Bresse were buoyed by the conviction that the Allies – so nearby – would soon be pushing the Germans out of their village and bringing an end to their ordeal. The fierce resistance by SS and regular German soldiers, however, slowed their advance considerably, and the Germans knew that every day's delay worked in their favour as the winter – already shaping up as a particularly cold one – delayed their progress even more. Nor could the overwhelming Allied advantage in airpower be brought to bear, as the relentless fog and thick skies provided the perfect cover for the defending Germans.

'The days follow and resemble each other,' recalled the boy. 'It rains in a torrent and blows a violent wind. Discouragement starts to settle into the town's population. When will we be liberated?' On the nearby battlefront, the weather continued to deteriorate, with General Tassigny later describing the conditions in Alsace that winter as 'Siberian', with temperatures of minus twenty degrees, strong winds and nearly a metre of snow.

It was developments further to the south of La Bresse, however, that sealed the fate of the town, as the French First Armoured Division led a push that would eventually threaten to surround the German positions in what would become known as the 'Colmar Pocket'. Caught in that burgeoning pocket was La Bresse and its neighbouring towns and villages. On 8 November, the Germans decided to pull back from the village, destroying it, house by house.

René, Gaby and Emma witnessed it all from their hiding place above. 'The Boches started to burn the village,' Gaby wrote to Barney, 'one house after another, starting at 8 o'clock one evening. The inhabitants were driven out – driven out into the snow, which was 60 centimetres deep, without any shelter. I counted between 80 and 90 houses burning simultaneously. I can assure you it was a terrible sight.'

Taking their revenge on both the Maquis and the French people who had resisted them so determinedly for four and a half years, the Germans decided to abandon one of their last footholds in France, leaving nothing behind but an empty, smouldering ruin. Street by street, house by house, cellar by cellar, the town's population were dragged up and out into the bitter cold. 'Many little children died in the snow on the sides of the roads, as well as the elderly,' recalled Gaby. 'All the men who were hiding were forced to come out, either that or burn with the house, a hard choice.' It was now, in the bitter November chill, that La Bresse's agony truly began.

From their vantage point at the *maison d'enhaut*, the three Mougel children could only watch helplessly as their beloved town, whose first building, the Church of Saint-Laurent, could be dated to 1303, crumbled in flames beneath them. The shelling had now stopped, as the American and French sensed the breaking of the German defences and prepared to advance up to take the town. The Germans were determined, though, to leave them with nothing, and what they could not loot they would destroy. Screams and choking smoke mingled in ghastly echoes around the valley. Lines of German lorries, arriving empty from the east, departed full of townspeople to add to their pool of slave labour. Virtually the only house they could see still standing was that of their lifelong family friends, two bachelor brothers, Henri and Robert. Then, to their horror, the Mougels noted a squad of Germans beginning to make their way up the long, rocky slope towards them.

'It was four in the afternoon,' recalled Gaby to Barney, 'and we were just having something to eat.' By this time, almost the entire village was in flames. The stench of burning furniture, clothing and bedding was unbearable. Emerging out of the smoke under a leaden sky, making their way towards the *maison d'enhaut*, the German soldiers truly resembled to the Mougels monsters of doom.

They had all known this moment would probably come, and had devised a plan. Emma went out to meet the Germans, smiling, ignoring the chaos of the valley below and offering to prepare them a meal. René and Gaby, meanwhile, rushed to a small pile of women's clothing they had prepared and put it on. At least from a distance, a female would draw less attention. Their disguise roughly complete, they exited through the back of the house and dashed to the haystack, burying themselves deep inside. The minutes went past. The two brothers lay there, silently listening to their own breathing but straining their ears for any sound of the Germans, hoping desperately that Emma's well-rehearsed charm had managed to fool them.

Suddenly, boots were heard coming down a flight of wooden stairs. Guttural words were shouted. Gaby risked the briefest of peeks from the hay, to be confronted with the sight of the German squad pouring into the barn. René urged silence. Then, the voices were closer, barely metres away. Some more shouted orders were followed seconds later by an ominous crackling sound and white smoke filling up the boys' hollowed-out cocoon in the haystack inside the barn. The Germans were setting it alight.

Behind them, they had left the rear barn door deliberately open for a quick escape. Crawling as quickly and as quietly as they could, the boys emerged from the hay, somehow evading the Germans, and dashed out the back of the barn, avoiding the flames, but now fully exposed in the open. Bolting across the field, the two brothers expected at any moment a bullet in the back, or at least a shout, but the edge of the woods, just metres away, drew them towards safety. Suddenly, René stopped. '*Arrêt! Arrêt!*' he cried, grabbing Gaby's arm. He had suddenly remembered their beloved goat and cow, which they had managed to keep safe thus far, and he could not bear the thought of them perishing in the flames. Incredibly, they headed back towards the barn. 'We could not let our cow and goat burn,' says Gaby, 'so we immediately returned to save them.'

Re-entering the flaming barn, the two boys managed to release the terrified animals from the unbearable heat, before escaping again themselves. This time, however, they were seen. '*Halt! Halt!*' they could hear behind them as they ran. 'We had a fifty metre start and as we could run quicker than them, we got away,' says Gaby. Why the Germans did not fire was something the boys wondered about for the rest of their lives. Their luck continued, as they were able to recover their animals and conceal them in the forest.

Emma, meanwhile, having failed to fool the Germans, raced down to one of the few houses not on fire: that of their friends, Robert and Henri. From there, she would never forget the sight of looking back up the mountain and watching her family's beloved *maison d'enhaut*, which she had known all her life, burning to the ground.

By 7 pm, only the fires that still raged across the village illuminated La Bresse. At this part of the letter, Gaby takes up his sister's story. 'The Boches rounded up everybody,' he says. 'They wanted to take Robert with them,' but Emma had other ideas. Henri had managed to escape, so as the Germans looted the house of their friends, one soldier with a revolver held Robert hostage in an upstairs room. Along with some other village women who had taken refuge in the house, Emma was forced by a barking SS man holding a rifle out into the freezing night. She was determined, however, not to let Robert be led away to what she sensed would be his death. Seizing her moment, she rushed back into the house and managed to cause enough commotion to distract the soldier holding him, as he emerged to investigate the shouting. It was just enough for Robert to find his way out of the room and disappear through a back entrance into the dark. Emma, too, chose her moment to bolt. The cover of the darkness that night proved a mighty ally.

Encountering Emma, Robert bolted with her through the chaotic streets of the town to the address of a stepbrother, who was sheltering with his family under the ruins of his own house. No one dared move again until the Germans had left.

René and Gaby had picked their moment to come down from the higher slopes, to which they had headed after fleeing the barn. In silence, leading their precious cow and goat, they made their way past the still hissing ruins of their *maison d'enhaut*, sensing that, should they survive this night, their lives would never be the same. Then, as if this November day could get any worse, the shelling began again. Hugging the flank of an old stone wall, they emerged into the terrible sight of what had been their village, the only home they had ever known. Although eighty centimetres of snow covered the ground, the flames lit it up like daylight. All the boys could now think of was finding their family, but, stumbling into a semi-wrecked house, they discovered some bedding and exhaustion took hold.

It was not until the late afternoon of the following day that their father appeared, having found a refuge somewhere at the other end of the village. Their mother and Bernadette, he told them, were also safe. The Boches, however, had destroyed everything. Though relieved beyond words at finding each other alive, the men of the Mougel family could only look silently around them with staring eyes and bleached faces at the ruin of their home.

'Down in the village,' continues Gaby in his letter, 'we found over 700 refugees in a huge cheese cellar. All livestock had to be abandoned in the snow. The only exception was Mickey our dog, who followed us everywhere but in those last hours I had to kill poor Mickey, because I could not feed him.'

The boys' mother was overcome with relief at the sight of her two sons, but it soon transpired that the whereabouts of Emma was still a mystery. The boys assured their parents that she was a smart girl and would be safe somewhere, and prayed silently that they were right. On a small sled, their mother had somehow managed to save a handful of possessions from their burning house. The five of them – mother and father, Gaby and René, as well as their sister Bernadette – stood in the snow looking at the contents of the sled in silence: a pathetic pile of odds and ends, all that remained of a family whose lives had, in a few hours, been shattered into a thousand pieces.

The Mougels then spent a miserable night in the cellar, along with several hundred other shocked and freezing townspeople. 'We could not sleep as there was no room to lie down,' recalled Gaby. 'The cold was terrible.' At one stage during the night, the Germans reappeared and shone flashlights around the room full of terrified faces that resembled more the dead than the living. 'The Boches found that there were still some men remaining, and they said they would sort them out in the morning.' The Mougels decided enough was enough, and that, come what may, they would leave the village that very day rather than die at the hands of these monsters who had descended upon them.

At daybreak, Gaby, René, Bernadette and their mother, Marie, and Papa Eugene ventured out into the most terrible dawn of their lives to search for the brave but missing Emma. Silently, they walked through the ruins of La Bresse, ready to hide at the first sign of any patrolling Germans. Virtually the whole town, they could see, had been burned systematically. When the Mougels saw that the house of their also missing friend Robert had remained intact, they approached it with caution, as they suspected it might be occupied by the Germans. But it was as empty as every other house in the village.

Later in the morning, the Mougels returned to their mother, who had somehow found out that Emma was safe, a couple of kilometres away at the hamlet of Grosse Pierre. Fearing the Germans would be returning soon, the Mougels and a small party of townspeople sneaked out of what was left of La Bresse, towards Grosse Pierre.

'We were fifteen persons,' wrote Gaby, 'and we were in a sad state. We ate potatoes cooked by the blaze of the houses.' Soon, however, the family was reunited. They elected to stay sheltering in the relative quiet of Grosse Pierre until they could be sure the Germans had gone, and that would not be for another eight freezing, terrifying days.

La Bresse was not the only part of the Vosges to be destroyed in the battle. In the eastern part of the province, the towns of Saint-Dié and Gérardmer were also devastated, firstly by French and American artillery, then by the Germans, who dynamited everything they could in their retreat. A postwar estimate put the overall damage at seventy-five per cent of the buildings across several towns, including 3700 homes, 2000 farms and 1700 industrial or commercial premises, resulting in 25,000 people rendered homeless.

La Bresse was by far the most damaged, resulting in the town having to be completely rebuilt. Of the 1018 buildings listed in 1936, 500 were totally destroyed and the rest damaged. The young boy whose reminiscences give us one of the only written eyewitness accounts of the devastation of La Bresse remembers the destruction of a mill in front of his farm. A 500-kilogram bomb the Germans were transporting on a cart was so heavy it became stuck in a meadow. The boy watched as they struggled to free it. 'In the evening,' he remembered, 'there was an enormous explosion that shook the neighbourhood. When we remove the protective covers from the window, we witnessed a fire that lit everything up like daylight.'

At the height of the destruction and the round-up of the population, 483 of the men of La Bresse were gathered in front of the church square and taken away on trucks towards Germany. Several thousand women, children and elderly were force-marched under shellfire through snow roughly five and a half kilometres east to a high point called the Col de la Vierge, where for ten days they were 'billeted' across farms without food or care of any kind. It was for them an unspeakable ordeal in which many died of exposure, brutality and neglect. Below them, their village burned. Here, recalled the boy, 'they will spend ten days at 400 per farm . . . dead with cold, hunger, and frozen feet. After this Calvary, they will be taken care of and evacuated by the Americans.'

The destruction of La Bresse continued until 18 November, when, the very next day, the Germans were finally forced out by the arrival of the Americans. At this point, 1200 exhausted, starving and desperate people who had somehow managed to survive amid the ruins of their town emerged from the rubble, to meet the astonished American and French forces who over the previous weeks had forced their way inch by inch up the mountain. Even they were shocked by what they saw of the destruction of La Bresse.

Gaby, too, remembers his liberation. In his case, he had the joy of welcoming French Moroccan troops, who signalled the end of his war but by no means the end of his difficulties. They warned him that the Germans were in the area and that it was not secure. As he wrote to Barney:

When we met the first French soldiers near the church, they told us that the Boches were still holding the Lac des Corbeaux area and all the mountains below my cousin's house. I think you will easily remember the place . . . I went down to the village to have a look and to get news . . . in four days La Bresse had been reduced to ashes.

By 22 November, the battle was over and the Germans had left. In almost constant rain, snow and mud, the US 7th Army, assisted on their far southern flank by the French First Army, proved to be the only army in modern history to defeat an enemy force defending the Vosges, but at a terrible cost.

The Mougels, along with hundreds of other residents of La Bresse, were evacuated to Cornimont, where they remained until the end of the war. 'I can assure you,' Gaby wrote to Barney, 'that we saved nothing at all except some clothes that we recovered, and two cows, which we have with us here in Cornimont. There it is: the story of my life since you left us.'

It was not the end of La Bresse. Temporary housing soon appeared, as did the bulldozers and reconstruction teams. In early April 1945, a ceremony took place where the bodies of those maquisards killed in the German attack back in

September were re-interred, attended by representatives from the British and US armies. Through the smashed main street, at the head of the procession, a banner was carried as the townspeople of La Bresse looked on in silence. It was a tricolour bearing the symbols of the 4th Group of the FFI – the Maquis to which Gaby Mougel and Barney Greatrex had belonged – and was borne proudly by their commander, one Jean-Paul Vitu, aka Bébert.

Gaby signed off his extraordinary letter to Barney with the warmest of greetings, apologising for not being able to send him some of the photographs taken of both of them during his time with them in France. 'The camera and films are in the ashes of La Bresse with everything else,' he laments.

After reading the letter, in his sunny, peaceful garden on the other side of the world, Barney sat in deep silence for a very long time.

EPILOGUE

Not long after I began to piece together the story of Barney Greatrex's war, his family handed me a box filled with some of the minutiae of a long and active life. Inside, arranged in logically sequenced bundles, was an array of letters, cards, newspaper cuttings, photographs, bits of uniform and other associated artefacts spanning Barney's childhood (his Knox Grammar school reports are universally excellent) to his final journey to the Vosges, which he undertook when well into his nineties.

Included among the collection are such items as the official notice of his promotion to 'Flying Officer, (substantive) effective 3.7.44' and a pamphlet printed for the benefit of serving sons of the Empire distributed by the Empire Societies' War Hospitality Committee. 'What do you like?' the writer asks. 'Fishing, Riding, Swimming, Dancing, Skating, Theatres, Cinemas?' The breadth of activities available to the thousands of men such as Barney Greatrex while in London was apparently boundless, although 'drinking in the local pub' seems to have been curiously omitted.

There is also a short but welcoming letter from the adjutant of Barney's unit, 61 Squadron, sent at the end of October 1944. 'My Dear Greatrex,' he begins. 'We have just had the happy news that you are safely back in this country! We have no news of the rest of the crew, and are very anxious to know if you can tell us anything about them – subject to restrictions, of course.' He then adds poignantly, 'I am afraid that, after all this time, there are very few people on this Squadron whom you would know.'

Somewhere near the bottom of the box was a smooth, fawn-coloured envelope of a quality almost unknown today, from which several items fell into my hand as I up-ended it. One was a card showing a photo reproduction of a pastel portrait of Barney, drawn by an artist of obvious and prodigious talent. It was done just a few weeks after his return from France, as he was preparing for his voyage home to Sydney. As I hold the photo in my hand, I am struck by the face in front of me. Here is the young Barney – finally in his flying officer's uniform, the single stripe positioned just above his 'Australia' shoulder flash. His skin is smooth and his thick, reddish hair neatly combed. Here is a man still in the prime of his life, but, with a subtlety only the finest artist can capture, his eyes hold a sadness that belies his youthful visage. Perhaps, sitting there in the studio in his RAAF blue, his war now finished, Barney felt once again the loss of those six men with whom he began it, and who, unlike him, would have no final voyage, and no homecoming. Perhaps the absence in those eyes is the yearning for a job left eternally incomplete, a void that can never be filled.

Clipped to the small picture is a letter, written in ink on embossed red letterhead that boldly states 'Homer House, Ipsden, Oxon', dated 28 December 1944. 'Dear Mr Greatrex,' the author begins in a flourishing hand. 'As I write I am half expecting Barnaby to pay us a second visit, if his last leave is extended, prior to his trip home. I have the photograph of the portrait I did of him and it is a perfect one.'

The author, and artist, was the painter and sculptor Eric Henri Kennington, one of Britain's most respected official war artists, and whose work now hangs in London's Tate Gallery and Imperial War Museum, as well as in sculptured memorials across the country. 'A vital, independent talent in early and mid-twentieth-century British art,' claimed his biographer, and a man who counted such figures as T. E. Lawrence among his closest friends, for whose seminal *Seven Pillars of Wisdom* he provided the illustrations. Having been a soldier himself in the Great War, his most famous work, *The Kensingtons at Laventie*, is a true masterpiece, depicting a group of soldiers at rest in the odd jaunty chaos of a World War I French village. The pale young faces peek out from their winter kit amid war's detritus, bored, restless and uncertain. Realistic and compelling, it was a style that marked all of Kennington's work over the space of two world wars.

It is not known exactly how Barney's father, Basil, knew of Eric Kennington, but the family suggests it may have arisen from his long interest in T. E. Lawrence himself – he apparently read *Seven Pillars of Wisdom* voraciously. However, the surviving final page of a letter to Barney in October 1944 urges him to follow up the contact he had made with Kennington and organise the portrait, which Basil was happy to pay for ('providing price not outrageous, say fifty pounds . . . please Barn, do this for us'). Kennington created many dozens of wartime portraits, especially of airmen, but seemed particularly taken not only by his depiction of Barney but by the subject himself.

'We are all hoping B answers my wire of yesterday by coming straight along for a day or two,' Kennington continues in his letter to Basil. 'He filled our house with fun and intense interest in the dozens of stories he told us.' Today, Barney's picture perhaps speaks most eloquently of how he was feeling at war's end. 'I hope you will think it like him,' concludes Kennington. 'I think it is just about the best I have done.' The portrait itself indeed arrived in Australia, carried under the arm of its subject, and still hangs in the Greatrex home, a prized family possession and timeless testament to Barney's war.

Delving on, I discovered another curiosity, the main reason for its inclusion among Barney's most prized keepsakes not being immediately apparent. On cheap and slightly crumbly wartime paper, a stray ink blot has left its mark on a small leaflet. Under a somewhat doubtful reproduction of the

RAAF eagle are the words 'Right Royal Cootamundra Navy' and the date 21 May 1942. It is the roll call – depicted in a comical nautical theme – of the graduates of Barney's navigation course, completed as part of the Empire Air Training Scheme's 22 Course at No. 1 Air Navigation School among the open flat plains beyond the Great Dividing Range at Cootamundra in New South Wales.

This event would have been the final time a great deal of these young men would have seen each other after many incredibly intensive weeks learning from scratch the difficult art of air navigation in a fraction of the time one would be allowed to do so in peacetime. Their 'ship' for the night appears to have been the '*P.U.B. Albion*', in Cootamundra's main street, and all the gallant crew were in attendance. The officers are all listed, including 'Skipper', Flight Lieutenant E. A. Jones (followed by the words 'the rest is up to you blokes'), '1st Mate, Flying Officer S. J. Brazier' (suffixed with 'which I don't intend to give you'), besides many others, all accompanied by in-jokes, the meanings of which have long ago been lost.

The joke continues onto the next page, where a menu has been created, no doubt employing the talents of the most comically creative cadets on the course. On the back page, all the graduates are listed, including 'Barnacle' Greatrex and the words 'Nocturnal Nausea', which hopefully amused the assembled lads with a remembered incident or celebrated misdemeanour. There are in total forty-nine names listed on the little program – each with an individualised epithet – and the reason Barney decided to hang on to it only becomes clear when reading the careful annotations he has added. On the left, beside each name, Barney has marked where each man was sent, either to the European theatre, marked 'UK', or the Pacific, which he indicates with 'Australia'. Despite his own country being under threat from the Japanese, by far the majority were sent, like himself, into the heavy bomber fleets of RAF Bomber Command. He has also chosen to note which men were offered the chance to become early officers via an 'on course' commission, with the words 'P/O' (pilot officer) in small letters to the right.

Then, obviously filled in at a later date in pencil, on the far right of the page beside the cadets' names, Barney has recorded their fates. In a long descending column, the word 'MISSING' is repeated over and over again. When one tallies up those young men who were sent to Europe, it appears that roughly half did not return. This list represents – in the most stark terms – the terrible cost of Bomber Command's six-year offensive, taking the lives of 55,000 young airmen. Perhaps Barney referred to it only occasionally over the years, gradually struggling to put a face to those names, a further reminder of his persistent, bewildering luck.

At a later date, someone has included in the collection photocopies of two letters of particular poignancy. One is from Barney's rear gunner, Paddy Rankin, to two close family friends, Al and Jean. Barney had last heard Paddy's voice as he conducted a grim dialogue with Wally Einarson, his pilot, while the German night fighter closed in under the cloak of the winter haze over France. An Irishman, Paddy had already earned a DFM and in the warm missive to his friends makes light of a recent motorcycle accident as well as revealing that he had requested to be taken out of training to resume operations. The letter is dated 18 February 1944:

... well here I am trying to have another go at old Gerry. I got cheesed training people and asked to come back which was granted for the asking. I have started with several on the big city (that was) and by the looks of things I shall finish on it too. By the way, I get my commission in a few weeks. I have seen all of boys including the AOC and all I am doing now is just waiting for it to come through. Not bad for a lad!! Remember when I heaved coal and swept the NAAFI floor? SSSSH! Don't say those things!

Accompanying the letter is Al's reply, filled with cheer and local family news:

Just a line you old 'Son of a Gun' to thank you for your very welcome and nice letter. Sorry old man to hear you had been in dock but I always told you that you'd damage yourself on a motor bike! Did you receive the photo of the wedding we sent you? So you have decided to have another bang at old Gerry – I wish you the best of luck and Happy Landings! Oh, Mrs Bennett, Fred and Len's mother has died last week. She was such a nice woman. Well cheerio Paddy and don't forget to write soon. Look after yourself Paddy Old fellow.

It is dated 26 February 1944. Even as it was penned, Paddy had been dead for twenty-four hours.

•

For Barney, like the vast majority of men who returned from World War II having experienced loss and trauma, the home-coming was not easy. His younger brother, Antony, who had also served with the RAAF in Australia and was not demobil-ised until 1946, thinks it was far more difficult for Barney than anyone suspected, including his family. 'I'm pretty sure he had something like a nervous breakdown,' he tells me. Antony's wife, Kathy, who has been instrumental in keeping Barney's story alive and who has methodically archived much of the material pertaining not only to Barney but also to the entire Greatrex family, agrees. 'I had brothers-in-law in the air force during the war and no one could appreciate what they went through.' What is classified today as post-traumatic stress disorder and all its associated treatments were, in 1945, still decades away, and millions like Barney were simply expected to shrug the war off and get on with their lives. Barney did his best, re-enrolling in his uncompleted engineering course at the University of Sydney, but it was not successful and he left it after a short time. 'Barney's parents were, like mine, quite Victorian,' says Kathy. 'Definitely not the sort of people who would have tolerated any sort of nervous trauma. They would have seen that as a weakness.'

Antony believes that the slight stammer Barney grew up with was greatly exacerbated on his return from the war, and continued to worsen as the years went on. Indeed, in a 2015 documentary on the wartime services of a dozen old Knox Grammar boys in which Barney recounts his experiences, it is pronounced, at times severe.

Both Kathy and Antony believe that Barney was severely haunted not only by what he had seen but particularly by the inexplicable nature of his survival. 'I think,' says Kathy, 'Barney was constantly asking himself, "Why me? Why?"' As Barney's life back in Australia outwardly reverted to normality, it was a question that only became louder and more unanswerable as the years went by.

Perhaps as a diversion, Barney after the war developed an interest in amateur theatre and joined his local troupe at Ku-ring-gai, in Sydney's north. Antony recalls a couple of brief and short-lived stage appearances, but Barney's real delight was the fantastical realm of theatre sets and props. One member of the group who did have the talent – and certainly the looks – to walk out onto the stage was a striking young woman named Jenny Mitchell. She and Barney struck up a friendship, and in 1950 were married. Jenny came from money, her father having a significant accounting business, and bought properties both in Sydney and Mudgee – the place, according to the family, that Barney came to feel happiest in.

The two brothers, Antony and Barney, became part of their father's engineering business in the 1950s, although Antony cannot recall Barney's initial role. 'Barney and I never argued, but we were never what you'd call great mates,' he says. Antony did not last in the family firm, but Barney, largely due to his input of funds to keep it afloat during lean times, eventually took it over. Having no children of his own, he eventually passed it on to his sister Pleasance's son Richard, who runs it to this day.

Richard and his brother Charles were a little in awe of their uncle, but they were wary of what they describe as his 'short fuse'. 'It took us a while,' says Charles, 'before we worked out a way of dealing with him.'

Like many veterans, Barney did not speak of his wartime experiences for many years after the events. Although his family knew the broad picture, the details were kept to himself. Working alongside Barney during his time with the firm, Richard became privy to some of the stories, but Barney was not the sort of man who was ever easy to push.

In the 1960s, Barney made his first trip back to France, piggybacking it with a business trip to the UK. For the first time since the war, he met once again with Gaby Mougel and walked across the almost unchanged hills and villages of the Vosges that he had come to know so well in 1944. La Bresse, however, was virtually unrecognisable, having been quickly and completely rebuilt after the war. Barney found that his legend had endured, and now the children of the wartime generation were able to meet in person the quiet Australian man who had dropped from the skies and become part of their struggle during the terrible nadir of the war.

Since then, several more trips were made, when the comradeships forged during the war were rekindled, culminating in Barney's final trip, which he conducted with his nephew Charlie in 2013. Even then, however, according to Charlie, Barney didn't give much away, even on a visit to the Choloy War Cemetery, where his crew now lie, a little to the west of Nancy, where they first encountered the German night fighter. 'Barney stood there, looking at the graves of his crew,' recalls Charlie, 'their white tombstones all beautifully lined up together side by side. Barney was very quiet, and didn't say much, just pointing out some of the names and who they were. I've often wondered what was really going on deep inside his head.'

One thing Charlie was reminded of was that they were initially not even buried in a proper grave but outside the local cemetery near to the town where they fell, the Germans not regarding them worthy of interment in consecrated ground. Here, however, in this quiet and beautiful corner of France, were the names of the men Barney had trained with, flown with and, for some reason that defied him all his life, survived:

Flight Lieutenant Johann Walter Einarson, D.F.C., D.F.M. – Pilot
Pilot Officer Allen James Collins – Navigator
Flight Sergeant Reginald Thomas Gill – Wireless Operator
Sergeant Maurice Leonard Worth – Flight Engineer
Flight Sergeant Phillip Llewellyn Jones – Air Gunner
Flight Sergeant Herbert 'Paddy' Rankin, D.F.M. – Air Gunner

The sole survivor of Lancaster LL775, O for Orange of 61 Squadron made several visits to the graves of his crew, but no more insight into the question of why he had survived them was to be found there. For Barney Greatrex, an ordinary young man from the suburbs of Sydney, the facts remained too overwhelming to explain or comprehend.

Barney's final logbook entry, penned months after that fateful flight, perhaps speaks volumes, not only for that night and the months following but also for the remainder of Barney Greatrex's long life. In the margin beside the entry for 25 February 1944, for the target they would never reach and from which all but Barney would never return, has been written the brief, simple, heartbreaking words, 'Rest of crew killed. I walked back.'

•

On 17 February 2018, five months after the publication of his story, Barney Greatrex was finally reunited with the crew of Lancaster O-Orange, after he passed away in northern Sydney, aged 97.

FOR SCHOOL AND COUNTRY

Background to the documentary

Beyond Barney Greatrex's family and the small community in the Vosges, few knew of his story for many years. It was only as Barney turned ninety-one that his tale of heroism, and a healthy dose of luck, reached beyond Mouacourt, La Bresse and Sydney's North Shore. His new-found fame started where he'd had his first exposure to military life: his old school, Knox Grammar, when a chance meeting led to the documentary *For School and Country*. No one envisioned that this passion project would one day inspire a book, sharing Barney's story with the world.

The documentary began through one of Barney's fellow classmates of 1939, Richard Miles, at the Anzac Day service at Knox Grammar on Sunday 2 May 2010. Richard was seated next to Angus Hordern, the son of a World War II veteran and formerly of the Royal Australian Navy and Army Reserves. Before the service started, Richard introduced himself to

Angus and pointed him towards the names on the order of service, his fallen classmates. Angus and thousands of other schoolboys had heard these names read over the years, but they really meant something to Richard. Richard and Barney were survivors from the class of 1939, losing nine boys of eighty-two from their year group in World War II. With seventy-three serving in the war, the loss ratio was one in eight.

Richard told Angus of a small tennis party in 1939 he still saw so vividly in his mind; his friends dressed in their tennis whites, innocently playing together. Richard could never forget it, for after World War II he was the only survivor of that autumn afternoon. Angus squeezed Richard's frail hand, lost for words.

Headmaster John Weeks began his address and in his opening lines said, 'What you do not value will not be valued.' Angus was moved, and resolved. At the end of the service, he turned to his new friend and committed to telling Richard's story and those of his mates. They decided that filming the veterans was the best way to engage younger generations and make them more appreciative of the supreme sacrifices made by so many who had gone before them. Richard felt an urgency; the number of his friends was thinning as time moved on.

A dozen 'old boys' were asked to share their stories. The veterans were ready to talk; they were all in their eighties and nineties, and had never really opened up before. Now, in their twilight years, they felt an urge to share their experiences.

Knox introduced Angus to Alex Lloyd, a recent graduate with filmmaking experience and a passion for history. Graduating from the school seventy years after Barney and his peers, Alex felt great reverence towards the men he was being asked to record on film and eagerly joined the team.

Twelve veterans were interviewed at length: sailors John Hordern, John Reid and Phil Stevenson; soldiers Ted Carter, John Hore-Lacy, Richard Miles (much to his humble protest) and Eric Thew; and flyers Barney Greatrex, David Nesbitt, Arthur Pardey, Lysle Roberts and Don Caldwell Smith.

Barney was the second veteran filmed, his first on-camera interview recorded on 13 May 2011 – barely a month after his ninety-first birthday. He had no qualms recounting his school days, wartime service and post-war life, but was clearly unaccustomed to doing so with strangers. He was gently guided through the first interview, Angus and Alex helpfully informed by the written account of his adventures that Barney had made after the war. The pair were instantly captivated by Barney's story. They visited him frequently to clear up details, digitise photographs or simply to enjoy Barney's reminiscences, whether they were on an experience as 'Jacques Clapin' or life at Knox under the headmastership of Neil MacNeil.

Barney's second appearance on camera was on stage at the Knox Prep School's Remembrance Day service in 2011 – 11/11/11. Nervous at first, Barney ultimately enjoyed telling his experiences to the crowd of seven- to twelve-year-old boys, who were gripped. At a smaller gathering after the assembly with some of the senior boys, Barney's quiet stoicism and humility finally cracked when he saw the awe and wonder that a crowd – besides the one at family gatherings – had for his tale. Posing for a group photo, he grinned and said, 'Make sure you get this picture in the yearbook!'

Angus and Alex were recording one remarkable story after another: platoon leader Ted Carter's fight against Rommel in Tobruk; Lancaster skipper Don Caldwell Smith's bravery in Bomber Command; the terror that Eric Thew and his platoon faced in the jungles of New Guinea; and Barney's time in France. The pair knew they had to do something bigger than they had first envisioned: a documentary. Alex, now working in the book publishing industry, happily took on the role of screenwriter.

The core team, going by the name Thistle Productions, expanded to include fellow old boys of Alex's generation: Thomas Kaye and Rohan Viswalingam. Alex's friends contributed design work and music tracks; Knox opened its archive of information, photographs and footage; historians were consulted and interviewed; and Dr Brendan Nelson opened the Australian War Memorial to the team. Headmaster John Weeks and the Old Knox Grammarians' Association threw their full support behind the project, including recording the Symphonic Wind Ensemble and school choir at studio quality to complete the soundtrack. The team undertook location shoots in Gallipoli, Germany, London and Singapore, and used photos from Barney's family trip to France in 2013.

Just as Richard had predicted, time caught up with his classmates. The first veteran to pass away was Angus's father,

John. Despite his grief, Angus invited Alex to film the funeral. The image of John's classmates John Reid, Eric Thew and Arthur Pardey laying poppies on the coffin was the documentary's closing shot, underscoring the importance of preserving these stories before they are lost forever – the reason the team began the project in the first place. The next to move on was Ted Carter, only a month after the release of the documentary.

For School and Country premiered within the Knox community in May 2015. The five-part documentary miniseries took Angus, Alex, Thomas and Rohan five years to research, film and produce. Dr Brendan Nelson launched the production as the VIP keynote speaker. Close to 2000 attendees watched an abridged version of the show for the launch, the audience made up of Knox students, the veterans, with their families and friends, and other special guests. These twelve men, on behalf of their classmates, finally had the spotlight. The heartfelt ovation for them after the screening never seemed to end.

At the lunch function afterwards, ninety-five-year-old Barney was delighted to discover that his wartime portrait had been used as the DVD cover.

The newfound recognition for Barney's story continued in June 2016, when he, along with four other Australian airmen, was awarded France's greatest decoration, the Legion of Honour, being given the rank of *Chevalier* (Knight). In a small but dignified ceremony at the French Consulate in Sydney, Ambassador Christophe Lecourtier expressed the same great affection for the Australian veterans that day as Barney experienced firsthand in 1944 as the famous '*aviateur Australien*'.

Barney was not the first in his family to be honoured for military service in France. Emperor Napoleon III created the Saint Helena Medal in 1857 to honour the service of those who had fought in Napoleon Bonaparte's *Grande Armée* between 1792 and 1815. One recipient of this decoration, certified by the Grand Chancery of the Legion of Honour, was Captain Andre Clapin, Barney's great-great-grandfather on his mother's side. To be honoured across the generations for serving on the same soil, despite living a hemisphere apart, was the final odd twist of fate in Barney's story.

Barney's new honour and the documentary's rousing reception led naturally to the idea of creating a book to capture these men's extraordinary war service in full for a national and international audience. But the life stories of the twelve veterans simply could not fit into one volume, so just one story had to be chosen. Once again, fate picked Barney out from amongst his esteemed and heroic comrades to be the subject of this book.

In 2016 Alex and Angus found an eager publisher for Barney's story in Hachette Australia and an enthusiastic biographer in Michael Veitch. Working together and with Barney's relatives, the complete record of this valiant airman's unique war service has now been preserved.

•

For School and Country captured the most amazing stories from twelve ordinary boys who downed books and went to war to protect Australia from the militarists in Japan, the fascists in Italy and the Nazis in Germany. Hearing the sacrifices of these boys and bringing their stories to light was the greatest honour and privilege for our team. We thank all who helped make this happen, especially Dr Brendan Nelson, John Weeks and James Brice. John Diamond, James Whiley, Jo Tait, Dr Karl James, Brendan O'Keefe, Christiane Gilbert and Len Traynor were invaluable history consultants; Richard Miles, Ian MacPherson and Edric Chaffer for selecting the veterans; and Lachlan Liao, Megan Bailey and Damian Ferguson were of immense aid with their unparalleled logistical talents. Thomas Kaye and Rohan Viswalingam, this would have been impossible without your dedication and skill. To the veterans we interviewed, thank you for speaking to us, and for serving your country with such valiance and humility.

Each veteran had an amazing tale, but there was one story in particular that had to be told beyond the documentary – the story of a boy called Barney. This book is the culmination of seven years of work, starting at that Anzac Day service in 2010. Warm thanks must go to Ashleigh Barton, chief advisor and dear friend. Barney's story would never have made the leap from film to page without you.

We are eternally grateful to publisher Matthew Kelly, editor Tom Bailey-Smith and their colleagues at Hachette Australia for believing in Barney's story and publishing it with such expertise.

This book could never have happened without Barney's very supportive family. Antony and Kathy Greatrex, Margaret Brownlow, and Richard and Charlie Mort all helped in spades.

Thank you especially, Charlie – mastermind of the 2013 France trip – for all the extra lengths to which you went.

We are forever indebted to the incomparable Michael Veitch – history aficionado, literary archaeologist and maestro author. You have captured Barney's story perfectly, and were always the man for the job.

Finally, of course, thank you to Barney Greatrex. A dear, kind and thoughtful man – and a bit cheeky too – it is a privilege to have called you our friend. It has been an honour to share your story first on camera and now in print. Thank you most of all for your service, especially the day you looked at the Lancaster schematics and decided that volunteering for the bomb-aimer position might be a good idea.

Alex Lloyd and Angus Hordern,
Thistle Productions
forschoolandcountry.com

SOURCES AND ACKNOWLEDGEMENTS

Telling the story of Barney's extraordinary war has been a genuinely collaborative project, first sparked by the interest and efforts of Knox Grammar old boys Alex Lloyd and Angus Hordern. Their hard work in assembling Barney Greatrex's history, culminating in their documentary *For School and Country*, was the point at which this story first came to public light. This was followed up by an important extensive interview conducted at the school, in which more of the story was revealed.

It then transpired that several years earlier, and at the urging of his wife Jenny, Barney had in fact written his own brief account, titled simply 'Barney's Story', which was also supplied to me and had been read by almost no-one outside his immediate family.

Secondary sources used include Martin Middlebrook's invaluable *Bomber Command War Diaries*, as well what must surely be the definitive account of Bomber Command's winter campaign on the Nazi capital, Middlebrook's *The Berlin Raids.*

Bomber Command, Max Hastings' grim 'warts-and-all' history of the controversial weapon of strategic bombing, was greatly utilised, and I was also quietly pleased to dust off my own childhood favourites, *The Lancaster at War* (Volumes 1 and 2) by Mike Garbett and Brian Goulding. These excellent works dating from the 1970s still give any observer the clearest picture of what it must really have been like to operate in Lancasters during World War II, and in particular provided me valuable information regarding the bomb aimer's precise role and the equipment at his disposal. Among Barney's correspondence, I noted, were several letters back and forth from Mike Garbett himself, requesting Barney's input into the books.

Much information regarding the operational history of the Jedburgh missions was derived from *Jedburgh Team Operations in Support of 12th Army Group* by S. J. Lewis, published in 1991 by the US Combat Studies Institute, and Robert Gildea's new unravelling of the complex story of the French Resistance, *Fighters in the Shadows,* was a much-sourced account.

On a personal note, thanks must go to the most knowledgeable Christiane Gilbert, who herself grew up in the Vosges, and from her childhood friendship with the Mougel family became greatly imbued in Barney's saga, even acting as his translator on several of his return trips to France. Meeting Christiane in Sydney gave me much new information and an insight into France's war of resistance against the German occupiers.

The wonders of the internet now provide a raft of material previously difficult to access, and I was amazed to discover the original 1944 report from the Special Operations Executive 'Jedburgh' mission penned by Lieutenant Colonel Prendergast himself, available in full in all its facsimiled foolscap glory. It is easily accessible via the UK National Archives online service.

I am enormously grateful for the support of Barney's family, particularly his nephews Charlie and Richard Mort, who have given much time and devotion both to Barney himself, as well as the preservation of his story. Charlie accompanied Barney to France to retrace his steps in the Vosges and to visit the graves of his fallen crewmen. Just weeks before publication, Richard discovered a previously unknown trove of photographs of Barney and his crew, which we have been able to include in this book's picture section.

I must particularly thank Barney's brother Antony – also an RAAF veteran – and his wife Kathy, who supplied invaluable information about Barney's early childhood, as well as the Greatrex family history in general, and whose enthusiasm and generosity towards myself and the project has been enormously appreciated.

Finally, I want to thank Alex Lloyd who, knowing Barney's story like few others, has been a tireless support in helping me bring it to light, gleefully chasing a lead or checking a detail and, in general, keeping me on track. Alex, I thank you.

Lastly, I must thank the team at Hachette Australia, particularly my publisher Matthew Kelly for once again giving me the chance to write about what I love – the stories of the men who flew in the great and terrible conflict that was the Second World War.

INDEX

MARCH 1942, THE JAPANESE ARE BOMBING DARWIN AND ADVANCING TOWARDS AUSTRALIA THROUGH NEW GUINEA.

In the midst of this dire military situation, RAAF 75 Squadron was born – and for 44 days these fearless but barely trained pilots fought a desperate battle at Australia's edge. In March and April 1942, the squadron bravely defended Port Moresby when Australia truly stood alone against the Japanese. This group of raw young recruits scrambled ceaselessly in their Kittyhawk fighters to an extraordinary and heroic battle, the story of which has been largely left untold – until now.

The recruits had almost nothing going for them against the Japanese war machine, except for one extraordinary leader named John Jackson, a big laconic Queenslander who led from the front and had absolutely no sense of physical fear. Time and time again this brave group were hurled into battle, against all odds and logic, and succeeded in mauling a far superior enemy – whilst also fighting against the air force hierarchy. After a relentless Japanese onslaught, the squadron was almost wiped out by the time relief came . . .

'should be part of Australian military folklore. ★★★★'

—*Adelaide Advertiser*

'Brilliantly researched and sympathetically told, *44 Days* is more than just a fitting tribute to brave but overlooked heroes. It's also a top read.'

—*Daily Telegraph*

FROM CHANGI AND DARWIN TO
KOKODA: THE TRIUMPH OF BRAVERY,
MATESHIP AND COURAGE THAT
SAVED US IN WORLD WAR II

THE
FIGHT FOR
AUSTRALIA
ROLAND PERRY

HACHETTE MILITARY COLLECTION

In the dark days following the fall of Singapore in February 1942, Australia faced its toughest battle yet. It was centre stage and under attack from seemingly invincible Japanese forces. Winston Churchill was demanding our best battle-hardened troops stay in North Africa, while President Roosevelt called for them to fight the Japanese in Burma. But Prime Minister John Curtin insisted they return to defend their homeland.

In this masterful and gripping account, Roland Perry brings to life the bravery of our fellow Australians: from the forces engaged in brutal frontline fighting in the jungle, sea and air, to the backroom strategic campaigns waged by our politicians, and the sacrifices made on the home front.

'I can unashamedly recommend this very readable book . . . it fills a major gap in Australia's history.'

—Major-General Jim Barry (retired)

'A very readable and engaging account of Australia's pacific war'

—*Australian Defence Magazine*

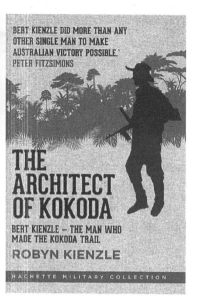

'BERT KIENZLE DID MORE THAN ANY OTHER SINGLE MAN TO MAKE AUSTRALIAN VICTORY POSSIBLE.'
PETER FITZSIMONS

THE ARCHITECT OF KOKODA

BERT KIENZLE – THE MAN WHO MADE THE KOKODA TRAIL

ROBYN KIENZLE

HACHETTE MILITARY COLLECTION

In 1942, when the Japanese had invaded New Guinea and the Australian soldiers sent to hold them back thought victory was impossible, one man, Bert Kienzle, changed the course of history.

This charismatic man, well-known locally for having run gold mines and plantations, was charged with the seemingly impossible task of establishing a trail across the forbidding Owen Stanley Ranges in just a few short months.

Out of jungle and mud, Kienzle carved a working transport route on which his handpicked teams of native bearers, the now famous Fuzzy Wuzzy Angels, would work alongside the Australian troops, ensuring they got the food, munitions and medical support they needed. The feats that these men performed were heroic, and their endurance as they transported supplies along the Trail unparalleled.

Bert Kienzle lived an amazing life, and the transport route he established — the legendary Kokoda Trail — made Australia's victory possible.

'This book was an eye-opener . . . should be read by all Australians'
—*ADF Journal*

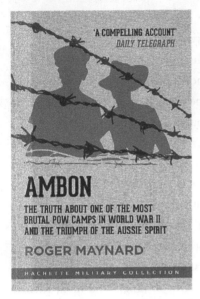

'A COMPELLING ACCOUNT'
DAILY TELEGRAPH

AMBON

THE TRUTH ABOUT ONE OF THE MOST
BRUTAL POW CAMPS IN WORLD WAR II
AND THE TRIUMPH OF THE AUSSIE SPIRIT

ROGER MAYNARD

HACHETTE MILITARY COLLECTION

In February 1942 the Indonesian island of Ambon fell to the might of the advancing Japanese war machine. Among the captured Allied forces was a unit of 1150 Australian soldiers known as Gull Force.

Several hundred Australians were massacred in cold blood soon after the Japanese invasion. But that was only the start of a catalogue of horrors and in this hellhole of despair and evil, officers and men turned against each other as discipline and morale broke down.

Yet the epic struggle also produced heroic acts of kindness and bravery. Just over 300 of these gallant men lived to tell of those grim days behind the barbed wire. In *Ambon*, survivors speak of not just the horrors, but of the courage, endurance and mateship that helped them survive.

The story of Ambon is one of depravity and of memories long buried – but also the triumph of the human spirit. It has not been widely told – until now.

'One of the greatest military debacles of World War II'

—Good Reading

'A compelling account of one of World War II's most brutal prisoner of war camps'

—Daily Telegraph

Clive 'Killer' Caldwell was a natural and brilliant pilot, a superb shot, and a born leader. He saw action against the Germans, Italians and Japanese, and remains Australia's greatest ever fighter ace.

Born and brought up in Sydney, it was obvious from an early age that nothing would stand in Caldwell's way. He bluffed his way into the RAAF, and then made sure that he was posted to exactly where he thought he should be.

His ability was unquestioned by all those around him, and he developed new tactics in aerial combat which contributed so much to Allied success. But he was never afraid of voicing his opinions to all those above and below him, be it about the training of pilots, or the equipping of Spitfires for use against the Japanese – or trying to run the show his way.

'Captain Clive "Killer" Caldwell single-handedly saved hundreds of Australian lives.'

—ABC News

'He was an ideal pilot for the rough desert war; tough, adaptable, inspirational . . . and an excellent poker player.'

—*The Independent*

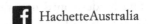

hachette
AUSTRALIA

If you would like to find out more about Hachette Australia,
our authors, upcoming events and new releases you can visit
our website or our social media channels:

hachette.com.au

 HachetteAustralia

 HachetteAus